1839-1908 Ouida

Santa Barbara etc.

1839-1908 Ouida

Santa Barbara etc.

ISBN/EAN: 9783337038984

Printed in Europe, USA, Canada, Australia, Japan

Cover: Foto ©ninafisch / pixelio.de

More available books at **www.hansebooks.com**

SANTA BARBARA

ETC.

By OUIDA

London
CHATTO & WINDUS, PICCADILLY
1891

NOTE

With the exception of 'Santa Barbara,' which was written for 'Les Lettres et les Arts,' all the stories in this volume are now printed and published for the first time.

CONTENTS

	PAGE
SANTA BARBARA	1
POUSSETTE	67
RINALDO	101
THE HALT	187
THE STABLE-BOY	211
LA ROSSICCIA	247

SANTA BARBARA

Santa Barbara

DO you know San Francesco della Vigna, in Venice?
Some say that its tall tower is the first point rising above the waves, which the returning Venetian sailor sees as he comes homeward from the south-east, over the foaming bars of Chioggia and Malamocco, one slender shaft lifted against the sky, calling him back to his city and his home. All the mariners and fishermen, who come and go over the Adrian waters, have an especial tenderness, an especial reverence, for Saint Francis of the Vineyard. There is no vineyard now; only one small square garden, with a cloister running round it,

arched, columned, marble paved, where the dead lie under the worn smooth slabs, and the box-edges hem in thyme, and balsams, and basil, and carnations, and thrift, and saxifrage, and other homely hardy plants which need slight fostering care. The sea winds blow strongly there, and the sea fogs drift thickly, and the steam and smoke of the foundries round about hang in heavy clouds, where once the pavilions and the lawns and the terraces of the patricians of Venice touched the grey-green lagoon; but this garden of San Francesco is still sweet and fresh: shut in between its marble colonnades with the deep brown shadow of the church leaning over it, and the chiming of the bells, and the melody of the organ rolling above it in deep waves of sound, jarred sometimes by the clash of the hammers falling on the iron and the copper of the foundries near at hand, and sometimes sinking to a sweet silence, only softly stirred by the splash of an oar as a boat passes up or down the narrow canal.

For the sake of that cloistered garden, a gondola came one summer every day to the landing-place before San Francesco. In the gondola was an artist, a painter of Paris, Yvon Dorât, who had seen the spot, and liked it, and returned to paint from it every day, finding an inexpressible charm in its contrasts of gloom and light, of high brown walls and low-lying graves, of fresh green herbs and flowers, and melancholy immemorial marble aisles. He meant to make a great picture of it, with the ethereal Venetian sky above all, and, between the straight edges of the box, a solitary monk passing thoughtfully. Dorât was under the charm of Venice : that subtle dreamy charm, voluptuous and yet spiritual, which no artist or poet ever can resist, and these summer months were to him as a vision of languor, and beauty and rest, in which the white wings of sea-birds, and the silver of gleaming waters, and the festal figures of Carpaccio and the golden warmth of Palma Vecchio, and the glories of sunsets aflame behind the Euganean hills, and the mystery of moonless nights, with the tide washing against the weed-grown piles of a Madonna of the lagoon, were all blended in that confusion of past and present, of art and nature, of desire and repose, which fills the soul and the senses of those who love Venice, and live in thrall to her.

Dorât was young enough to feel this spell profoundly, and old enough to be glad that he could feel it, and to welcome it as a lingering breath of youth, as in the heat of the midsummer nights he welcomed a stray breeze blowing down from the Paduan hills, across the still waters by Murano. In Paris he was famous, wearied, feverish, sated: in Venice he was a student still, a pupil still, a lover of all lovely things, content to sit at the feet of Titian, and Giorgione; happy to dream his days away, where silver sunlight poured through a canopy of vine-leaves, on a group of naked children, playing like young dolphins in green water, or a fleet of boats, red, yellow, orange, ruddy as so many flames, glided by a grassy isle, or ruined marble mole.

In Paris he could not live a day without all the refinements and ingenuities of what some call vice, and some call pleasure; in Venice he was content merely *de s'écouter vivre*, dreamily, and harmlessly, penetrated with that divinity of beauty, which is the very lifeblood of the true artist, and that humility which alone contains the germ of greatness.

'Je me sens si jeune ici,' he wrote to a friend in Paris: 'je me retrempe corps et âme dans cet air pur, dans ces eaux ensoleillées. Laissez crier les gueuses et les cabotines, je n'ai pas besoin d'elles ; j'ai la Sainte Barbara qui se donne à moi.'

And he had come to the cloister of San Francesco every morning for a fortnight, to pourtray its cool greys, and browns, and whites, its simple green leaves, its poor lonely monks, he who was wont to enrapture Paris with pictures of nude women and drunken revellers, and daring visions of Greek and Egyptian orgies, and scenes of oriental sensuality, and strange landscapes burning with the scorch of Asia and of Africa.

He meant to call this picture merely 'Le Passé.' The pavement of flat moss-grown tombs, the shadow of the high church, the homely fragrant flowers, the peaceful colonnades, did they not embody in them, and symbolise all that the modern world has lost of silence, of leisure, of simplicity, and of faith? He had no faith of any sort, but he envied those who could still bask in its illusions: and in a solitary country house, upon the dreary moors of Morbihan, with stormy seas boiling between black rocks and long winters enshrouding the cruel coasts in mist and snow, his mother, a lone woman, prayed for him night and day. All his great triumphs had been but as mere terrible forecasts of hell to her superstitious piety, and on none of his works had her pained eyes borne to look: this picture of the past should be painted for her, he thought, since to her, as to the monks, the past was still a present and its legend a reality.

It was the harmonious proportions of its colonnades and the subdued sweetness of colour in its garden which had first drawn him there; of its symbolism he had only thought later, one day when the chanting of the lays within the church had come to his ear; they had been singing from a mass of Palestrina's. It is only in the old obscure churches of old historic towns that one can still hear all the beautiful music of the old masters, whose scores lie dust-covered, yellow and moth-eaten, in organ lofts and sacristies, their melody left mute and neglected between the leaves, whilst the world runs after braying chords and borrowed motives which have dethroned melody.

It was August, and August is very warm in Venice; all that wide shadeless plain of shallow rippling sea draws down and reflects tenfold the sun, as in a mirror, and there is no retreat from the heat except inside the water-gates of the palaces or behind the leathern curtains of the churches; out of doors, everywhere, even under the deep vault of the Rialto bridge or under the drooping trees of San Trovasio the strong heat penetrates; and here in the cloister of Saint Francis at noonday Dorât, who had ceased to paint because the light was too strong, and who was unwilling to leave the place as yet, felt his eyelids grow heavy and his hand become slow to obey him.

All things invited to repose; the cool marble parapet of the cloisters, the drowsy hum of the bees rifling the stocks and carnations, the monotonous chant of the choristers repeating their lesson, the silence which prevailed everywhere else, for at midday the foundry hammers ceased; and Dorât, resisting his indolent impulses but a moment, strolled to the cloister on his left, and threw himself down on the marble ledge in the shadow. There he in another moment fell asleep; the hum of the bees and the hymn of the choristers lulling him to slumber as a song sung low lulls a child. Soon the chanting ceased, and all was completely still. There was no sound except his own even breathing and the buzzing of the bees in the little garden; the monks were mumbling over their midday fish and bread in their refectory; the sun poured down on the brown brick wall of the church, and the flowers drooped under the strength of its rays. Dorât slept on undisturbed, his head on his arm, his limbs outstretched, his head handsome as the Antinous of Canova, his face pale from the habits of his life, his slender and graceful limbs indolently posed as he dreamed on in complete unconsciousness.

From a crevice in the marble beneath him a little head peeped out, and a darksome form crept towards him; not the gay green innocent frolicsome shape of the lizard, but the wicked black head of an adder. In these old walls all manner of poisonous as of harmless creatures dwell, and no seat or couch is more dangerous than the rest which an old wall in Italy offers to the tired and thoughtless traveller.

All snakes, large and small, love the noon sun; and this adder came out after the manner of her kind allured by the basking heat. Did she know what she did, or did she not know? Who can tell? Man knows what he does when he slays; but these others—who can say that they know what they do, though often they are wiser than we? She looked out of her hole and enjoyed the great heat which fell on her flat pointed head; and then she emerged more fully into the light, and saw the hand of a man which hung down over the ledge of marble and lay idly on the ground; the slender supple delicate hand of the artist which creates beautiful things and has power in all its fingers to call up visible scenes from worlds unseen by his fellows. Then it seemed good to the adder to touch this hand, and she crept close to it on her belly and wound herself carefully round it and upward to the wrist. But her touch and her clasp were so light that the sleeper did not awaken, and she drew her head back as a child recoils before making a leap, and darted her tongue out like a little arrow of death, and showed her double range of fine small teeth like pins.

But before those teeth could reach and penetrate the flesh, another hand seized her by the throat, gripping her so tightly that she could not move, and threw her on the ground, and then with a stone killed her. The noise of the stone falling on the marble pavement awoke Dorât; he raised himself on his left arm, and looked with astonished eyes up into the white warm light above him.

'Santa Barbara!' he murmured; for the woman who stood above him resembled marvellously that picture which he loved, and which he had gazed on that morning for the hundredth time where it hangs in the shadow of the side altar in the church of Sta Maria Formosa.

'It is bad to sleep upon old walls, they harbour dangerous beasts,' said the woman, gravely, in the soft liquid Venetian accents. 'See, Signor, I killed her, or very surely she would have killed you.'

'You have done me a service indeed; I was asleep and dreaming of Sta Barbara,' said Dorât;

he was still but half awake, and he looked dreamily at the little black crushed adder lying on a slab of discoloured marble. Was it possible? One touch from that small creature, one drop of venom from its fangs, and all the power of his brain and cunning of his hand might have been dulled and dead for ever!

The idea seemed so strange to him that he was absorbed by it for a moment. The next his eyes, still dim and heavy with slumber in the heat, saw only the face of his saviour, a face like Sta Barbara's, of the old noble warm-hued Venetian type, with strength as well as beauty in its lines, and dusky golden hair, and a mouth like a carnation. She was a woman of the people, she had a black shawl worn over her head as Venetian women so often wear one; a linen bodice and a woollen skirt; but these poor clothes could not conceal the magnificent lines of her form and the mingled grace and strength of her limbs; whilst her throat and bosom and arms were those of Veronese's Europa.

'All the types in one!' he murmured to himself, feasting his eyes on this incarnation of womanhood till the ardour and abstraction of his gaze called up a vivid blush over the cheeks and brows of the young matron, who, half offended, half diverted, frowned and laughed and turned away. 'By the Virgin, how you stare, 'llustrissima!' she murmured, as she drew her shawl closer about her breast. 'It is well for you that my man is away over the seas.'

The homely words recalled Dorât to himself; he rose and thanked her warmly for the service she had done him, and begged to know to whom his debt of life was owing.

'I am Veronica Venier, and my husband is Zuan Tron,' she answered. 'Yes, Venetians both, what else should we be? I live close by, in the Campiello dei Merli, where the well is, with the marble angels; they say it is very old, and people come and sketch it. You are a painter too?'

'I am,' said Dorât, 'and I may come and see the well with the angels?'

'Surely, it is in the Campo; it is not mine. Any one may see it. But why do you lie and sleep here? Why are you not at home if you wish to sleep?'

'The heat overcame me, and but for you I

might have wakened from my siesta only to sleep for ever in the grave. May I ask how you came here, in a monkish sanctuary?'

'I came to bring some linen to Cattina, the sacristan's wife; and she gave me leave to gather some lavender; I often come here; the monks say nothing.'

'They would indeed have ceased to be men if they could object!'

The calm deep blue eyes of Veronica gazed at him without comprehension of the compliment.

If she seemed Barbara and Europa to him, he seemed to her a being of another world, so delicate, so slender, so sweet-voiced, so unlike the gondoliers and boatmen and sailors who made up her family and her neighbourhood and her world. She stood a moment, reflecting, in the hot sunlight with her bare feet on the marble pavement and the tawny gold of her coiled hair burnished in the light. Then she stooped and picked up a bundle of lavender which she had dropped when she had seized and stoned the adder, and nodded her head in farewell.

'Do not sleep on old walls again,' she said carelessly; and turned to leave the cloister.

'Wait a moment,' murmured Dorât; 'tell me where I can find the Campiello?'

'Three turns from here, one to the left and then two to the right; you cannot miss it.'

'And take this,' he added, as he slid his watch into her hand; 'take this, to remind you that I owe it to your courage and presence of mind if time has not wholly ceased to exist for me.'

She took the watch and gazed at it in admiration; it was a gold chronometer of great value; but after looking on it in admiration for a moment she gave it back to him.

'I want nothing,' she said with some coldness. 'You owe me nothing either; and if Zuan were to hear that I took payment for doing my duty he would give me the rope's end when he came home.'

'The brute!' muttered Dorât, but he did not force his gift or his presence on her.

'I will give you some other memorial of this morning,' he said with tender grace as he raised her hand to his lips and kissed it reverently. That action surprised and pleased her; she felt the homage of it and its difference from the rough wooing of Zuan Tron.

'Addè!' she said to him, drawing her hand away; and with her sheaf of lavender in her arms she went out of the cloister.

Then he let her go, watching her superb walk as she passed through the garden with that mingling of poetic analysis and of sensual desire which, together and inseparable, characterise every artistic temperament.

Dorât was accustomed to leave his easel and canvas and colours with the sacristan of San Francesco; when he left them there this day an hour or two later, he questioned the old man as to the history of Veronica, the wife of Tron. The man had little to say in answer; she was the daughter of Ruffo Venier, a coppersmith; Tron was a working sailor in a coasting brig. They were poor folks; she was not twenty years old; she had had one child, it was dead; she was a handsome wench, yes, but there were others as good to look at, and in the Campo the neighbours thought that she gave herself airs; what sort of man was Tron? well enough, honest, hard-working, good, but violent and apt to be jealous; he had only sailed two days before with wood for Greece; those brigs were slow but sure. Then the sacristan pocketed a fee and took in the easel, and a little later said to his wife that Veronica had saved a foreigner from an adder's bite.

'More fool she,' said his wife; 'we never do a stroke of good in this world but what it turns against us and comes and bites us.'

'That is true,' said the sacristan, washing Dorât's brushes, 'but,' he added with a chuckle, 'this adder will be more likely to bite Tron.'

In the afternoon Dorât walked down the street of the Merceria, that busy crowded narrow alley which has some looks and sounds of the bazaars of the East in its colour and confusion, and entered a jeweller's shop well known to him; a dusky den where gold and silver, coral and agate, pearls and diamonds, and all kinds of filagree work in precious metals shone and gleamed in the deep shadows.

Thence he selected a necklace of great price

from its purity of ore and rarity of workmanship; a gold serpent so flexible that it curled like a living snake and seemed almost imbued with life as its emerald eyes sparkled in the dark. He paid for it and put it loosely in his pocket, refusing the case in which the jeweller wished to enclose it. Then he went to his gondola waiting at the water steps between the pillars of the Piazzetta. An hour or two later, as the heat of the day cooled, he had the gondola moored to the ring in the landing stair of the Campiello dei Merli, an abandoned little square, one of those green places where in the Venice of old the citizens used to keep their sheep; surrounded now on three sides by palaces gone to ruin and having in its centre the well with two kneeling angels, of which she had spoken, which was said or supposed to be the work of Tullio Lombardo.

Poor people alone occupied these once noble houses; their rags of many colours fluttered from the ogive windows, and half naked babies tumbled in numbers on the short turf. His Barbara, his Europa, lived here! To Dorât, used to luxury and ease, it seemed an outrage against nature and against art, that a creature so beautiful should dwell in such squalor and in penury, with all the meagre and dull atmosphere of poverty.

'Can I see Veronica Venier, the wife of the sailor Tron?' he asked the people of the Campo who had come to gaze at him. They answered Yes, and her name, abbreviated into 'Nica! 'Nica! awoke the echoes of the old dilapidated walls. She came in answer out of an arched stone portico, her head uncovered, shading her eyes with her hand from the blaze of the sunset light; he thought that she had expected him, for her clothes were of a better kind than those which she had worn in the morning, and in her breast there was a knot of red carnations.

'I have come to see the angels of the well,' said Dorât softly, 'and also to bring you this little thing in memory of to-day.'

She was leaning against the marble side of the well, and the neighbours and children were gathered round, staring and listening, as Dorât with a sudden movement which took her utterly by surprise clasped the golden snake about her throat.

'Ah,' she cried quickly, and with that quick rush of blood under her fair skin which made her beauty so much greater.

Dorât, turning to the neighbours, said: 'She saved my life from a snake this morning; is it not fit she should wear its souvenir? And snakes bring good fortune, they say.'

'Good fortune, indeed,' grumbled one old crone, 'if they hang your neck about with gold!'

Veronica, raising her arms, tried to unclasp the gold snake from her throat, but in vain; it had closed with a spring and her fingers could not find its secret. Dorât, smiling, stood and watched her unavailing efforts.

'Do not be unkind to me,' he murmured, 'it is but a trifle, a toy; keep it, I entreat you. It has a grander place there than if it were on the throat of any princess. Keep it in memory of me.'

Veronica stood irresolute; a beautiful figure with her raised hands still behind her throat, and shadows of longing, of irresolution, of pleasure, of fear, of embarrassment and of natural pride all passing over her expressive countenance, while the children hung on her skirts to stare, and a clove pink fell from her breast on the stones. Dorât stooped and took up the flower. Then, being an unerring artist in the arts of life and of love, as in his art of painting, he gave her no chance to repent or to refuse, no opportunity to debate or to protest, but bowed low to her as to any great lady and left the Campiello while she still stood irresolute, the golden adder clasped about her throat; the children and the women clamorous around her, and on either side the angels of the well kneeling with folded wings as the sculptor had left them there three hundred years before.

Veronica stood there as in a dream, listening to the soft plash of the gondolier's oar as he descended the narrow side-canal, now tinted with all colours and glowing with the crimson reflections from the western skies.

The carnation dropped from Dorât's hold into the water as he shifted the cushions to stretch himself at ease.

Poor women in Italy often possess jewellery that is both good and handsome, as heirlooms, or as marriage portions, but Veronica came of people too poor for her to own anything more than the silver earrings which Zuan Tron had given her on her bridal day. Her father and brothers were workers in one of the smelting furnaces; and Tron was but a common sailor who brought home little from his voyages; she had a room or two which she shared with Tron's sister, and she made a little money for herself by washing linen. Her name was the old ducal name of the Venier; and, maybe, she had their blood in her; maybe her ancestors had worn the pearl-sown robes and golden bugole of Dogaresse, and gone in state to hear Mass at San Marco; but, if so, the traditions of such grandeur were all lost under the accumulation of the centuries, and in the darkness of ignorance and poverty. She was only a poor sailor's wife; a woman who beat linen with wood in the canal-water and hung it on a cord to dry.

Therefore the golden adder made her heart leap in her bosom with elation and triumph; and yet—and yet—she was a proud woman; and an innocent woman; it was not well for her to keep it, she knew that.

When she unclasped it from her throat at night, she laid it on her pillow; and all the night she could not rest.

It was a night of rainless storm; the heavens were filled with lightning; and the vivid flashes came through her unshuttered casement, and lit up the little snake with its emerald eyes, as it lay on the rough hempen pillow where the rude head of Zuan Tron had so often reposed. With the first flush of morning she slipped the necklace in her breast, and went out and finished her washing, and spread the linen on the stones of the Campo to dry.

Then when it was noonday she took her way to the cloister of San Francesco. Dorât was again there painting; he saw her entrance with a smile; he mistook her errand; he felt a passing irritation, a vague distaste; he did not care for a woman who offered herself.

'She might have waited,' he thought, as he rose with some words of welcome and flattery.

But she did not heed his words; she took the gold adder out of her bosom and held it towards him.

'It is beautiful,' she said, with a hot colour in her cheeks, 'but it is not for me; give it to your *dama*; I want no payment.'

Dorât was so surprised that for an instant he was silent, gazing at her in stupor; a woman forego a jewel!—she could not be in earnest.

'I will not take it,' he said angrily, 'it is yours. Throw it in the canal if you choose.' Then, as the sun, shining on her, showed him the full splendour of her fair skin, her burnished hair, her flower-like lips, his tone melted and changed, and grew passionate and supplicating. ' Keep it, keep it, not in payment, but in remembrance. Did you not save my life from that little poisonous black beast? I have no *dama*; all women that I have ever possessed are as nothing now that I have seen you. Do you know how great your own beauty is?'

Veronica heard him with a vague terror, but with a strong confused sense of power and of pleasure. Men had told her often of her beauty; but not in this way, or in these words.

'I cannot take it,' she repeated with embarrassment, clinging to that one idea which had brought her thither, and powerless to express her feelings, as the uneducated always are. 'I cannot take it. Tron would see it when he comes home and he would beat me. I came only to bring it back here, because you are a stranger and I know not where you dwell, or where you lodge even here. There is no need for you to have any gratitude. I merely took the little beast off your hand. Cattina would have done the same had she been near.'

Dorât looked at her in silence; he wondered if her rejection of it was sincere; he believed but very little in the words of any woman. .

'If you be too proud to take a gift from me,' he said, with affected mortification, 'will you be content to earn it? You can do so easily.'

Her large calm eyes, the eyes of the Sta Barbara, lightened with pleasure and expectation.

'Earn it? But I could never earn it! you mean, I suppose, by washing your linen; but it would take years.'

'No; you can earn it in a week, if you will.'

'How?

Unconsciously to herself, her whole face spoke the wistfulness and eagerness of her longing for this toy; her breath came and went rapidly; her whole form seemed tremulous with a childlike yet passionate desire.

'Let me make a portrait of you,' said Dorât simply.

'Of me?—But I am nothing!' she exclaimed in her ignorance and her surprise. 'Why should you want to make a picture of me?'

Dorât smiled; he saw her words were quite sincere.

'Because you are a beautiful woman,' he answered; 'you do not seem to know it or to care about it, but it is so. If you will come to me a few hours now and then, you will have more than earned the necklace, since you wish to earn it; and your husband, when he sees it, will have no cause to blame you. Will you not do this little thing for me?'

'Perhaps,' she said, slowly and doubtingly, for the idea was strange to her; she was of the city of Tintoretto and of Titian, but of pictures she knew nothing, though she knelt before them sometimes and said her prayers.

'You wish me to come here?' she asked.

'Here at first if you please,' said Dorât, and he looked away from her as he spoke, 'but afterwards you must come to my studio. I cannot finish a portrait in the open air.'

'But you are making this picture of the garden in the open air?'

'This is different. Tell me, will you let me paint your portrait? Just as I saw you first, standing with the sun shining about your head and the sheaf of lavender lying at your feet. All the great world shall see it, and will see in it that the women of Palma Vecchio and of the Veronese live still in Venice.'

She was silent; the world conveyed no sense to her; she had never been farther over the waters than to the islands of Murano and of Mazzarbo when the fruit was ripe, and, though she was a mariner's wife, she did not understand what other countries and other nations meant. But she understood that Dorât thought her beautiful; and she would not have been a woman born of a woman if she had not felt the thrill of that consciousness in her innermost being.

'You will come?' said Dorât softly.

'Yes,' she said slowly, 'I will come.'

'And you will keep the necklace?'

'Not till I have earned it.'

From that resolution he could not move her; she would not take the little golden snake till she had earned it, though her whole soul sighed for it.

He had perforce to let her go that day, for she was in haste, being wanted by her sister-in-law.

'You will come back to-morrow?' he asked her persuasively.

'Yes: to-morrow,' she said calmly, and then with her ' Addè, 'cellenza,' she went away from him across the sunlight down the marble arcade of the cloister.

Dorât watched her with languid eyes, amorous and yet cold; he was a man who could wait. He put the gold adder in one of the drawers of his colour-box; one day very soon it would be round her throat; what matter a day sooner or a day later when one is certain to succeed at last?

And yet the calm noble simplicity of her in her strength and beauty sank with a certain profoundness of impression into his mind, sated, selfish, and sensual though it was. 'She is a grand creature,' he thought, 'despite all her ignorance and poverty and her frankness of desire for that jewelled toy.'

He painted very little that day, but sat and dreamed in the sweetness of the garden, dreams of things which his youth had desired, and the visions of which had been hustled and hurried away by the rush of those passions and follies and ambitions and achievements which had filled his years since the world had made him famous.

'Santa Barbara se donne à moi,' he murmured, recalling the words of his letter to his friend. 'Je ne croyais pas avoir si bien dit!'

And within a yard or two of him the little dead body of the adder lay under the saxifrage leaves whither the sacristan had swept it with his broom the day before; a sun-dried, wrinkled, shrivelled little thing, looking like a small burnt branch, a shred of leather. Its work was done.

The picture of the cloister and the garden was

laid aside, and waited; with its canvas turned to the wall in the sacristan's room.

The portrait of Veronica grew in its stead; a portrait taken in the fulness of the daylight with that strong sunshine shed over it in which Dorât excelled; the marble pavement under her feet, the rosy saxifrage and the yellow tiger lilies behind her, and above all the blue sky with boughs of oleander in white blossom crossing it.

'The pose is a little too much like Sta Barbara's, and the *pâte* a little too much like Cabanel's,' thought Dorât, who was quickly disenchanted with his own creations. 'It is not a Titian nor a Veronese; it is only a Bouguereau!'

But it was beautiful, and it was not the portrait which he wanted to gain, but the woman; he was an artist indeed, but he was beyond all a voluptuary.

Seven mornings she came to the garden in the warmth of the forenoon, and stood for him with the sacristan's wife and children looking on, and the monks, who were sociable and not hermits, came now and then also down the middle aisle and talked of what was being done as became friars who had paintings of Gian Bellini and the Veronese on the walls of their church hard by; the gardener monk who came thither with his spade, and rake, and shears, and water-pot, was in especial eloquent.

'It would make an altarpiece, my son, and you might give it to us,' he said, 'only you have put such a profane look into it; it will not be a holy picture if you do not correct that; and myself I wonder why you paint new things at all; the chromo-lithographs in the shops under the Procuratie are so very fine; there is a reduction of the Assumption of our Titian there that I would sooner have myself than the original, for the colours are brighter and the size more sensible.'

'Your government has had the Assumption daubed over until it is hardly better than a chromo-lithograph, and you are verily wise as your generation is wise, my father,' said Dorât, angrily as the rotund figure of the monk, clothed in brown and with a hoe on his shoulder, came between him and the sunlight.

'I cannot paint here,' he said impatiently to Veronica a little later, 'I cannot paint here with these chattering fools about us; you must come to my studio to-morrow.'

'Where is that?'

'On the Fondamento of the Malcanton. You know the house where the fig-tree hangs over the wall.'

'But will it be well? Cattina said but yesterday to me: "See, I am here and the children and the holy men come and go, and so Tron will not mind much when he returns, but beware how you go to his house by yourself"—she meant your house.'

'Do not heed Cattina or any one, and what of Tron? He cannot be here yet. He is gone to Greece, you say, and those heavy-laden brigs sail very slowly.'

'But he will come back, sail they ever so slowly, and——'

'You are afraid of him?'

'I do not know.' She did not know; the poor are too ignorant to sift, to analyse, to classify, and to docket their emotions and sensations as cultured minds do theirs.

'Why did you marry him?' asked Dorât, with impatience and scorn.

D

'I do not know,' she said again. His questions disturbed her, as stones thrown into a well of still water trouble its clear surface.

'I will tell you,' said Dorât ; 'you were a girl, and girls are curious, and vain, and inquisitive, and the first man who comes is welcome—was it not so ?'

'Perhaps,' she said, with a blush which came and went. 'Zuan is handsome,' she added with pride, 'so strong and tall ; you would want to paint him if you saw him.'

'Ah,' said Dorât with irritation, 'it was his good looks and his straight limbs which tempted you, then.'

'Perhaps,' she answered again, but she answered uneasily ; she was perplexed and troubled by this search into her motives and feelings. Zuan was handsome, but he was rude and violent ; he swore at her in his wrath as he swore at the ropes and the sails when the waves were running high and the brig labouring through a white squall along the coasts of Dalmatia or Albania.

Dorât looked at her where she stood in the transparent light ; her head and arms uncovered, her swelling bosom confined by the white linen bodice she wore, her whole aspect that of one of those strong and fertile women with whom the quays and bridges and calle of Venice had been full in the days when Giorgione and Veronese and Titian had found their saints and goddesses in the maidens drying their golden locks seated in high air on their wooden *altane*, and sketched their Madonnas from the young matrons suckling their big-eyed babies in the noonday heat under the vine-bower of a *traghetto*.

'You must come to me in Malcanton,' he said abruptly; 'I cannot paint here, with these people about, and in this glare of light. What should you fear? No one need know. If they do, it would not matter. No one will see your picture here. It will go with me to Paris.'

'What is Paris?'

'The heaven of women and the smelting-house of genius. You do not understand? Of course you do not. That is what is so divine in you. You might be Eve or Lilith living in a virgin world.'

He spoke dreamily, to himself rather than to

her; and drew out the drawer of his colour box in which the gold adder lay, and turned it over with his hand carelessly, as if seeking the colours which lay beside it.

Veronica's eyes fell on it; and her heart heaved under the linen of her gown.

'Come to my house,' said Dorât softly, 'come to-morrow to Malcanton.'

She hesitated a moment and glanced towards the sacristan's wife, who was washing carrots and peeling onions between two of the marble columns.

'I will come,' she said in a low voice; 'but do not let Cattina know.'

'Cattina shall not know, any more than the adder that lies dead in the saxifrage.'

Then he added a few touches, a little colour, to the portrait he had made of her, so that the monk and the woman might see him at work; and somewhat later let her go away from the garden by the narrow passages which turn and twist behind the church, passages full of teeming families, curly-haired children, fluttering rags, scarlet runners clinging to strings, little vines which flourish seemingly without soil, and here and there in the dirt and confusion and squalor, a brass vessel of beautiful shape, a marble lintel of beautiful moulding, an iron scroll-work balcony fit for Desdemona, or an ogive window with some broken fresco-colour on it, under which Stradella may have played a serenade in the moonlight.

Dorât put the necklace once more in his pocket and went to his gondola.

'A daughter of the gods, a sister of the saints,' he thought, 'and yet won by a little gold beaten out and curled about by a jeweller's cunning! They are all like that, all; the *cabotine* sleeps in every madonna of them all.'

Veronica, meanwhile, who knew the multitudinous mazes of her city by heart, went on fast through the narrow ways and over the small bridges straight across the city, until behind the Grimani Palace she reached the church of Sta Maria Formosa.

There she entered and crossed herself, and knelt for a few moments, then rose, and asked one of the vergers where the famous picture was. Being told, she went to the first side altar on the right of the entrance, and gazed at the Santa Barbara until her eyes were green blind.

'Like me! Like me!' she thought. She knew nothing of pictures, less even than the monk who preferred the chromo-lithographs of the shops, but she could see that this saint was beautiful, and he had said that she, a poor common woman, a sailor's wife, resembled her!

She sank down on her knees before the altar and tried to pray again, but could not; her heart beat too tumultuously, her brain was in too great a confusion of pride and of pleasure. She was like this great and heavenly creature! like this famous picture which strangers came from far and wide to see!

'Had it been painted from the saint herself?' she asked of an old beggar, who was near when she rose from her knees.

The old man chuckled a little, decorously, as beseemed a reverend place. 'Not it; they do say it was painted from Violante, the painter's daughter, who was a love of Titian's. Titian was in luck; she must have been a rare one, and fine and strong, too.'

Veronica went out of the church with a dizzy sweetness dazing her mind and soul, and took her way homeward by the lovely bridge of Paradise and under the *vista superba* of great Colleoni. When she reached the Campiello dei Merli, it was late; her sister-in-law was scolding vigorously, the children were crying, the neighbours were quarrelling, the fish was burning in the frying-pan, the washed linen was lying in a heap on the kitchen floor, un-ironed and unstarched. It all struck on her painfully, with a sudden perception wholly new to her, of its penury, its noise, its coarseness, its squalor, its misery.

She had never felt them so before. For to that which is for ever about us, we are both blind and deaf until some ray of light from another world than ours is shed upon our darkness.

The calm green garden, the cool white cloisters, the sweet penetrating voice of Dorât, the homage and the eloquence of his eyes, all seemed to her very far away, far as a dream of the night.

'Have you sold the gold snake and brought us the money?' asked her sister-in-law.

'I gave it back to the gentleman a week ago,' said Veronica, in a low, unsteady tone.

'More fool you,' said the other woman.

The following day she did not go to the palace in Malcanton.

On the day after that, whilst it was still early in the forenoon, she was beating her linen in the canal water, leaning down from an old black boat of Zuan's under the slender shade of an acacia tree, when the strokes of a gondolier's oars came near to her and she saw Dorât. The gondola paused by her.

'Why are you unkind to me?' he murmured, with his hand on the side of her boat. She grew very red, and with her wet fingers hurriedly drew together the cotton folds of her bodice which had opened as she leaned over the side to dip her linen in the water; she felt that her hair was loose, her face and body were heated.

'Why are you so unkind to me?' he repeated. 'Without you I can do nothing with this portrait which might be so beautiful.'

'There are many other women, and I am busy as you see.'

'Leave those rags and come with me. There is no other woman in Venice who has the face of Santa Barbara and the form of Europa. Come.'

'With you? Like this? Oh no, oh no!'

She spoke in infinite distress, her hands unconsciously wringing out the folds of one of Tron's rough blue shirts.

'Well, come by yourself if you will, but soon— I mean whilst the morning light holds. *Mia cara*, what use is it to have saved my life from the little snake, if you poison it to me yourself?'

'You laugh at me when you say such follies,' said Veronica, with a flush on her face, half of anger, half of humiliation, yet with a pleasure in her soul which was stronger than either.

'No,' said Dorât softly, 'I speak in all seriousness. Your beauty haunts me. If you will not let me capture it at least in semblance on canvas, my days will be useless and your memory joyless to me. You know nothing of the world, but there are great cities in it where I can make men worship your effigy. You know nothing of books, but I think the public reader in Venice still reads aloud Ariosto to the people sometimes, does he not? Ariosto, one saint's day, met a woman wearing a robe embroidered with golden branches of palm; and that palm-bearer changed the ways of his life for him; so you have changed mine.'

The dulcet and poetic flattery, which was none the less sweet to her that she only most imperfectly comprehended it, sank into the very soul of Veronica as she listened, shrinking back from his gaze under the boughs of the mimosa acacia. At that moment the shrill voice of Tron's sister called to her from the Campiello.

'Do not let her see you,' said Veronica in terror. 'Go, go, pray go; she is a cruel woman, and Zuan bade her watch me.'

'Come, then, where she cannot watch you!'

'I will come,' murmured Veronica, as she heard the heavy step of her sister-in-law sounding nearer and nearer over the stones.

'Have you not done yet, Nica?' cried the woman; a fine wife you make for a poor sailor. If Zuan hearken to me, he will bring you nought home but a rope's end. A few shirts to dip, and you are all the morning at it! Did my brother marry you to keep you like a duchess?'

'Come to me, and you shall have in recompense what you will,' said Dorât. Then he made a sign to his gondolier; and the man backed with a single sweep of his oar between some great black barges moored there, which screened him from the sight of the sister of Zuan Tron as she came down, breathless, blousy, dishevelled, and bursting with invectives, to the edge of the stones where the acacia grew.

But Veronica did not go that day, nor the next to that. Her resistance increased his desire and his resolution a hundredfold. He followed her, he interrupted her, he besieged her; what was it he asked? So little! Only a few hours of morning light that he might make her beauty as famous to the world as it was dear to him. Whenever she went to pray in the churches near, which she did often, for Venetians are pious and humble children of the Church, he was there in the mellow incense-scented shadows, and his presence filled her whole existence; she could not sleep or work or eat for that one thought ; she was a creature of simple mind, of clear conscience, of perfect honesty, but in her nature there was the capacity for strong passion, for romantic illusion, and to these he appealed irresistibly.

Zuan Tron's wooing had been brutality not love; had she known it, Dorât's desires were no less brutal and were no more love. But they were veiled in the soft dreamy colours of art, of apparent deference, of sweet persuasive solicitation, and they seemed to her as the warm and soft south wind seemed after the bitter blasts of the north from the mountains. The contest was unequal, as unequal as the contest of the lutist and the nightingale in Ford's great poem. The lutist had all the resources and endurance of art and of artifice; the nightingale had only its own little beating heart and throbbing throat.

The days passed and she did not yield ; and the cloister garden saw neither her nor Dorât.

'That great gentleman is always after you ; if you brought home money, at least it might be worth while,' said the sister of Tron; 'if you brought home money, may be I would say nothing to Zuan when he comes back.'

'You are a vile woman,' said Veronica, with all her face in a glow of shame and rage ; ignorant of how much the gold coins of Dorât had already to do with the relaxing of her sister-in-law's vigilance. But she was restless, feverish, ill at ease ; she had strange dreams when she did sleep ; and it was in vain that she besought the guidance of Sta Barbara.

Sta Barbara had been a princess and a warrior, her chastity decked in armour, and the splendours of wealth around her, with her cannon and her tower, emblems of her strength. What could she know of the temptations assailing a poor sailor's wife ?

'You are cruel to me,' said Dorât, and repeated it so often that the ignorance of her mind and the tenderness of her nature blent together in a sense of tormenting reproach ; she believed that he suffered; his pallor, his restlessness, his heavy eyes, his feverish movements seemed to her like the suffering of the soul, and all that he told her she believed. Indeed for the moment he was sincere ; in their desires men lie like truth because they do not know that they are lying; what they wish for is to them, as to children, the universe for that one moment, and they are honest when they vow it is so.

'Will you come once more at least to the cloister? if you will not to my house,' he asked; 'what can you fear? Zuan Tron himself might see you in the garden, what could he say? We are hardly ever alone. It is a sacred place.'

'I will come once more then there,' said Veronica reluctantly; and yet with all her whole being in a tumult of longing fear and joy. It could not be very wrong or perilous, she thought; the children ran in and out, Cattina was the sacristan's wife always near, usually some monk paced through the aisles. There could be no risk of harm in going there, she thought.

It was a brilliant morning when she reached San Francesco on the morrow. Rain had fallen in the night and washed all things fresh and fair. The herbs in the garden filled the air with pungent sweetness. Some lizards swayed themselves on the blossoms of the rose laurels. Some pigeons scratched amongst the thyme and basil.

'I thank you for this at least,' said Dorât gravely

and with deference ; the portrait of her, in its shadowy unfinished suggestion, stood on an immense easel within one of the arcades. He placed her in the attitude of the Sta Barbara and, himself almost turning his back on her, and only looking at her furtively from time to time, painted on steadily without heeding the woman Cattina who came and looked on till she was tired, or the gardener monk who was digging in one of the borders, or the sacristan who said that the picture would be a better one if Veronica borrowed his wife's best feast-day gown, a fine blue gown with red and yellow ribands attached to it.

Dorât answered them no single word, and they talked till they were tired, and went away unnoticed and displeased. It was noon when he had worked two hours ; the drowsy heat lay like a weight upon the eyelids ; the green leaves lost their verdure and drooped ; the monks went in to the monastery, the shutters were shut in the sacristan's windows, and the church itself was closed ; entire silence reigned everywhere.

Dorât turned and laid down his palette and his brushes and looked at her ; she coloured over all her face and throat under that gaze which seemed like a very flame of fire stealing into all the recesses of her soul. She had stood still like a thing carved in marble for two whole hours ; a sense of oppression, of faintness, of dizziness came over her, strong though she was in her sea-fed vigour and youth.

'I am tired and thirsty,' she murmured ; 'may I go ?'

Dorât did not answer ; but he came towards her till he was so close that his lips brushed her hair, and with a touch soft and swift as the touch of the living adder had been, his hands stole round her throat, and clasped the golden adder around it. Then, unresisting, she sank into his arms.

. . . . . .

'Santa Barbara s'est donnée à moi,' thought Dorât a month later, 'et que puis-je en faire, mon Dieu?'

. . . . . .

The warmth of the summer passed ; the rains came, and oftentimes the white fogs drifted in from the Adriatic and shrouded the sculptures of the Salute, and the golden domes of St. Mark's as in a vapour of snow ; the noons were still hot and the waters still were beautiful, with fruit boats and barges piled high with grapes coming in from all the isles, and filling the city with their regal purple and gold. And in the studio on the canal of the Malcanton a great picture was finished in which his fullest genius and mastery of colour had found expression ; the portrait of a woman with the head of Sta Barbara and the body of Europa. Painted with singular rapidity and strength, it had the vitality of a sudden passion in it ; it lived, it breathed, it spoke ; it was the incarnation of Woman.

But he had given a high price for it. He had created a passion in another over which he had no control, one of those intense unreasoning absolute passions which can only exist in natures which are all sense and emotion and over which the mind has no dominance and in which all reason is dumb.

He had destroyed in her the calm of ignorance, and the simplicity of unconscious chastity ; and there had arisen in their stead one of those violent delirious exhausting tempests of love, which is ecstasy to a lover for a little time, and then appals, enthralls,

E

wearies, and burdens him, and clings to him, fatal as the shirt of Nessus.

She was a beautiful woman, yes; but when her beauty had been made wholly his, and studied, devoured, and known in every line both by his art and by his senses, her mind could say nothing to his, and he asked himself with a sigh what should he do with this adoration which he had called into being?

He had no love for her; and the violence, the immensity, the absorption of the love she felt for him terrified him. He had desired a summer week's caprice, a conquest for his art and for his senses, and she dreamed of an eternity of union. All the ardours dormant in her had awakened into life, and clung to him with a force which was commensurate with the physical strength and the splendid vitality in her. Sometimes he felt as if the adder she had killed had taken resurrection in her, and clasped him and curled round him and drew away his very life until he swooned.

He had forgotten the sheer animalism of the untutored human creature, and the intense avarice and jealousy and greed of love in a woman whose intelligence is a blank. And he was himself unreasonable. He had had no rest until he had banished her modesty, her serenity, her peaceful ignorance of passion, and yet he was dissatisfied now because she was no longer the same woman who had looked at him with those tranquil eyes of Palma Vecchio's saint.

The chill of the autumn was on the air, the mists of the autumn made the sails limp and wet, the lagoons drear and rough, the golden altars of the churches dim and dull; and Venice held him no more in her sovereign charm; he grew restless for movement and change and the cities and companionship of men. 'All of her that I care to keep is here,' he thought as he looked at the picture, 'and what can I do with the living woman?'

And he felt unkind, ungrateful, almost base; yet the poet is right:

> How is it under our control
> To love or not to love?

If he took her away with him, he knew well what the issue would be; the old, old story; the terrible idolatry on one side gnawing ever stronger on neglect and coldness, the indifference on the other which would become, under exaction and reproach, impatience, intolerance, and even at the last hatred, the cruellest hatred of all : that which spurns what it once fondly sought.

He knew it so well, and he was sorry ; for in so far as he could feel it, being of the temperament he was, he had a compassion which was almost affection for this woman who had saved his life whilst he slept in the cloister garden, and who had seemed to him on his awakening half a goddess, half a saint, and whom he knew now to be but a poor daughter and wife of rude men, a poor child of ignorance and toil, with whom his mind and his thoughts had no affinity, however closely their hearts might beat together. And how to tell her this ? he who had made himself her earth and heaven ? whose own paradise indeed she had even been for a few short summer weeks in the sweet languor of the Venetian air ?

She had saved his flesh from the sting of the adder, and he had placed in hers the dying sting of a deathless desire.

It was harsh, ungenerous, ungrateful, but he knew that he must leave her, that he would leave her, as soon as the first north winds of November should blow the sea spray over the stairs of the Ducal Palace and wash the rosy feet of the pattering pigeons in its courts.

The thought of Zuan Tron was unpleasant to him, but not intolerable as it would have been earlier in the year.

He did not feel for her that love which creates jealousy, either of the past or of the future.

What he most feared of all was that she should quarrel with her husband, and lean wholly on himself. But how could he say that to her when she came to him up the marble water steps of his house in the moonlight with such surety and ecstasy of love in her eyes?

'My poor Veronica, it would have been well for you if you had let the adder do its work on me that day,' he murmured once to her. But she would not understand. She smiled and sighed, that sigh which means that joy is beyond words. How could she tell that this adoration, this ardour, these embraces were not love—were merely the play of a grown child to whom no plaything could long suffice? Zuan Tron might kill her when he came home; that she knew; and sometimes the terror of his vengeance ran like ice through the leaping warmth of her veins. But she put that thought from her. She was not twenty years old and she was happy. To other eyes she was only Veronica Venier, the wife of Tron; but to herself, because to her lover, she was a goddess, a queen of heaven, even as the Barbara was in her immortality, even as the Europa was with her white breasts and shining hair. She had drunk deep of the philtre of vanity and passion: and when she trod the stones of court and calle she walked as one whose winged feet tread on air. Was she not more than mortal? Had he not found her fair?

'Thou art a fool, thou art a fool! But I have made solid money out of thee, and though the gallant will go with the summer, these pieces will stay behind him,' thought her sister-in-law, counting over the bright gold and the crisp notes which she had had from Dorât, and which she had laid up with her feast-day clothes with sprigs of Easter-blessed olive to keep thieves away. Zuan would be none the wiser when he came home that thieves had been at his treasure; sailors went and came and were long away, and must take their chance of what was done in their absence.

'He will be back at Ognissanti,' said Veronica once, and her eyes had a look of appeal and terror in them as they gazed into Dorât's. He looked away from them.

'Ognissanti is not here yet,' he answered, 'and ships do not always reach the port for which they are bound.'

'She is a good brig, and they know every knot of their course as I know the turns of the calle,' she said with a shudder which passed over the fine smooth skin like a cold breeze that blows over the sun-warmed waters.

'We will show him your portrait when he comes,' said Dorât, and smiled. The Othellos of life had no terrors for him; this one would no doubt take gold as his sister had taken it.

'He is only a working sailor, is he?' he added.

'Well, we will buy him a brig of his own; then he will be owner and skipper in one, and he will be always away on the seas, and you will be at peace.'

'No,' said Veronica abruptly, 'you shall not do that.'

The coarseness of the cultured mind stung and wounded the instinctive honour of the untaught nature. Then with passionate tenderness and entreaty she threw her white arms, the arms of Europa, about his throat.

'Take me away before he comes,' she murmured, 'take me to your own country, your own city, anywhere, before he comes.'

'Are you so afraid of the brute?' he asked, evading her prayer. Veronica was silent, her face hidden on his breast. Then she said slowly: 'I am afraid, yes; for as the Madonna lives in heaven, so surely, if he try to touch me *now*, will I strike him dead, stone dead.'

Dorât started and looked down on her, troubled as he was always troubled by the violence and intensity of her feeling for him. Then he smiled and caressed her.

'O my angel! he is not worth that, nor am I. We are in the city of Desdemona and of Stradella indeed, but those great passions are not of our day nor of my world. Leave me to deal with your husband. He shall not trouble us.'

He felt a coward and treacherous as he spoke. He knew that this was not the recompense she merited, not the devotion that he had promised; he was conscious that in contrast with the greatness and veracity of her love for him, this egotism must seem feeble, ungenerous, pitiful, coarse. But he could not force himself to say otherwise. He dreaded with the intensity of long selfishness the burden of her passion, the tumult of jealousy, of reproach, of violence which would come with the arrival of her husband if the truth were made manifest.

He had no physical fear, for he was a brave man physically, but he dreaded unspeakably the ridicule of the world, the harassing emotions of untutored and uncontrolled temperaments, and he intended to go away where these could not trouble or pursue him. She would be wretched for a while; women were always so: but with a season that would pass away, and she would learn wisdom and resignation to the inevitable; and he would come to her again some time in spring or summer; he had a certain affection for her, and she had been his Sta Barbara, his Europa. She would always merit some remembrance.

Veronica said nothing more that day, but on the sensuous beauty of her mouth and in the lustre of her eyes there came a look which left him uneasy; the look that he would have given on canvas to a Clytemnestra or a Medea.

'O furious Moor! have you left your sombre spirit breathing on these waters?' he thought as he passed Othello's house in going to the Zattere. It was a spirit not in unison with his own. Like all men who love pleasure he shunned and dreaded passion.

It was now late in October.

The days were short but luminous still when the mists did not drift in from the lagoons of the Lido, or from the marshes of the low-lying lands beyond Mestre and Fucina. Boats still came in with rosy sunrise reflection shed on their orange sails, and took their loads of autumn apples and pears and walnuts to the fruit market above Rialto. But soon, very soon, it would be winter, and the gondolas would glide by with closed felze, and the water would be a troubled waste between the city and the Lido, and men would hurry with muffled heads over the square of Saint Mark when the Alpine wind blew, and the strange big ships would creep on their piloted course tediously and timidly through the snow-storms to their anchorage in the wide Giudecca.

And Dorât would be away. How to tell her that he was going? How to plant that knife in her generous breast? How to banish from those adoring eyes that sleep which he had ceased to care to watch? He was not heartless, and the knowledge of how cruelly he would hurt her hurt himself; nor could he wholly forget that in the cloister garden, this woman, whom he knew he would desert, had saved his life.

The days passed, each a little shorter, a little colder, than its predecessor; and the sea-gulls and curlews, finding food rare on the northern waters, came in thousands nearer the city.

One morning Veronica went from his palace in the Malcanton to go as was her wont to mass, for it was a holy day and the bells were chiming from the spires and domes, and the coloured banners were hanging above the church doors, and the sound of sonorous symphonies and chanting choristers echoed over the canals.

Dorât lay still on his bed and gazed at her portrait. It was a great picture; a picture which would make all men envy him. Where it stood in the distance in the studio on to which his chamber opened, the brilliancy of the morning light illumined it; it looked as she had looked when he had seen her first in the cloister garden. Barely ten weeks had gone by since then, but she no longer looked to him like that. Yet she had true beauty in her face and form, and she loved him—great heavens! how she loved him!

'Voilà le mal,' he thought sadly, with the cruel wisdom of one who has been too often and too much loved, the sorrowful satiety of experience.

All was silent around him. There is but little traffic that passes by Malcanton. The tolling of all the distant bells had not ceased; high mass was being said in all the churches. He stretched his limbs out as he had done on the marble ledge of the cloister colonnade; he slept again, profoundly.

An hour had gone by when he was awakened by the voice of Veronica. In terrible agitation she cried aloud to him as she hung over his pillow.

'Wake, oh wake! his brig has been sighted off the Tre Porte, a sailor has told me so this morning. By evening he will be here in the city; do you understand? They have seen his brig coming in by the Tre Porte!'

Dorât, astonished, and scarcely awake, gazed at her where she knelt beside his couch, flung down beside it in a vehemence of emotion which shook her from head to foot.

'Do you mean your husband's ship?' he asked her, still drowsy and bewildered.

'Whose else? Take me away, take me away! He shall not touch me, he shall not look on me! Do you hear me? He will be in port by evening?'

'Yes, I hear you.'

Dorât raised himself on one arm and looked upon her with pain and trouble. He understood her; but how could he bring her to comprehend him?

'Why do you have such fear of this man? It is needless,' he said persuasively. 'He need never know, he will never know, if you have common prudence; and I will be always his best friend and yours, my dear child. Tron may be a brute, but brutes are tameable; the human brute is always tame when he smells gold, and you know that I am rich. I will spare nothing to make your life easier and happier; all things can be managed by money.'

He paused, startled by the expression in her eyes; her hands were clenched on the satin coverlet of the bed.

'You must take me away,' she muttered; 'you must take me away, far away, very far, before the brig comes in at Ave Maria.'

'I cannot do that.'

'Cannot—why?'

He was silent, embarrassed, and not knowing how to reason with the unreason of passion.

'Why cannot you? You love me,' she said, with a vibration of ferocity and suspicion in her tone.

'I love you certainly,' he answered, with a passing sigh for the falsehood which would have been, in some sense, a truth only a few weeks earlier. 'But I cannot take you where I go. You would be wretched, and I too. I should have told you this before, but I thought you understood that—that—in a word, it is impossible. I will come and see you here, every summer. We will be as happy as we have been. But you must be reasonable, dear. Tron will never know. You must meet him as you have met him before. Do you not understand? It will be painful to you, but women can always act if they choose. We will show him this picture and you will tell him you have sat for it, and then he will not wonder that we are friends, and I will buy him the best vessel that is building in the yards. Veronica, do not look like that; we will be together every year as we have been now. Only be prudent. I abhor tragedy, and all scenes that are painful.'

She rose slowly from her knees, and stood erect

beside the bed and gazed down on him; it seemed to him as if her eyes blazed fire, and the fire entered into his very soul and searched out and searched up all its littleness and poverty.

'You would have me live with him, whilst I love you?' she said slowly, while her white teeth closed on the red fulness of her lower lip.

A faint flush of shame passed over his face; the tone of the words cut him like a scourge.

'I shall not be here,' he murmured, 'and you must be prudent till we meet again; you are a noble creature, and very dear to me, but you do not understand.'

'I understand.'

An immense scorn flashed over all the beauty of her face, and quivered in her tremulous nostrils, her breathless mouth, her agonised eyes. Without a word she left him. At last she understood but too well: all the coldness, and tyranny, and cruelty which lie in mere desire were laid bare to her. Her hands clutched the golden adder which was always, sleeping and waking, round her throat, but she could not unclasp it.

'He never loved me, he never loved me!' she muttered, as she went through the lofty rooms, down the staircase, and out on to the marble water-steps.

The full light of day smote her on her eyes as with a blow. He had never loved her, but she had been his; no other should touch what he had embraced. There was no escape for her possible but in death; by death alone could she keep inviolate what had been given to him.

Her husband would be in the city at night-fall. She would have killed him if her lover had cared, but he did not care, and her own life was hateful to her.

The palace in Malcanton was quite silent and empty; there was not even a bird in the leafless branches of the fig-tree to behold her.

'He never loved me!' she said once more between her shut teeth; 'but I am his—I am as dross in his eyes to be passed on to another—but I am his; Zuan shall never touch me.'

So, knowing well what she did, she descended to the lowest of the water-steps, and thence stepped calmly from the lowest stair into the cold, yellow,

F

sluggish water itself, and threw herself forward, face downward, upon its slimy breast.

It was but a few feet deep, but deep enough to drown.

The mud soon choked her; the thick gliding current soon stole over her and sucked beneath it her shining hair, her white bosom, her beautiful limbs.

And when the brig came into port that evening, she was lying dead on Dorât's bed, with the green weeds of the canal caught in her clenched hands, and the little golden adder clasped about her throat.

POUSSETTE

Poussette

POUSSETTE was a little lady. She was seven years old. She had various races blended in her, but the result of the union, if incorrect, was charming. She was small, and very gay and agile. She was covered completely with fine silky waving hair of the palest buff colour; and she had big hazel eyes set in her little face with sunbeams always dancing in them. Poussette was a dog, and not even a thoroughbred dog; but she was aristocratic in her appearance and her tastes, and was as pretty a creature as ever carried a heart of gold on four little canine legs; flying hither and thither in animated rapture, with the happy conviction that the world is full of joys and kindness with which all dogs are born, and which they cherish until the hand of man has beaten it out of them.

Poussette had never been beaten or even menaced, so that the world was really to her a very delightful and merry play-place. From her earliest recollection she had belonged to the same human being; and this person, whatever he might be to others, was good to her, even though he had called her by such a naughty slang name as Poussette. His heart was tender for Poussette, though it was hard to everything else, as the heart of the gambler becomes through the withering dryness of an ignoble passion which is like a desert wind.

When he was in his darkest moods and bitterest hours his temper was sullen, and all his acquaintances feared him, for at such times he was quarrelsome and he was known to be an expert shot and fencer. But Poussette never heard a rough word from him. Underneath all the harshness and foulness which had overgrown his original nature, there remained in him some tenderness and some pity, and such as these were, they were given to Poussette. '*Plus je connais l'homme, plus j'aime le chien*,' has been said and felt by many worthier and greater persons than he.

The master of Poussette, like many another man, had been meant by nature for better things than those to which he had chosen to descend. He was of old family, was good-looking, talented, and gifted with that power of charming others which is as precious as a magic wand; he had been once of fair fortune and high ambition; and the accursed fascination of play had killed the ambition, scattered the fortune, and undone all the good deeds of nature. He was now, at thirty-eight years of age, a gambler, and nothing else. He had lost his estates, his position, his opportunities, his reputation, and his own self-respect; and the friends of his youth, when they saw him on the boulevards of Paris, or even of Nice, crossed over to the other side.

'We are *gens tarés*, Poussette,' he said to his companion; and Poussette cocked her pretty ears as joyfully as if to be *taré* were to be robed and crowned.

He told himself that he did not care when those who had been his contemporaries at the College of Louis le Grand no longer liked to be seen even to speak to him in the streets, but in his inmost soul the slight hurt him; for he knew that it was his own fault that he was not as they were: deputies, diplomatists, landowners, colonels of cavalry, heads of great families, men of honour and of worth, men of use in their generation. When a boy of sixteen he had fought the Prussians with fury and admirable courage as a franctireur in his own forests of Vallarec; the forests were his no more. He sometimes wished that a Prussian bullet had killed him then, under the shadow of his own great oaks, in his stainless and valiant boyhood. For he had wit and dignity enough left in him still to make him despise that which he had become, and to make him most esteem those who most despised him also.

Poussette disliked the pavement of Paris or of any city; she had been born on the Corniche in one of the fishermen's cabins and knew her way all about the coast, and everyone knew her, from the croupiers of Monte Carlo to the boat-builders of St. Jean. For several years of late she and her master had rarely left the vicinity of the Casino. More than half his life was spent at the tables, and Poussette waited patiently for him under the palms in the gardens. Children with cakes, women by their caresses, vainly endeavoured to beguile and attract her. Poussette was never to be seduced from her post. Often she was hungry, thirsty, sleepy, tired, but she never stirred until she saw her friend come down the marble stairs.

Sometimes when fits of shame and black despair were on him, and he had scarcely a franc in his pocket, he tore himself wholly away from the place, and went and lived for awhile in some fishing village, miserably and morosely ; but to Poussette these weeks were ecstasy ; her friend was all her own in them, and she trotted through the rock pools, and scratched in the sand, and basked in the sun, and slept on the rough pallet of a hut as happily as she had done under the satin and gilding of the beds at the costly hotels. Sometimes these periods of retreat would last weeks, months, sometimes a whole season, but whether they were short or long, whenever any money came to him from the remnants of land which he still possessed, or from some clever article which he had sent to the Parisian press, Vallarec at once returned to the gaming-tables. Sometimes he strove against his passion, hating both it and himself, but in the end it was always stronger than he, and the long waiting of Poussette under the palms of the Casino would begin again.

Her vigils did not make her unhappy, because she was a sunny-tempered, patient, contented little soul; but when she saw the features she loved contracted and overclouded by desperation and humiliation, then her loyal heart was vexed and her mind was troubled; she could not tell what ailed him, but she knew that something did. At other times, when hazard favoured him, which was rarely, he abandoned himself to those pleasures and consolations which neither pleased nor consoled him; and then Poussette did not understand at all; something was wrong, but what, she could not tell; yet when the noon sun looked in upon his troubled heavy feverish morning sleep, it always lighted up the little form of Poussette sitting up, mute but eager, waiting his awakening.

'If there were only a woman like you, Poussette, who would always bear with one, and never ask questions!' said Vallarec to her more than once. And his conscience smote him when he did so, for he had met such an one once, and he had used her ill. Poussette did not know what he said, but she knew that he meant something in her own praise, and jumped on his knee, and rubbed her soft ear against his.

One day he became involved in a quarrel. It had its origin in a trifle, but became embittered into seriousness and ended in his sending his *témoins* to meet those of his adversary, who was one of the best fencers in Europe. The meeting was fixed to take place outside a Belgian town. 'It comes *à propos*,' he said to himself, for things had so gone with him that he had only a few hundred francs left in the world, just enough to take him to the place of meeting, and pay for his funeral afterwards if he were killed. He believed that he should be killed. He was superstitious, like all men whose life is hazard. He wished to be killed. He was tired of the game. He was impatient of the remorse and regret which at times assailed him. For change it was too late. The gold of his youth had been scattered like dropped sand behind him. It was not in his power or that of any other man to gather it up and make it into coin. He wished to die; he believed that he should die; he was an admirable fencer, but his opponent was one of the two or three men in the world who could give him points. So much the better, he said to himself; there was only one creature who would regret him, Poussette.

The thought of her possible fate troubled him, haunted him, she was so small to be left all alone in the world; they would cart her off to a *fourrière*, or consign her to a torture table. He had a servant, indeed, a clever rascal, who had been true to him hitherto because Vallarec up to this time had been a master both amusing and indulgent, if often sorely pressed for money. But he knew his Leporello to the core, and knew that, he once dead, the rogue would sell Poussette for half a bottle of cognac and a packet of cigars.

'What can I do with you, Poussette?' he said to her, as she sat on her little hind legs before the marble balustrade facing the sea. In twenty-four hours' time he believed that he would be lying stiff and stark in a clay-field in the neighbourhood of Lille. What would then become of Poussette? Who would give her the cream off the coffee tray, the truffles off the cutlets, the little white roll out of the napkin? Who would care a straw whether she lived or died?

He thought of every friend and acquaintance he possessed, and could remember no one of whom he could ask so much as to take care of a little spoilt nondescript dog. The men would not be bored by such a bequest. The women would promise— oh, yes, they would promise anything; but that would be all. He had no illusions. He knew that a beggared man has no friends, and a dead man has no mistresses.

Then suddenly to his memory there recurred

the recollection of the one woman whom he had treated worst of them all.

Marie Desjardins had been one of the most promising pupils of the Conservatoire, and had already commenced with success her public career, when for her misfortune she had met himself. To please him she had abandoned her art and sacrificed her future. He had requited her ill. She had been the one woman who had loved him as Poussette loved him. It is the ideal love; but it is not the one for which men are often grateful. Its devotion makes them too sure, and perfect security begets satiety. Ten years had passed now since he had left her abruptly and brutally for a woman who was not worth the dust which her foot touched on a summer day. He knew what had become of her. She was living at a little house which she had inherited in the small town of Bourg (La Bresse), and gave lessons in singing and recitation: she, who, if he had never crossed her path, might have been one of the idols of the world. He told himself that it was not his fault in any way, that she might have returned to her career had she chosen; she had been only twenty then; but he knew that he lied to himself when he said so. When he had left her he had killed the artist in her, as the bird's song ceases if the bird's wing is crippled.

'Very likely she had only a small talent,' he said to himself to stifle his remorse. But he knew that the reasoning was ungenerous and that it was untrue, because her talent had been great, great enough to move the admiration of the most fastidious of critics and the most severe of audiences in the brief season during which she had been heard at the Grand Opera. So many years had gone by since then; years filled for him by the egotism of a base and destructive passion. He had forgotten her long and cruelly. But at this moment her memory returned to him. She had always been gentle and kind to all creatures; she would, he felt sure, be good to Poussette. There was time to turn aside and go to Bourg on his way to Belgium, and he went, taking Poussette with him.

It was late in the afternoon when he reached that quiet town covered up under its abundant foliage which was now in the first freshness of earliest summer. He found that she lived in an outskirt of the Faubourg St. Nicolas, and walked thither. The baseness of what he was about to do did not occur to him. To seek a woman out after so many years only to ask a favour of her was an act which in another man would have struck him as odious and mean. But his sense of shame was lost in his desire to save Poussette, and moreover the life which he had led had dulled his sensibilities and destroyed the finer instincts of human nature in him. He had become indifferent as to whether what he did were right or wrong, were just or unjust, so long as it fulfilled his immediate purpose.

The little house in which Marie Desjardins dwelt was at the end of a grassy lane, deeply shaded by limes and sycamores. It was hardly more than a cottage, but it stood in a large and shady garden of which the odours of the lilies and the mignonette were blown on the west wind to him as he approached it. 'You will be well there, Poussette,' he said to the little dog, who was running gaily along the grass, not knowing the fate which awaited her. The garden was enclosed by a high hedge of privet;

there was a small wooden gate in one part of the hedge; he unlatched the gate and entered, Poussette trotting before him, curious as to this new scene, and delighted with the garden, which was a labyrinth of blossoms and of boughs. Rain had fallen in the earlier day, and the sunshine sparkled on the moisture of every blade and leaf. The path from the gate turned suddenly and brought him in sight of the house itself, old and low with latticed windows and deep eaves where swallows nested, and a thatched porch buried under tea-roses and honeysuckle. It was so calm, so fresh, so innocent, a poem of Verlaine's came to his mind :—

> Le ciel est par-dessus le toit
>   Si bleu, si calme !
> Un arbre par-dessus le toit
>   Balance sa palme.
>
> La cloche dans le ciel qu'on voit
>   Doucement tinte ;
> Un oiseau sur l'arbre qu'on voit
>   Chante sa plainte.
>
> Mon Dieu, mon Dieu, la vie est là,
>   Simple et tranquille ;
> Cette paisible rumeur-là
>   Vient de la ville.

> Qu'as-tu fait, ô toi que voilà
> Pleurant sans cesse?
> Dis, qu-as tu fait, toi que voilà
> De ta jeunesse?

Verlaine's life had been drowned in the same swirling waters of vice and folly as his own.

Out of the fragrant darkness of the path a woman came towards him: tall, grave, fair, clad in black. He knew that it must be Marie Desjardins, and for the first time a sense of his own monstrous selfishness and insolence in seeking her out thus, came upon him. Dazzled by the sunshine she looked at him at the first indifferently, seeing in him only a stranger; then, as he drew nearer she recognised him, the blood rushed to her face and ebbed away, leaving her deadly pale; she stood still in the grassy path.

'You!' she said faintly,

Then he felt ashamed. He said nothing; only remained where he was, instinctively uncovering his head. Poussette paused also, with one paw uplifted; puzzled, inquisitive, dubious.

There was silence between those who long before

had been lovers: a prolonged silence in which the burr of the bees in the chalices of the lilies and the chattering of the swallows under the eaves were audible.

They looked at each other, mutually moved by a strong emotion; noting how time had changed them both, him the more by far, for the woman's calm and simple life, passed in pure air and healthful pursuits, had kept her younger than her years. He was the first to speak. He moved towards her with embarrassment, as though he were a boy instead of a worn-out man of the world.

'I have done wrong to come here,' he said in a low voice. 'I beg your pardon. Are you—are you —well and happy?'

'You did not come here to ask me that, I imagine,' she said coldly: the tone had scorn in it, but her voice trembled; his appearance there shook her life as a tree is shaken in a hurricane.

'No. I came to ask you a favour,' he answered humbly. The enormity of his intrusion there seemed to him as he spoke so inexcusable, so odious, that he loathed himself. She did not answer, she did not endeavour to aid his explanation: she stood under the drooping tea-rose boughs of her doorway, mute, cold, still; as still as though she had been made of marble.

He looked at her, hoping for some word from her which might make it easier for him to continue, but she did not speak. His presence there seemed to him monstrous, insolent, grotesque, unpardonable. He hastened to complete his errand and leave her in such peace as she possessed.

'Marie,' he said humbly, and his voice faltered over her, 'this little dog has been my only friend for seven years. I am going on a long journey, I shall never return; I know no one who will be good to her; I thought of you; you were always good.'

He paused, made dumb by an unusual emotion which he could ill control. Poussette looked up in his face as though she understood; she was troubled, her tail drooped. Marie Desjardins did not speak. Was she offended, he wondered, or touched, or outraged, or disappointed? Her countenance and her attitude told him nothing.

'Will you do it?' he asked at length. 'If not—I must kill her.'

'Where do you go?'

'That I cannot tell you.'

'Is it impossible for her to go with you?'

'Yes. I do not wish her to suffer.'

She was silent again, looking at the little figure of Poussette, who, anxious, wistful, and afraid, stood gazing upward in her master's face. Then she said at last; 'If you be in any extremity and have no other way—yes—leave her here; I will take care of her.'

Tears rushed into the weary eyes of the man before her; he loathed himself in that moment with a deadliest scorn.

'I thank you,' he said simply.

He lifted up the little dog and pressed her closely to his breast, and kissed her on her forehead. Then he set her gently down upon the garden path, and dropped one of his gloves upon the ground, and motioned to her to guard it.

Poussette lay down beside the glove and folded her little soft forefeet upon it. She was used to the order; and only her large hazel eyes, dewy and dilated, expressed her wonder and alarm at being bidden to stay thus in an unfamiliar place.

He bowed low before the woman whom he had wronged, and without any other farewell, with one backward look at her and the little dog, he turned and went out of the garden. Poussette lay still, obedient and faithful, her paws folded on the glove, a great terror and a great anguish gazing helplessly out of her pathetic eyes.

Marie Desjardins, as she heard the click of the gate in the hedge behind him as he passed out into the road, sank down on the bench beside the porch, and wept bitterly. She had long thought her heart dead, and the peace of the grave her portion; but now, lo! it lived again, and its life was only hopeless, writhing, poisoned pain. How cruel—with what refined and insolent cruelty!—to seek her out after these many years in her humble seclusion, and once more banish for ever the resignation which she had attained, the poor pale simulacrum of content which she had striven to believe was happiness!

He, meanwhile, went on through the blossoming

brightness of the little tranquil town and reached the railway station as the train for the north was about to move; in another moment it bore him away from the green and pleasant places which had touched him for a moment into passionate regret.

The following day the duel was fought. Contrary to his presentiment and to all probability, he wounded his adversary severely and was not himself touched.

'All luck has left me,' he said bitterly. He had wished to lose his life; it was of no use to him; he had thrown away all which had made it worth anything; an intolerable sense of fatigue was on him; even the passion which had been his ruin had ceased to move him much. Yet he returned to it instinctively, through habit rather than will.

The thought of Marie Desjardins was often present to him as he had left her in the green and quiet garden. He felt glad that Poussette was there, safe with a woman, amongst flowers and leaves. She would never be hungry, or tired, or ill-treated; she would live out her little life in comfort. But, unknown to himself, Poussette had been the tie which had still united him to the simple and healthy things of existence. Again and again he had done for Poussette what he would never have done for himself, ashamed of his softer feeling, but yielding to it for her sake; that better influence was now no more upon him, and unopposed the viler instincts in him had all their way unchecked. He missed Poussette as he had never dreamed that he could miss the presence of anything. The remembrance of the little dog patiently waiting for him in her faithful affection had often made him tear himself from the gaming tables for her sake, had often drawn him out for her sake to country places in the hills and down to the more solitary seashores. Poussette had been the one innocent thing in his existence which had had power to arouse in him still some unselfishness, and some emotion beside that of the feverish lusts of play. He was sincerely glad that she was where she was, in peace and safety, but he missed her.

He remained at the tables day and night, leaving them only for brief intervals when he was absolutely forced. He had only five gold pieces when he returned to Monte Carlo from Belgium; nothing else in the whole world; all that he had possessed was gone to the devil of hazard; he had lost everything, even the miniature of his mother; and he had no longer any power to compose anything for the press which would fetch money. There was an anæmia of the brain upon him; he could not sustain any line of thought long enough to write a page.

With his five napoleons which he had staked at roulette on the evening after the duel, he had won fifty; with the fifty he had continued to play, leaving the roulette for rouge et noir. At first he won continually, then he lost largely, then he won and lost in those maddening alternations in the coquetry of which lies the horrible sorcery of gambling. Play, like Madame de Maintenon, loves to keep her wooer '*jamais content, jamais désespéré,*' until he yields, the king his crown, the gambler his life.

He won large sums, and then played them back whence they came. Three weeks passed away thus like one long nightmare. He saw everything through a red mist, splashed with black specks.

People looked at him in apprehension. He had been well known there so many years, but he had never had this look upon his face before. He had eaten scarcely anything all this time, and slept but very little; his sleep, such as it was, being only a repetition of delirious dreams of series and of syndicates which should break the bank. There was no Poussette to awaken him, with her little soft head against his lips, and her low smothered bark of appeal which said plainly, 'the sun has risen; so long, oh, so long, ago!'

He played on and on and on through twenty days and nights, hypnotised by the vacillations of chance, getting on his features a look of almost brutalised imbecility. He had a vague dominant desire which came now and again over him: he thought, 'If I could win a hundred thousand francs I would go back to Marie Desjardins.' He had seen at a glance, that she forgave him, that she loved him; he longed for the rest and comfort of her presence. As a beggared man he could not go to her; she was poor as the world counts money, but she was rich compared to a cleared-out gambler, to a *raté* who had not anything which he could call his own except the clothes he wore.

That thought, and the memory of the green peaceful garden in which he had left Poussette, swept over him now and then like the gust of a fresh west wind. Then they passed away; and he was left to his semi-delirium, playing mechanically and seeing everything red, splashed with black aces. The authorities of the bank watched him with uneasiness. He had the look of a man who would bring a scandal upon it.

It was not so long since the Marquis de Vallarec had been one of the most noted and admired figures at Monte Carlo, but now they knew that he was ruined, out and out, and they watched him as they would have done a beggar, could a beggar have passed through their gilded portals. There was a rumour current that he had sold his dog for the five napoleons which he had brought there last, and on which he had won at roulette. The story gained credence, for Poussette was no more seen.

On the evening of the twenty-second day he lost his last coin.

He looked round him with the desperate hunted gaze of a wolf at bay; understood that he could stay there no more, and left his place: the people who had been nearest him eagerly closed up around the table, and the momentary vacuum was filled up without a second's delay. The game went on uninterruptedly; the players gave no thought to him. Only one of those observers who watched all which went on, on behalf of the bank, noting the look upon his face, whispered a few words to another person, and that person followed him at a distance, keeping him within sight.

Unconscious of the espionage, Vallarec went out through the glittering halls so familiar to him, through the gay group of fashionable visitors, through the chatter and the perfumes and the artificial light, and descended the stairs into the grounds; the orchestra in the concert room was playing the march from the 'Mage' of Massenet, and the music echoed dizzily through his brain; he felt drunk, worse than drunk, imbecile.

He had not a farthing in the world, and nothing left on which to raise a franc except the little revolver, ivory-mounted, which he always carried in the breast pocket of his coat.

He walked on, stupidly, to the marble bench set beneath a group of aloes and sheltered by mimosas where little Poussette had so often waited and watched for him. The gardens were wholly deserted; he sat down and leaned his elbows on his knees and his head upon his hands. It was a brilliant starry night, the sea was throbbing under the moonlight, the earth was at her loveliest. He had no eyes for her beauty, he was only devoured by his own misery.

As he sat thus the emissary who had been bidden to follow him approached and stood near, and with a certain timidity murmured an offer of aid, of money, of any facility desired, if he would leave the principality before morning.

Vallarec started as if he had been stabbed by a knife, and rose to his feet.

'For what do you take me?' he said, haughtily, staring at the messenger in amazement; the words spoken in his ear had been like a douche of iced water on a brain in stupor.

The other man thought doubtless, 'I take you for what you are: a desperate and cleaned out gamester,' but he was awed by the tone and the glance of the fallen gentleman, and muttered a vague apology. He did not dare to insist upon the errand confided to him, and slunk away into the shadows of the shrubs and trees.

Vallarec laughed low and drearily to himself.

'They are afraid I shall kill myself on their territory and get them into evil odour. They would pay for my transit to Paris, and perhaps give me a week's board wages as well—how kind! *Gentils seigneurs*, I will leave you a parting gift, the gift of my body, and if it frighten all your clients away out of hell, so much the better. My death will have been of more use than my life.'

Then, fearing that he was watched by the detectives from the Casino, and might be interfered with, he walked slowly away from the bench and along the gardens.

He thought of Poussette as he left the marble seat where she had so often watched for him, and he felt glad that he had placed her in safety.

His mind was clearer; the insult of the offered assistance from the bank had given him a shock which had cleared away the semi-insanity of his fury and despair; he was exhausted both from sleeplessness and want of food, but he was sane once more. He knew that he had left in the gaming-hell behind him his honour, his intelligence, his past, and his future. What was there left to live for? Nothing.

Not even Poussette! he thought with a weary smile.

Poussette was doubtless at that hour sleeping in the little cottage under the sycamores and limes of Bourg; perhaps sleeping on the breast of the woman whom he had forsaken, but who had never forgotten him.

'*On passe au côté du bonheur sans le savoir,*' he thought, recalling the words of an author whose name he could not have remembered. How true it was! he sighed heavily, thinking of Marie Desjardins as he had seen her first, in the flush and promise of her gifted and trustful youth.

He walked onward through the gardens and

left them, and traversed the lanes which led to the house where he had his one poor chamber. The door stood open, for the air was hot, not fresh and dewy as it had been in la Bresse. He went up the staircase unseen and unheard to his room which was under the roof. The little casement of it was also open and looked out to the sky and the sea. There was a letter lying on the table, but he did not notice it. He went straight to his valise, unlocked it, and took out his revolver; the pistol case and a little linen were all which were left in it. He drew the charge and loaded it again with great care; he wished to die at once and without torment. He looked for a moment out to the silvery skies and the silvery sea which were the last sights that he would ever behold. Then he lifted the revolver to his temple and felt its chill metal touch his flesh; in another moment he would have been a dead man.

But the door was pushed aside; a sound of panting laboured breath, and hurrying feet, came to his ear; instinctively he laid aside the pistol, and turned towards the doorway. Covered with dust and mud, dragging herself feebly along the floor, making little low breathless murmurs of delight, Poussette staggered up to him, strove to lift herself up on to his knee, and failing, fell back into his outstretched hands.

She had found her way to him alone from Bourg to Monaco.

'My little friend! my little love!' he cried to her, raising her bruised starved body in his arms and covering her wistful face with kisses. Her eyes one instant gazed up at him in mute and unspeakable adoration; then a sigh of a joy too intense to be borne fluttered through her little form, and with that sigh she died.

. . . . . .

Had he opened the letter lying on the table he would have seen that she had been lost from Bourg fifteen days earlier and that all efforts to trace her had been vain. Care, affection, indulgence, comfort and repose had been powerless to reconcile her to exile from her master; the peace of the peaceful garden had given no peace to her; she had never consented to accept her exile; she had been restless, unhappy, intolerant of restraint; separation, however softened and gilded, had been unendurable to her. Her faithful soul had kept its love within it, and had brooded on its loss, refusing to be comforted. When opportunity had made possible her escape, she had gone out into the unknown, unfriendly, unmerciful world, and with her own little wits unaided had found her way back to her beloved. How she had accomplished her pilgrimage none could ever know. A little thing, so small, so humble, so defenceless, all alone in the brazen brutal world of men. Her swollen and bleeding feet, her emaciated body, her rain-soaked, mud-cloaked fur alone spoke piteously of all she had endured. Alone, and with no guide but what men called her instinct, she had made her odyssey with greater courage than the great Odysseus himself.

Hunger, thirst, cold, heat, terror, cruelty, blows, bruises, unsheltered nights, unnourished days, had been her constant portion. Perhaps here and there one in ten thousand had seen the little travel-stained trembling panting thing with some degree of pity, and had given her a draught of water, a scrap of bread, a kindly touch. But oftener we may be sure she had been hooted at and stoned and left to starve, and always hindered, never helped; for she was a dog, a creature only fit for the furrier's knife or the scalpel and the poisons and the red-hot iron of the scientific torturer. The earth had had no pity for her, and had torn her feet, and chilled her body, and left her stomach famished; the heavens had had no pity for her, and had poured on her their icy rains, their piercing winds, their scorching sunrays, their harsh blazing light which showed her little creeping figure to the human devils of the streets. But she had persevered; she had found the right way through strange places and strange people, with no defence, no guide, no assistance; her only friend her own indomitable spirit, her only support that great tenacious love which can move mountains. The same genius which steers the swallow straight over desert and ocean to his summer nest, beneath some northern cave, the same marvellous and mysterious power which brings the nightingale, year after year, from the reeds of the Nile, and the roses of Hindostan, to the same green nooks in wood or garden by Arno, Loire, or Thames, had led her along roads she had never traversed, amongst crowds unkind and unknown, through peril and trial, in continual dread, and loneliness, and inability to ask for aid or pity; and with all the pangs of want and fear gnawing at her heart, home here to the feet of the one man she loved.

And looking in his face she gave one sigh of rest and joy : then died.

Earth has no guerdon for such as she. She had spent her little life—her all—lavishly, and unrewarded.

Her grave was made in the green garden at Bourg. Could she know, she would be content; for by her death she saved her master.

RINALDO

Rinaldo

SAN DOMINICO was, only a few years since, still a peaceful and poetic place, keeping close its memories of Dante and Fra Angelico, and of Boccaccio and of his ladies, and lying still and shady under the maternal knees of the Fiesolanian mountains. Its one-arched bridge, which long ago used to bristle with the lance-heads of the riders of Hawkhood and the reiters of Barbarossa, still spans the stony bed of the dried-up waters; and the deep shade of those cypresses and cedars, which not so long ago sheltered the leonine head of Savage Landor, still falls across the sward of his lawns ''twixt Afric and Mensola.'

But that is all which remains of the old pristine loveliness of the place; the axe of the peasant, the pickaxe of the builder, the greed of the money-grubber, the frightful follies of the jerry-builder, have defaced and devastated it, and the jangling bells of electric wires break in on its stillness, as the tramway trains scurry on their noisy way up and down those historic slopes. Haste, cheapness, and vulgarity—the three devils which possess the body and soul of the present age—have come even up here under the shadows of the wide woods of Doccia and the topaz and amethyst hues of the Apennine spurs; and the green world in which the lovers and the ladies of the Decamerone loitered, and laughed, and made the air musical with canzone and lute, is no more to be found save in a few leafy nooks hidden away behind grey walls, as if ashamed of their own beauty in a time which only adores dust and dirt, hurry and cunning, sham and stucco, quick profits and ill-gotten gains.

In one of such nooks as these, which still hold their place, silvery with olive and dark with cypress and ilex, there is a small square stone house, very old, very poor, which leans up against the back wall of a villa, and has above it a hillside of yellow sandstone, and around it fields intersected by fruit trees and maples. The road is far away, and from it nothing is seen of the hurrying tramway trains or the crawling carts which go up through San Dominico to Fiesole itself. The fields belong to the villa; and the cottage is all alone, with a little plot of ground of its own, and no relationship to its statelier neighbour on the hill.

Its owner is a lawyer in the city, and its occupants are, or were, a mother and grandson, with a small female child; poor people, exceeding poor people, who gathered together with difficulty the one hundred francs a year which the landlord exacted for their dwelling; fifty francs, twice a year, paid six months before it was due, after the Florentine custom and obligation, is a heavy toll on the livelihood of those who labour hardly for every scrap which they put in their mouths and every rag with which they cover their bones.

The old woman, Nonna Tessa, as she was called by everyone, had once been a well-to-do peasant on that same hillside, but her son had been but a boy of twelve when his father had been killed by a steam-engine running on the then newly-made railway at the foot of the hills, and his grandfather had died a little later of bronchitis and fever one hard winter time. The land they lived on had just changed hands when this last death took place; the new owner had not been disposed to leave a good farm to a lonely woman and a mere boy; they had received notice to quit and had come then to this little cottage to make a living as best they might. Those who have been peasants on the same soil all their lives consider it to be a great downfall and humiliation when they are forced to become mere day-labourers or hand-to-mouth gainers of their daily bread. Tessa, who was a brave and industrious woman, tried to make ends meet by washing linen, plaiting, spinning, and chicken-keeping, and the lad Rinaldo worked on the little plot of ground, and did odd jobs on the farms near, and at the stables where the diligence-horses were changed, and went into the city on errands for anybody who would so employ him, and was always cheerful, good-natured, active, and gay. It was exceedingly difficult, however, to make enough to live upon, although their wants were few and their patience extreme. The years went on, and 'Naldo grew a man and Tessa an old woman ; and, as they had not enough for themselves, he was foolish enough to take a third mouth to feed. He married, and brought a girl as poor as themselves to the little stone cabin above the olive trees. She was the daughter of a blind cobbler, and carried with her no dower whatever except her shining brown eyes and her broad happy smile. She died in childbed two years later and left a little boy behind her, who in his turn was called Rinaldo, 'Naldo, or Naldino, in the mouths of the country people.

The elder Rinaldo at thirty years old looked fifty, for he worked so hard and ate so little; he was always on his legs and out in all weathers ; and the soles of his bare feet were hard as horn, and the skin of his face and throat was burnt brown and lined like a crumpled autumn leaf. But he kept his gay and pleasant humour to the last, and was quite content with his lowly lot ; he could run into the city as fast as a hare scuds before the hounds, and could labour at odd jobs all the day through on nothing but a bare crust and a pipeful of tobacco.

His mother, though she said little about it, never ceased to regret her old life on her goodly farm. To be only a hind for daily hire seemed to her a sorry fate for her beloved son. She could see, across the valley on the opposite hillside, the long grey buildings with their red-tiled roofs where she had passed all her early womanhood; and her heart was full of longing for them, though twenty years had gone by since she had come down for the last time through the familiar fields, her boy carrying their crockery and hardware upon his back, and she some hens and a cock under her right arm and a big bundle of linen under the left one.

There the place which she had left lay, unchanged on the sunny mountain side, its blue smoke curling upward, its gable ends dotted with pigeon holes and brushed by flying doves; its pear and peach trees and walnuts standing up thickly all around it, and yet never more would she sleep under its roof-

tree and reign as mistress in its vast old kitchens.
Another family was there; a noisy, numerous, ever-
multiplying family; greybeards and beldames, sons
and grandsons, women of all ages, children of both
sexes. They were good enough people; honest,
steady, laborious; she never said an ill word of
them, but the pain of her exile was as great to
her as though she had been driven out from there
only a day before, and the iron of banishment in her
soul never ceased to harry and wound her. If, instead
of marrying that poor useless penniless creature,
her son had found a mate in some well-to-do rural
household, perhaps they might some day have gone
back thither; who could say that they would not?
But he had set his heart on a poor feckless,
friendless lass, and it had kept him back from ever
rising up one step above the humble lot to which
he had sunk. It was nobody's fault; if anyone's, it
was that of the stupid, newfangled, monstrous
machine which had struck her good man his death-
blow. What would you? What will be will be,
said Nonna Tessa with a sigh. But her handsome
boy had become a battered and weather-beaten

man, fixed in his dull place, like a mile-post in the ground, and he had been forced to toil, toil, toil on a half-filled belly all his years, instead of eating bread from the corn he sowed, and gathering fruit from the trees he pruned, as he should have done, and as his fathers and grandfathers always had done before him ; and before he was forty he died of lung disease, leaving on her hands his young son eighteen, and a little dark gipsy-like female child, offspring of a second and equally improvident marriage.

'Never mind, granny,' said the younger Rinaldo, who had grown up tall and fair and comely. 'We are happy as we are, as long as we can keep the cottage, and there is the Morianinina.'

He was really happy, a good cheery, peaceable, humorous, lissom lad, trudging about in snow and mud, as in sun and wind, and never thinking of blaming God or man.

The Morianinina or the little Moor was his small half sister, a bright quick brown-faced motherless child.

'We have always enough to eat on Sundays,'

he said to the little girl. 'Many poor folks never get a bellyful once, no, not once in the whole twelve months.'

This was the way he looked at life, without being sensible that there was any credit or courage in his cheerful content, and he wished the little brown-skinned, black-eyed Morianinina to share his cheerfulness. Times were hard; and he was often cold and hot, pinched by north wind and scorched by noonday sun, hungry and tired and wet and aching, to bed with empty stomach and up at dawn to begin the day's fatigues afresh; but he was happy despite it all. There was the old grandam, and there was the merry child, and Rinaldo, when he knelt and crossed himself on the bare stones of the church at mass, said his paternoster in unaffected gratitude. Whilst he himself had health and strength, whilst his grandmother was hale and well, whilst the child was good and merry, he felt that life was worth the living. He could not reason about it, nor weigh its claims and failures as educated people can; but the sense of contentment went with him, making his rough lot pleasant, as a singing brook will make a steep and stony path seem gay to the tired wayfarer who treads it.

When the months of February and August came round in each year, sometimes his heart did fail him; they are dreaded months to all Florentines; they are the times in which rent is due. Happy are the *possidenti* who have no rent to pay! Happy are those who own the roof which shelters them! Except to those, the almond blossom of February, the water-melon of August, bring terror and carking care with them for all, since they are the signs of the fatal dates on which the rent money must be forthcoming, or the home be broken up and lost.

To gather together the six months' rent is the preoccupation of many a day and night to the Tuscan poor. The soiled crumpled paper money is saved so hardly, stored up so cautiously, visited so anxiously, lest thieves should break in and steal it before the momentous day of its payment shall arrive! When you want anything, everything, all the days of your life; food, fuel, clothing, boots and shoes, a shirt to your back, a sheet to your bed, bread in your pot, meat in your soup kettle, when maybe a sick woman lies on your mattress, and a hungry urchin is crying for a meal, it is hard work indeed, it is an effort almost beyond human nature, to amass and hoard up that rent money, and leave it untouched whatever you suffer. To do so is one of those agonising trials of the very poor which none but they can feel and fathom. The rent was the spectre which kept Nonna Tessa wide awake in long winter nights when sleep was so much needed to make her forget her thin coverlet and her aching rheumatism. The rent was the nightmare which haunted the deep noontide slumber of Rinaldo, when he lay at rest in hot midsummer days amongst the wheat-sheaves or the bean plants, on the grass of a dusty roadside, or on the straw in a stable loft.

The little stone house had been their home now for a score of years, dear, sacred, precious; if they lost that little hut, there would be nothing for them but to descend to the dreary desolate existence, called *a dozzina*, life in the hired chamber, sleep on the hired bed, all sanctity and privacy gone, all peace and family seclusion ended. The little grey stone cottage was the one thing which gave them dignity in their own eyes, and gained them respect from their neighbours : dividing them by its privacy from the sorrier herd of tramps and vagrants, and homeless labouring folk. And every year the same terror lest they should fail to pay the rent and so lose it hung over them always; for were it unpaid, they knew that the notice to quit would be served on them without pity, and the cottage let to others over their heads; aye, were they even but a single week too late in payment.

In the winter the diligence helped them to make up the money; and in the summer, the fig-tree. When the roads were bad, the wheels of the vehicles often needed help to get out of the ruts and mud, and when the season was good the fig-tree bore a fine crop. It was the only tree which belonged to them, standing in their little plot of ground, striking its roots far underneath the walls and out towards the fields: a goodly tree, with white criteria flowering about its roots in spring, and the hens and chickens pattering, and the little brown child playing, beneath its branches in all seasons.

Rinaldo moreover had another anxiety at his heart of which he said nothing to anybody, but on which his thoughts brooded long and often. He was twenty-three years old and he was in love. Higher up on his hillside, stood a house with one big old ilex tree in front of it, and a lonely neglected garden facing the setting sun. The house had seen better days, and the garden had once been rich in flower and fruit; but the one served now as a dwelling for many poor families, and the other was now only a wild tangle of bush and briar, honeysuckle and elderberry, straggling roses and self-sown groundsel.

It was an old place, and could have told many tales of war and rapine, of lust and carnage ; and the red tide of conquest had rolled by it many a day, to pour in desolating fury over the fertile vale below. But the only thing about it which Rinaldo knew or cared for was a lancet window high up under its broad-eaved roof, where the face of his sweetheart could often be seen, and a south wall where the honeysuckle ran riot, on which she often sat when twilight fell, watching the lights shine far

far away in the evening shadows where the distant city lay. She was a fair girl with ruddy lips and rippling hair the colour of a fresh fallen chestnut; her fingers were almost always nimbly working at a tress of straw, and her feet in warm weather were bare where they hung down amongst the grass, for she was well-nigh as poor as he: but she was set high above him in his sight and his mother's, for she was the daughter of Matteo Lencioni, the Procaccio.

In the first mild evenings of spring, he was wont to stroll up there while the nightingales were singing in every clump of bay and thicket of wild rose, and lean his tired back against the old house wall, and look up into his Nita's light hazel eyes, and forget that he was ragged and hungry and poor, that he worked like a starved mule, and was never sure one day of gaining his bread for the next. He was young, he was strong, he was sanguine, and though his shoulders ached and his thighs throbbed with the fatigue of the past day, his heart was as light in that evening time as the white petals of pear and plum blossom, which the wind blew like snow along the side of the hill.

'She is not for you. She will be never for you,' said his grandmother often, who was wiser than he. But he heeded her not; and returned to the light of the gold-brown eyes as the nightingale returns to the rose-bush which it built in last year.

In the old ruined garden, there was a shrine with a stone Madonna and child half hidden in honeysuckle, and the long dark green tresses of capsicums; and there, timidly, furtively, he and she plighted their troth to each other. They were never wholly alone, someone was always within earshot; the house held many women, and one or other of them looked after the girl when her father was away. But like all lovers they were quick and fertile in invention, and escaped observation now and then; and one dusky evening, when the moon was only a slender crescent, and the mountains and the clouds were blent in one, and the only light was a glow-worm's under a cabbage leaf, they were unnoticed for a few moments, and he said tremblingly, 'If I might tell thee?'—and she said wistfully, 'If I might hear thee?'—and without more words they kissed each other and then knelt down in the wet grass, and asked the Mother of Love to smile on them.

Love is a rude thing amongst the poor; rough as their labours, coarse as their food; Rinaldo was not better nor gentler than his fellows. But in that moment, before the Madonna's shrine, he, poor, simple, dull toiler as he was, became for a moment a poet.

He took up the little glow-worm out of the grass, and held it tenderly in his hands.

'I am poor as this little worm,' he said, with a quiver in his voice. 'But there is a great light in my heart as in his; it shines through the blackest night; it is my love for thee.'

Then he set down the little beast, and left it to creep on unmolested under the honeysuckle coils, and he held the hands of Nita clasped in his own against his breast.

'They say that the ladies in the town wear precious stones that glitter like that worm,' murmured the girl, as her eyes followed the pale green light beneath the leaves.

Rinaldo let go her hands.

His mind was not awake or analytical enough to know why it was that the words jarred upon him in his momentarily exalted and emotional mood; but they disappointed him and chilled him.

'Women's thoughts are always with gewgaws,' he reflected sadly; and he, alas! he would not be able to buy her even a sham gold chain or a string of little seed pearls, but only a plain brass hoop for a wedding ring. A wedding ring! The mere idea of it brought him down from his ardour and dreams and set him face to face with harsh facts.

Would ever Matteo let him stand with her before the altar?

Matteo was good-natured and cordial with him whenever they met, but between that kind of good fellowship and the acceptance of him in a closer relationship there was a wide difference; and that he could ever bridge over the difference between them seemed to him hopeless. But his temper was sanguine, and love is always confident in its own rights and triumphs. It looked like madness, indeed, for him to dream of it; he who had the old woman and the small child to keep, and little or nothing on which to keep them or himself. But such improvident unions are made every day, the lovers trusting to chance and their own right hand to get them bread and set a roof over their heads. If prudence ruled the world, the priesthoods would have but little to do so far as the sacrament of marriage would go.

Rinaldo was no sillier or more selfish than his fellows when he said to himself that he would try and win her father's consent to his suit. With a timid spirit but a hopeful heart he saw the old man the next forenoon standing gloomily at the side of the road, watching the laying of wires and plantings of posts for an electric railway along the highway which he had trodden so many thousands of times in fair weather and in foul.

The old Procaccio was a small, grey, bony man, worn very thin in the incessant movement which his calling entailed, and battered and browned by exposure till his skin was like a shrivelled yellow leaf of December. He had been a cheery humorous companion in the days of his youth and earlier manhood, but things had gone ill with him, and now that his teeth were few and needed tender meats, he had to eat more bare dry crusts than in his boyhood, when they had been as strong and white and sound as a young dog's, and had been able to crack and crunch plum stones and almond shells. The sense that life, like food, grew daily scantier and harder to him, made his temper bad and his words bitter. He had always been a man of mark amongst his fellows, and now of later years he knew that he had lived too long, and this knowledge soured him.

The Procaccio is a man who does the errands of a district, or of a commune, carrying letters and parcels, buying small articles on commission, taking messages to and fro for the country people who are too busy to go on such errands themselves; at once carrier and postman, go-between and ambassador, pedlar and agent, gossip and money-changer. He is out in all weathers, foul or fair; he usually trots on sturdy legs grown by habit as quick in movement as if they were made of mercury and steel; he is always fond of gossip and generally fond of wine when he can get it, which is often, for no one grudges him a glass; he knows the affairs of all the countryside, their loves and hates, their ways and means, and though very generally he cannot read, he never by any chance makes a mistake in the delivery of what is confided to him. In the districts which have no regular communication with the towns except through him, he is a person of importance, more esteemed and more trusted than the postman, almost as much so as the priest. In the Fiesolanian highways, diligences and tramways have already robbed the Procaccio of his proud position and rendered him almost a nullity, but still in outlying hamlets and in the more distant nooks and spurs of the hillside he is the person most employed and esteemed whenever there is any errand to be done or message carried.

The old man who had been the Mercury of these hills above San Dominico, in days when the lordly travelling carriage of rich strangers and the strings of charcoal or baggage waggons were the only vehicles moving up and down the curves and inclines of its roads, had been in his early years in incessant request and employment, carrying many written and oral communications, and bending under the weight of numerous packets and parcels and small boxes. To many a household along that sunny mountain slope his going and coming had been the sole connection which they had ever had between their own ingle-nook and the world which lay beneath the glittering vanes and empurpled domes of the city which they could see in the plain at their feet,

> Where white and wide,
> Washed by the morning's water-gold,
> Florence lay stretched on the mountain side.

'Folks were happier in those days,' said old Matteo with the obstinacy (or the wisdom) of old age ; 'they bided at home, and stuck to their own soil, and ate and drank the food and the drink which they had baked and brewed with their own hands. They were not always careering along strange roads, and swilling stinking chemicals, and spelling out rubbishy news sheets, and bothering their brains with other people's business as they all do now. If they had a letter written for them it was really because they had something to say, and if they had anything bought for them they gave sound silver pieces, and they got sound solid goods in return. A man's Sunday jacket of velvet would wear a lifetime then, and so would a woman's woollen gown. Now it is all cheap and rotten; easy to come by and quick to go; fine as poppies and nasty as stinkwort; from the stamped cottons the wenches wear, to the dried weeds the lads stuff in their pipes; it is all cheap and rotten, cheap and rotten, and the stomachs turn and the heads turn with them. What do the trumpery clothes, and the doctored drinks, and the hurry and scurry, make of the folk? Poor, bow-legged, weak-kneed, gawky things who must get up behind a steam-engine, and be carried, like so many bales of wool, every time they want to stir a step from their doors. In my days men were up at red of dawn and trotting sturdily from hill-top to town gate, never dreaming of wanting other help than Shanks' mare, and back again by sunset or by moonrise with their business done; the sweat on their foreheads indeed, but not an ache in their whole body. Nowadays, Lord love you! only see the shame of it! They must all huddle together in a pen behind a smoking chimney, and be carried wherever they want to go, cooped up and cramped like fowls in a crate too small for them. Do you wonder the lads are stunted and bandy-legged? Do you wonder the women frizz their hair up in a touzled clout, and so long as they have a smart brooch on their breast, never care that they've holes in their stockings and a rag for a shift? In my days the girls wore the flax and the wool which they spun, and the boys footed the highroads merrily on their bare feet.'

'Father cannot forgive the iron horse,' said his daughter.

When first the iron lines had been laid down in the centre of the roadway for the iron horse to run on, Matteo had stood for hours together staring at the men laying the woodwork and the metal rails between the hedges of elder and briar-rose; seeing in those ugly bars and wires the ruin of his own small calling and the greater ruin of the people's health and manliness.

'What a poor thread-paper creature a man must be who cannot tread his score of miles on his own two legs!' he said now with the natural scorn of one who all his life had gone to and fro in all weathers untiringly.

'Are ye all born cripples?' he said bitterly to the lads who were like him watching the laying of the metals for the electric folly which was to replace his old foe the steam one. 'Are ye all come into the world withered, like a dry gourd, or lame like a shot quail, that ye must need lightning to carry ye up and down over your own native hills? The mothers that bare ye must blush for you! Before I would waste a groat on that new hobby I would wear the nails off my toes on the stones!'

The lads laughed, lazy like all their generation, and to tease him said that they would be able to save the price of the fares in the shoe leather which the new steed would spare them.

'Wear the soles of your natural feet as thick as hide like mine and ye won't need shoes at all' said the old Procaccio, setting his bare heels down on the flint and mud of the road, heels made so tough and horny by long walking that they could tread sharp stones unfelt, and crush a scorpion unstung, and stamp down an adder's head at a blow.

'Well, we shall save time by the steam waggon at any rate,' said one of the younger men.

'What is the use of "saving" time when you do nothing good with the time?' retorted Matteo scornfully. 'What do you do when you get down in the city? Burn your stomachs with made-up wines in chemists' shops, and your mouths with chopped dung which you call tobacco? Stare at the lottery offices and buy a dream-book at the wizard's? Your legs would take you down to the town full soon enough for any good you do there.'

Rinaldo, who was standing near, said timidly, 'There is not much time saved by these steam-brutes either. I can go cross country to town quicker than they can run, taking into account all their stoppages and accidents. I beat the Sesto tramcars the week before last; beat them clean by fourteen minutes.'

The Procaccio nodded approvingly and glanced with pleasure at the sinewy limbs and steel-like muscles of the younger man. 'You'll be Procaccio after me, 'Naldo, if so be as any Procaccio is wanted at all in times to come,' he said with a friendly nod as he walked away on his sturdy old legs with his head hung down and his heart heavy.

'The lads and lasses will always be going gadding to city,' he muttered, 'and the pence will burn their pockets till they're spent, and the soup will burn the pipkin at home, and the worm will eat his fill in the weedy fields. Gadabouts never kept house well, nor well drew plough yet, since the world was made.'

And he went mournfully away; weighted by his prescient sense of youth's inferiority, and by the burdens of his own old age.

In his earlier manhood he had made ends meet very regularly and fairly, for his services were in constant demand and were amply paid: food was then cheap, wine was then wholesome, and life was then easy. But an open-air occupation is apt to leave a man stranded in old age when rheumatism stiffens his joints, and those changes which others call progress carry the tide of existence beyond him, and leave him altogether aside like an old hulk bedded in a beach.

Some employment old Matteo still got, but

people thought him rusty and slow, and were apt to give their postbags and their parcels to the conductor of the tram-waggons. Those whose farms and cottages were high up above the main road, were still glad of his services indeed, but to do their errands took him far and long, and, although he hated to confess it even to his own thoughts, his knees refused to mount those steep paths and stony ascents which in other days had been no more trouble to them than they are to the limbs of the goat.

On this day Rinaldo followed him, and overtook him and touched his arm.

'You spoke well and truly,' he said shyly, for he was always in awe of Matteo. 'The calling is gone all to pieces with these steam beasts on the roads, and the folks all flying here, there, everywhere, every day. And I fear me you find the hill-work try you sorely now you are no longer so young as you were. If you would like me to do it for you I would with pleasure, and you need not give me a penny; it would be all done for friendship and goodwill.'

Matteo turned and looked at him. 'It is only

a fool or a trickster who works unpaid,' he said ungraciously.

Rinaldo coloured to the roots of his fair curls. 'I am neither, and you know it, good friend,' he said simply. 'I have time on my hands, worse luck for me, and I will gladly go for you wherever it tries your strength to go.'

'Humph!' said the old Procaccio doubtfully. 'You mean you will slip into my shoes when my feet are laid shoeless in mother earth?'

'I was not thinking of that,' said the younger man truthfully. 'If I can be of use, use me. I am only a poor devil, but I am strong as you know; and the people's papers and money will be as safe with me as they are with you.'

'Oh, as for that, everyone knows you are an honest fellow,' answered Matteo. 'No one ever said otherwise. But a motive you have in your fine words; there is always a motive in a man's smooth words, just as there is the sting as well as the honey in a bee's tail. Out with it, lad! Didn't I say to you just now that if any Procaccio at all is wanted after me, you're the best fitted for it of them all?'

Thus encouraged Rinaldo grew redder and redder, stammered and was mute; pulled his hat off his curls and put it on again; kicked up the pebbles on the hillside path, plucked off a bit of bryony and nibbled it aimlessly; then gathering up all his courage in a rush he muttered: 'The truth is—I love your daughter.'

'I feared as much,' said old Matteo, gruffly, in a tone which fell like a stone on the warm and trembling hopes in the younger man's breast.

'Lord love ye!' he added furiously, standing still in the road; 'are ye mad, crazed, daft, my lad? Be these times for marrying and giving in marriage? Could Nita and you make up wherewithal to be sure of a loaf? Are you not beggars both? Have I not lived from hand to mouth all my years, and do not you do the same? Love! Love! Go to, you poor fool! Will love fill your soup pot with beans or give you oil to moisten your crust? You are a personable boy, and she a comely wench; but will good looks last long in foul fortune? Can a shapely body be fed upon air? Holy blood of Jesus save me! Was ever such madness known? My girl has hardly a rag to her back, and this lad is as lean as a church mouse, and has one old woman and a mere babe to keep as it is!'

'Nita loves poor Morianinina,' said Rinaldo very humbly.

'Wenches always say that beforehand,' grunted the Procaccio.

'I am sure it is true,' said the younger man, 'and the little child loves her: who would not?'

'Do you call that love, jackanapes?' said Matteo harshly; 'to lead a young woman to a fireless hearth, a breadless platter, a bed of dry leaves, and a house chock-full already? Love! a pack of selfish rottenness and villany! Get out of my way with your lies and your trash!'

Rinaldo's face grew pale under its ruddy tan.

'That is harsh, Matteo,' he said with patient temper. 'Is Nita so well off now that she may not come to need a stout arm to work for her? You know best whether she is or is not. But I fear—I fear——'

'You hope, you mean,' said the old man, harshly. 'If my lass were as I should have been able to keep her twenty years ago, it is not the like of a poor boy such as you who could pretend to her. Nay, nay, 'Naldo,' he added in a gentler tone, for he saw the pain and affront which he had given expressed on the young man's candid and guileless countenance. ' Nay, it is no crime to be a poor man ; poor am I, and poor I shall always be, and the very foot-paths we tread are no more our own ; and from bad to worse we shall all go. But to wed in poverty is to triple it ; and if there be not bread for one eater, why risk the bringing of more hungry mouths into a world chock-full as it is? Put this thing out of your mind, my lad. Nita is no more for you than if she were a king's daughter.'

'I did not think you so harsh, Matteo,' said Rinaldo, his eyes filling with tears as he spoke.

'One is cruel to be kind,' said the old man, whose heart was kinder than his words, and who had a soft place in it for this well-built simple fellow who strode over the ground with such a lithe firm step as recalled to the old Procaccio the days of his own youth when he had gone from hill to valley as easily as a swallow sweeps from mountain tower to city eaves. The girl might do still worse, he knew; she might take up with some loon from the town who would mew her up in a stifling garret, and leave her in rags while he drank in wine-shops. He glanced doubtfully at the poor suitor who had already a mother and a babe to maintain.

'If you were only in regular work,' he said, with a little relenting in his tone. 'But no, no, not even then;' he added hastily, 'I cannot give my girl to misery, and there are warm men and solid ones wanting her as well as you.'

'So I know,' said Rinaldo humbly. 'But she favours me more than those.'

'Men are always dupes and dolts with no more head than a pin,' said the old Procaccio, harshly. 'She will walk with you, talk with you, and laugh with you, but she will do no more, mind that.'

'And the errands? May I not help you? You are not strong as you used to be,' said the younger man, with a sound like a sob in his throat.

'There are few errands to do, and those few, please the saints, I will do myself still for many a year,' said Matteo, offended and infuriated at the youngster's persistent and ill-judged reverence to his own age, whilst he thrust his ash staff angrily down on a heap of broken granite on the road; no man likes to have it taken for granted that age or infirmity unfits him for his daily calling.

Then he turned round and looked the young man full in the face.

'You poor blind simpleton! You think you know my girl? Because she has pretty yellow eyes, and red lips that pout and smile, you think she will sing you a love song all the summer and all the year? Pooh! get out with you for a fool! Nita is no shepherdess of a moon-sung *stornello* to be fed on the mere pipings of a wooden flute. When she gives herself for good she will want in return a silk gown on her back and baked meats on her platter. When you are older you will find out that women are all like this. Don't fret. You are a good lad. Put this nonsense out of your head and I will forget all about it, I promise you, and will speak a fair word for you with the neighbours so that you shall stand in my shoes when I be gone.'

Then he would hear no more of his daughter,

were it ever so, but struck across the fields with a gesture as though he waved aside some importunate gnat which teased him; and Rinaldo was left alone, his heart throbbing with anger and sorrow.

He went with a sick heart home to his cabin under the fig-tree. The child ran to meet him with joyous cries, and the old woman laid by her distaff and smiled all over her wrinkled sunburnt face, but he put them both gently aside and sat down on the rough bench by the door with a heavy sigh.

'You have spoken out, and had "nay" from Matteo?' asked Tessa, anxiously.

Rinaldo nodded, and his head drooped lower and lower on his chest.

'I knew how it would be,' muttered his grandmother. 'My boy, what could any man in his senses say otherwise? Is this a house to which to bring home a bride?'

'She is ill off as she is; she is used to want and to work.'

'Ay, but want and work with children tugging at your breasts, and your breasts empty and dry from want of food—that is worse. Matteo does well to save her from knowing it; a girl does not think of a woman's woes.'

'How would it be with her if he died to-night?'

'He wishes her well placed, so that when he dies he may die in peace.'

'A woman is well where her heart is.'

'Nay, not if her body pine.'

She, herself, knew all the long slow dreary toil and pain; the days which were all alike, the nights wakeful from hunger and sorrow, the carking care of children when there was no milk to still their cries, the wearing dread of the morrow, the ever-present sense that all industry, all travail, all prevention, all sacrifice, would not at the end prevent the lonely and unpitied death on the wayside stones like the death of a starved stoat.

To him, despite all hardships, the possibilities of the future seemed fair; but to the old peasant who had sixty years behind her, life had been but a hard taskmaster.

Suddenly she turned her dim watery eyes upon him.

'If I went from you,' she said slowly, 'if I went

elsewhere, maybe you would have room for the girl. I can go—somewhere—anywhere, and you will be free, my lad. To be sure you must keep the child; but mayhap she would not mind that. It is I who am in the way.'

Rinaldo started to his feet; a sense of his own selfishness smote him with remorse. He laid his hands tenderly on Nonna Tessa's shoulders.

'Never while I have breath,' he said with warmth. 'Never, oh never! O granny! could you think it of me that I would earn Paradise itself at the price of seeing you take your old bones amongst strangers? You have been good to me all my days. Whilst I have bit or drop for myself you shall share them. Matteo is a just man if hard; he would never ask me to do such a vileness.'

'It would be human nature,' muttered the old woman. 'When the foal grows a colt he wants his dam no more: he goes to frolic with the mares in the pasture. I am only a drag on you, my lad; though it may not be for long.'

'May it be years and years,' said Rinaldo, with sincere fervour; 'if your seat were empty, granny, there would be an empty place in my heart, and it would ache and ache and ache, and no smile of woman would still it. What we have seen from our cradle we want till we get to our graves.'

'And that is true, my lad,' said Tessa, gravely, for there was always within her the yearning for her old home, so near, there, over the side of the hill, and yet, to her, lost for ever.

'Jump me, 'Naldo, and do not cry!' said the little brown baby, pressing her curly head to his knees.

Rinaldo, always good-natured, lifted the child above his head and swung her up into the white blossoming boughs of a young pear-tree amongst the tender green and against the bright blue sky. The white pear flowers, the dark, ruddy child's face, the blue radiant air, made a glad picture above his head, but he saw it dimly through his tears.

The old woman, the little orphan, the lowly home, these were his portion, in these his duty lay; he felt that never would there come thither to him the girl who sighed for the stones which shone like the glow-worm. She had kissed him in the moonlight amongst the honeysuckle flowers under the Madonna's placid smile, but she would never share his daily lot.

Matteo had spoken; and believed, with the credulous self-sufficiency of age, that his mere word would suffice to put out the marsh-fires of an imprudent and unwelcome love. He rated his daughter soundly, and threatened to mew her up in a convent if she dallied and toyed with a penniless lad like the one whom she now favoured; he watched her sharply for a few weeks, and sent her to her room at nightfall, and took away the pence she made by her plaiting; but after a little time his zeal cooled, and he forgot to look after her in the long light evenings of the early summer, or to learn what she did in the days of his absence, when he was trudging along the hillsides or through the streets and lanes of the city.

In such hours she and Rinaldo met as lovers ever have done since the world was young; met hastily, furtively, fearfully, but all the more sweetly for that. The soft owls flitting through the shadows, and the nightingales singing under the bay leaves, were their accomplices and confidants, and kept their secret. Anita, when she went with her father to Mass, her golden eyes cast down, and her rebellious hair plaited and wound close to her head, looked the most docile and shy of maidens; and the old man was satisfied that she obeyed him in letter and spirit.

'Nip a folly in the bud and it is done with, without fret and fuss,' he muttered to himself complacently, assured of his own shrewd wisdom.

'You need only be firm with children to bend them just as you choose,' he said aloud with perfect contentment to the priest of the church of San Domenico, who, having seen farther than he into the darkened mirror of the human soul, gave but a qualified assent to the opinion.

The working days were always full from April to November; and when the sun went down behind the opposite hills, leaving a dull grey haze of heat spread all over the valley, Rinaldo was so tired out this midsummer that it was only the wings which passion lends which could have borne him up the hillside on the chance of hearing the girl's naked feet come brushing the dry grasses of the footpath while the night crickets chirped shrilly to the moon. It was only a chance, and five nights out of seven he would watch and wait for nothing, for if her father sat smoking on the wall, or the women who lodged there were loitering and chattering in the road, she could not steal away unseen, but was forced to sit patiently by the old man's side plaiting her strands of straw till the ninth hour tolled from the church clocks down in the vale below, and lights were put out and house doors bolted.

These hillsides in spring and summer evenings have infinite repose and beauty in them. They have the solemnity of the mountains and the softness of the plains. The curves of the many mountain spurs fold and slope tenderly into each other in dream-like confusion and harmony. Beneath the cloud-like foliage the nightingales sing and the owl hoots. Until the moon rises, swallows hunt circling through the shadows, and bats, their mimics, wheel and whirl in rapid gyrations which have not the swallow's grace and calm. Distant voices echo now and again from hill to hill, coming from forms unseen.

The scent of pressed thyme, of bruised bay, of fallen rose leaves, is everywhere upon the air. Against the luminous sky cypress groves and ilex woods rise black and solemn, holding the secrets of dead gods and murdered men within their depths.

The months of summer were the busiest of the year to Rinaldo.

In summer all those whose labours are irregular and gains uncertain are in request and can be sure of occupation from sunrise to sunset. There is water to be fetched in casks for lands which are springless; there is hay to be mown and stacked, and grain to be reaped and threshed, there are errands to be run for the idle people who are basking in the villa gardens, there are hedging and ditching, carting and marketing, there are not hands enough on any of the farms for the field work then, and any man who is hardy and useful may be sure to make his day's wage every day and to get his meals as well from the peasants with whom he works. In the summer, there can be saved up and laid by enough to pay the autumn house rent, and something too left in store for the hard mid-winter weeks. But this summer his joys and his fears troubled his reason; he set his sheaves head upward, which is never done in his country; he left the bung out of his water-barrel, so that he arrived with it empty, and once when he was sent into the city for groceries, he brought salt for rice and soap for sugar. But his neighbours knew that he was moonstruck with his first love, and laughed at him and forgave him.

The days were long and hot and toilsome, but the noonday rest was good when sleeping in the shade of a stack or a hedge, and the evenings, though his limbs ached and his strained sinews throbbed, were filled with that delighted expectation which is the lover's heaven.

His grandmother saw his distraction with a quaking heart; but she was afraid to say much lest it should look as though she were selfishly afraid for herself and the child. After all, she thought, this fever would pass like all such midsummer madness; Matteo would never give his daughter to a poor lad; no real harm would be done; such love-crazes blow away into air as the golden dandelion flower changes into snowy gossamer, and melts away upon a puff of wind.

Rinaldo was sure that his love was returned, but that knowledge, though sweet, could not content him. The brief twilight meetings, the hurried words, exchanged in fear and trembling, were but meagre food for his passion and left him discontented and disconsolate, and he had an uneasy sense of the coquetry and capriciousness of Nita's nature. Many a trifle showed it to him, blind though he was with the glamour of illusion. The first figs which were ripe on his tree he gathered one day, and put in a basket with green leaves, and carried to her at twilight. She smiled, and set her white teeth in the rosy pulp of one, but she said with a grumbling little sigh, 'If it were only the precious stone like the glow-worm's lantern!'

Rinaldo sighed too, more heavily, for he would have given his right arm to be able to hang her about with all those collars and armlets of glittering gems of pearl, of coral, of silver, of gold, which he saw whenever he crossed the goldsmiths' bridge in the city.

'Look you, Naldino,' she said coaxingly, 'Nerino's Maria has had such a nice brooch from her *damo*;

a big, big thing, all colours and rays and set round with golden flowers; and yet he is poor, quite poor, as you know; he is only a working smith, but he loves her—yes—he loves her!'

'Not as I love you, my Nita,' said Rinaldo, stung with jealous hatred of the shoeing smith.

'Humph!' said the maiden doubtfully, and she threw aside the fig which she had tasted and felt the green smooth skins of the others doubtfully. 'They are not ripe,' she said slightingly; 'you may take them back to your old sow at home.'

'They were the first of the year,' stammered Rinaldo, 'and I wanted so to bring you something.'

'One can gather figs as one walks in this month anywhere,' she answered unkindly. 'It is not hard unripe windfalls which you would bring to me if you were like Maria's Nerino; it would be something solid and fine and worth showing. Maria's Nerino sold his Sunday coat to buy that brooch!'

And she began unkindly to cast fig after fig down the grass path, putting a cruel scorn of the humble gift into the careless action.

Your father said I was a fool to think you would

be true to me!' said Rinaldo, with a sharp anguish at his heart.

'Did father say that?' she asked, with a passing smile.

'Aye truly, he did; he said you would want a silk gown on your back and roast kid on your platter! And alas, alas! my dear, I shall never be able to give you aught save a cotton print and a dish of beans, and perhaps not always even that!'

Anita was mute, rolling to and fro one of the despised figs with her foot.

'If you were alone we could do well enough,' she murmured.

'Alone!'

'Yes; as you ought to be. If your grandmother went away and the child, we could do well enough; father would come round then.'

Rinaldo grew very pale.

'You know,' he said in a hushed tone, 'they are part and parcel of me; if I die they must do as they can, poor souls, but while I live, I am theirs, they are mine. Why will you say such cruel things Nita? You do not mean them.'

'I do mean them. If you loved me you would see as I see, you would have no thought but of me; if you loved me you would get rid of the old woman and the child, then you could come and live with us, and take up father's business after him, and we should be as happy as the day is long; but you do not love me; you are only made of words, words, words—and unripe little figs!'

And she kicked the basket over with her small bare toes, laughing sulkily, and set the fruit which remained in it tumbling amongst the grass.

'O Nita!' he cried, with a cry of such pain that it stopped her in her unkind trivial sport.

She looked at him, and her golden eyes shone with pleasure at her power. She threw her arm about his throat and laid her cheek against his for a moment. 'I was only joking, and father is a fool,' she whispered. 'But bring me a brooch like Nerino's Maria's, for I cannot sleep for the envy of it; and then we will wait like good children for what may happen, and the Madonna will be kind, and smooth the way for us!'

'If you loved me you would not care for gewgaws!' he said sadly, his whole being yielding to the seduction of her caress, but his reason chiding and doubting her greed.

'Bring me them, and you shall see!' said Anita sliding out of his hold, and flying down the hill through the gloaming, as a hare scuds under the dark leaves when she hears a dog stir, for she heard her father calling from the road below.

Rinaldo stood, and looked down on the poor despised green fruit trampled into pulp in the grass. A vague hateful sense of what her father had meant in speaking of her came upon him, but he thrust its doubts away. All women were vain creatures, so all the ballads and fables said. She was not more so than all the others; she was young and foolish and wanted to enjoy one of those little triumphs which are so dear to the female heart. He was her *damo*, though their wooing was secret; to whom should she look for gifts if not to himself? And he had never been able to give her anything; not even a blue ribbon for her hair or a silver gilt circlet for her ears! He had thought that she would understand and would not mind, knowing as she did how things were with him. But it was natural that she should despise the fruit and think meanly of him.

Suddenly the girl looked back, returned, and laughed in his melancholy and tragic face; she paused a moment before him, caught up one of the figs, nibbled at it for an instant, and then thrust it against his lips.

'I have made the sour thing sweet for you, my sulky one!' she said in his ear; and then darted away through the gloom. Rinaldo passionately kissed the fruit where her lips had touched it.

'If only we could go before the priest!' he said more than once restlessly. But it was impossible. No priest would have dared to wed them secretly and without the consent of the father and the preface of the civil rite.

In the old time, he had heard tell, that if two lovers only kneeled down in church or chapel at High Mass during the elevation of the Host, and joined hands and pledged themselves, it made a marriage solemn and binding, though secret. But those days were over. Love, like all other things, was caught and caged and clipped, numbered, registered, and licensed, and made to pay taxes to the public purse. Yet the idea of that old romantic stratagem haunted him. It seemed to him as if, were she so to kneel down with him at that solemn moment, she would belong to him more completely than she did now, would be unable afterwards to go back from her promise and plight herself to any other.

He unfolded his daring thought to her, and was laughed at for his old-world fancies. But he clung to the idea and returned to it again and again, whenever they got a few stolen minutes in the sultry odorous eves amongst the yellowing grass and the chirping crickets.

'If only you would meet me in the city some Sunday,' he said to her again and again. 'It would be easy. You go sometimes to see your Aunt Zaida. We could go into some church and kneel down and join hands at the elevation of the Host. It would be a sacrament.'

'It would be nothing at all,' said the girl with contempt.

'But I should feel as if you were mine!' he

urged, 'you would feel as if I were yours. The saints would know; that would be enough. We cannot go to Mass here together, but there in the town we might.'

'Would you give me a necklace if I did it?' said Nita, with a saucy smile; 'a necklace and pins for my hair? Blue stones or red; something very good?'

'I would buy you every stone in the jewellers' shops!' he cried, so dazed with rapture that the greed of the condition never struck him.

'If it bound lovers together in the old time, it must bind them so now. To be together when the Host is raised, and to kneel down hand in hand when the priest blesses the people, it is enough to wed us for time and eternity!' he added, with kindling eyes and an awe-stricken voice.

'Hush!' said Nita with a flushed face and a bashful smile. 'Father forbade us, you know, even to think of each other. To be sure it would mean nothing, and I could have Aunt Zaida with me; but no—it would never do; it would be wrong; we should jest at the Holy Spirit.'

'We should not jest. We should give all our

lives to each other,' said Rinaldo with passion and earnestness. 'It would make me feel as if you were mine, and you would not take Tonino's trinkets after laying your hand in my own before the priest.'

The girl smiled; in her own thoughts thinking what silly geese were men. Tonino was a sturdy wheelwright of Careggi, who paid his court to her on holy-days and feast-days.

'I see no sense in what you want and a deal of danger; father might come to know,' she said stubbornly, 'and if I take Tonino's presents, it is no business of yours; you give me nothing yourself, except figs!'

'You know I have nothing!' said Rinaldo, stung to the quick.

'You must have something sometimes, for you pay your rent.'

'There is the rent money—yes. We deny ourselves sorely to put it by——'

'But you deny yourself nothing to give me pleasure!'

'I would cut the heart out of my breast to give you pleasure!'

'Pooh! those are words. Tonino gave me these.'

She shook her pretty head and made some little silver bells in her ears tinkle a tiny chime.

'I will choke him dead like a dog!' swore Rinaldo. 'How dare he!—the great slouching black-skinned brute!'

'He is big and brown as a man should be. You look like a girl with your pink cheeks and your yellow hair.'

'You do not love me! You hate me, or you could not torture me so!'

'How can I love you? You are so mean, so cold, so niggardly; you are always thinking of saving money.'

Such scenes were renewed again and again; she teased, tormented, caressed, ridiculed, flouted, tempted, and excited him until he was mere wax in her hands.

The girl laughed at him, and chided him, and said such ideas were rusty and romantic follies; no one did such things as that nowadays. His heart was set on one thing, hers on another; the end of all her coquetries and his entreaties was that she agreed to do what he wished on one condition. She would meet him down in the town, and go into church with him during High Mass, but he was to buy for her whatever she liked out of the shops on the jewellers' bridge.

The baseness of the bargain never struck his mind; he was too intoxicated with the certainty that what appeared to him a sacred and inviolate bond would thus be formed between them. He knew it would not be a legal tie as law was ruled in those days, but it had held good as a marriage in times better than these, and a true marriage it seemed to him that it still would be.

When she should have knelt down by his side in the press of the people, and their hands should have met, and they should have bowed down their heads while the Host was raised, they would be indissolubly wedded, so he thought; no jealous dread of the black-browed wheelwright would torture him any more. They would belong to each other, and nothing would be able to part them.

When she had promised to do this thing, Rinaldo

was stupefied with joy. He scarcely knew what he did or what he said. Men joked him, he did not care; his employers scolded him, he did not hear. The long, hot, light days went on in a blaze of sun and of delight. He worked very hard, he worked early and late; but his heart sung in his breast like a bird in pairing-time.

She could make his hard life sweet for him as she had made the fruit by the touch of her lips; but would she do it? Did her father know her better than he did? Would she give her playtime and amorous fancies to him, but her solid troth to some other for sake of smart clothes and baked meats?

When he went down the hillside, home, the evening had waned into night, the round moon was golden amongst dark clouds, the ebon shadows of the fig-tree and of the little stone house fell black across the white and dusty highways. All around was still, except for the chirp of crickets in the dry grasses, and the soft hoot of the small moth-hunting owls.

In the moonlight he saw the old woman sitting on the bench before the door, and the little brown form of Morianinina cast down on its stomach beside her in the deep repose of slumber.

'Why is not the child abed?' he said, irritably, for the sight of these two who filled and over-filled his house were unwelcome to him at that moment.

'It is hotter in bed than up; I had not the heart to force her; you know she always likes to see you come in before she sleeps,' answered Nonna Tessa, surprised to see her boy's face so overcast.

'Am I to suit my hours to meet a baby's whims?' said Rinaldo with increasing irritation.

'No, dear, no,' said his grandmother, meekly. ''Tis only the child is fond of you, and it isn't worth while to flout any love—'tis a rare thing in this world.'

The child, roused by their voices, gathered herself up on her hands and knees and shook her rough hair out of her eyes. 'Is 'Naldo cross?' she said timidly to the old woman. 'Won't he carry me in to bed?'

'Not I, I am not a brat's nurse!' said the young man fiercely, and he strode past the bench in at the open door.

In the middle of the night, when his grandam and the child both slept, he went to a corner of the shed where the hens were kept and the faggots which were used for firing, and the tools which had belonged to his father, and he turned the wood aside and pulled up a brick and took out a broken pipkin. In the little pipkin were some dirty five-franc bank-notes, a little silver, and a good number of bronze pence. It was the money for the rent, fifty francs exactly.

As long as he could remember anything, the money for the rent, in its slow accumulation, had always been kept out of sight there in that corner of the shed under the brambles and dry bracken. As a boy he had hung on to Tessa's skirts when she had gone to count it over; and the mystery and magnitude with which it had been then invested in his eyes hung still about that dark corner now that for several years it had been his own earnings which had been buried there, and his own hands which had had the right to lift them up and count them.

Looking over his shoulder quickly as though he

were a thief, he turned the hoarded money out on to the battened earth of the shed floor. One, two, three, four, five, six—he began to count it over as he had done nearly every day before to make sure that the sum was right. Put all together, paper, silver and bronze, there was the money exact; fifty francs, scraped together with hardship and privation and endless toil; bound to be paid to the man in the city before the twenty-fourth of that August. The season was now July; the tenth of July; and the weeks which lie before a rent day are always weeks which scamper with cruellest haste and have shorter span in them than any other weeks of the year.

The money was certainly his to take, but if he took it or part of it, how could he ever make it up again by the end of August, barely seven weeks time? He counted it all out, and laid it before him on the ground, whilst the startled hens took their heads from under their wings, and stared with their little round eyes at the oil wick, wondering if it were sunrise.

Every piece of the money had, as it were, a drop of blood, a tear of labour and sorrow, on it; to put by this, he had gone without a pair of boots for feast days, and to set aside that he had done without a draught of watered wine at noondays; even every penny had a physiognomy and a story of its own: to put together all these stout, dirty, defaced pieces of metal, how many sacrifices of appetite and longing had he made! One coin in especial, a silver coin of ancient date, which he knew again by a little cross which he had scratched on it, had a whole day's history in it for him, for he had gone down into the town with an empty stomach and had come back fasting, that he might add it to the store in the pipkin. How well he remembered the day, a soft glad day of the last Lent, with narcissus and lilac everywhere, and all the town bells ringing; how his empty body had yearned, and how his dry throat had gasped as he had passed the wine-shops and the food stalls, gripping hard that silver coin, and carrying it unspent all the way home, sick with a day-long hunger, but still so glad and proud!

'Dear lad! Good lad!' Tessa had said when he had thrown it down on the table with a laugh, and set his teeth ravenously into a dry hunch of bread.

He sat on the mud floor now, with his oil wick beside him, and spread out all the money slowly.

It represented for him and his, half a year of safety, of shelter, of peace. If he spent it, never again would he be able to gather up such a sum by the day it would be needed. Out into the dust or mud of the road would go the old woman, the young child, the familiar sticks of furniture, the rough beds on which they slept the heavy slumber which follows on toil.

All the respect and self-respect which go with a home, inviolate and unshared, would be gone; there would be nothing for the future but the noise and shame of a hired lodging.

And it was not even wholly and solely his own. Amidst it, part of it, was the money his grandmother got for the eggs, and by the bees; nay, there was even one bright half-franc which had been given to the child by a stranger for some field-flowers, and which she had brought to them in glee and pride, crying delightedly, 'Morianinina too can help to pay the rent.'

No. It was not his to take. And yet Rinaldo,

M

with the first blush of shame which had ever dyed his cheeks red, swept the various moneys all together into his left palm with a hurried action, slid his hand into his trousers pocket, and holding the pocket tightly with a nervous grip, kicked back the faggots and branches over the now empty hole, and blowing out his light, went noiselessly out of the shed and up to the loft where he slept.

At break of day he was out of the house.

It was a feast day, that of the Purification. Some bells were ringing for matins, but the chimes came from the firwoods above Majaino; and no other as yet replied to them. The air was clear as glass and cold, with that delicious coldness of summer dawns in Italy. No one was stirring, the hills were bathed in cloud, the plain far below was hidden in vapour. Rinaldo stood and looked at the familiar outlines of the landscape with a strange, vague fear upon him; he felt as if he had committed a crime. The old woman and the little child were lying asleep. He felt as if he had cut their throats in their slumber.

'It is my own; it is my own,' he kept saying

with his hand tight clenched on the money. But he could not persuade himself that it was truly his, since it had been earned by mutual toil. It had had a common purpose. It was a common property; theirs as much as his. He felt as if the little silver piece which had belonged to the child, burned his fingers as they closed on his pocket where the coin lay.

'What folly!' he said angrily to himself. 'It is all mine; I keep the child and I keep granny. Any trifle they may make comes to me by right. It is all mine.'

But although he said so, the sophistry did not satisfy him.

He was by nature essentially honest, and he knew that, though the law could not have touched him for it, he had done a dishonest thing. But though he repented, he did not atone. The money weighed like lead upon him, but he did not think once of turning back to put it again in its hiding place. He could not bear to think at all. The spectre of the August day to come, when the rent should be due, and there would be no money forthcoming to pay it, pursued him like his shadow as he ran down the road which he knew so well that he could have travelled it blindfolded.

There was no reason why he should go so early into the town, but he felt that he could not meet Nonna Tessa's eyes, nor even bear to see the little brown face of Morianinina lifted to his own. It was still earliest morning, and the streets were empty, and the houses closed, when he reached the jewellers' bridge, and sunrise, rosy and radiant, was shedding its light over the reaches of the river; the little shops on the bridge were unopened, and their green wooden shutters covered them like so many closed Noah's Ark boxes. He sat down on the parapet under the arches, his hand all the while on the money, his heart heavy with shame and yet beating wildly like a caged bird's wings with longing and with hope,

He knew the city well, having come thither often; and yet it seemed strange to him and hostile; its silence oppressed him; it seemed like a city of the dead; he had eaten nothing, but he did not think of that; he thought only of the coming of Anita.

Slowly the light broadened on the river, and the blue smoke rose from the chimneys, and the windows and doors of houses opened, and mules and horses with their carts came over the roadway, and itinerant sellers carrying their wares screamed to the housewives to come down and buy. All the morning life of the town awoke and the many bells pealed from spire and tower, seeming to call to each other like friend to friend.

Amidst all the noise and stir and confusion which seemed to him so harsh, after the sweet melodies of his own bells, Rinaldo sat immovable under the arches waiting for the jewellers' and silversmiths' shops to open. At last, one by one, the dusky shutters were taken down, and the little queer square dens with all their treasures close-packed and their back windows like port-holes showing glimpses of the water, were opened to the passers-by. Rinaldo's eyes felt dazzled at all that glitter and glisten of gold and silver, with the blue of turquoises, and the pale rose of coral, and the jewels of reliquaries and chalices shining there in the full sunshine of the morning within those little dusky cabins. The shops were to stand open until noon, and the money was in his breast pocket. Would she never come? Would she fail him after all? His gaze strained to see her through the crowd. He sat staring at the southern entrance of the bridge by which she was sure to come.

'She cannot doubt that I love her now?' he thought, while his pulses beat, and his ears grew full of the noise around and his conscience stirred in him fitfully, restless yet sluggish, like a drugged watchdog.

At last he saw her; the sun shining in her amber-like eyes, a black veil thrown about her head; a smile playing upon her rosy mouth. She looked from right to left; much at the jewellers' windows, a little at the loitering people, not at all at Rinaldo.

'Nita!' he cried with a shout of joy, which drew all eyes upon him; then she saw him and came up to him quickly.

'You have the money?' she asked.

His heart fell.

'Yes,' he said moodily; 'yes; I have brought it all. But——'

'How much is it?'

'Fifty francs. But——'

'It is so little, Aunt Zaida!' said Nita with vexation, turning to the little dirty old woman who accompanied her.

'It is all I have on earth. A king could not give more than his all!' said Rinaldo piteously.

She shrugged her shoulders, and turned from him to gaze at one of the windows.

'You had best make haste to buy, or the young man's mood may change,' whispered the woman whom she called her aunt.

'I make his moods as I please,' said Anita, pettishly. 'Oh, the beautiful, beautiful things! Look at these corals, and those big red stones, and these blue ones, and that necklace and cross in filigree! Oh dear, oh dear! We can get nothing worth getting for fifty francs. If you had only your pockets full of gold, 'Naldino!'

'We shall miss the first Mass,' murmured Rinaldo impatiently; his thoughts were far away from the jewellers' windows.

'Pooh-pooh!' said Nita, scornfully; 'there is more

than one Mass in a morning. Let us go in; say not a word, 'Naldo; leave Aunt Zaida and me to bargain.'

Rinaldo followed them in and out, of shop after shop, standing behind them whilst they admired and expatiated, wondered and cheapened, handled this and tried on that, taxing the patience of the sellers severely, and straining that of Rinaldo almost to bursting. At last the momentous choice was made; tired out with her own hesitations, and broken-hearted because she could not buy all she saw, she decided at last on a set of coral; the thing of the most colour which she could find come within her price; it consisted of earrings, hair-pins, and a necklace all of red coral in silver-gilt filigree.

'It costs seventy francs the set,' she said to her lover. 'Pay for it. Aunt has beaten them down from a hundred and twenty.'

'But I have only fifty francs!' he muttered in sore distress, feeling the seller's eyes upon him.

'Give your watch in; they will take it, I think,' said Anita, and she plucked out of his waistbelt an old silver watch. It had been his father's, and in direst stress and strait of poverty he and Nonna Tessa had never dreamed of parting with it. They had often gone supperless to bed, but the old watch had always ticked the night hours by their bed.

'The watch! Oh, not the watch, Nita!' he stammered, piteously. 'I can never go home to granny if I have lost the watch.'

'Tell her it was stolen in the streets,' said Anita, and she handed the poor old silver case to her aunt while the Jew seller waited with the set of corals in his hands.

In a few moments more the watch was tested, weighed, priced, and gone; Rinaldo had paid away also the fifty francs; and the set of coral was in the possession of the Procaccio's daughter.

'It is a poor thing compared to all the jewels,' she thought discontentedly; 'but at least it is much finer than Nerino's Maria's brooch.'

The jeweller was meanwhile looking at the youth who had paid for it, with an amused and compassionate smile.

Rinaldo was confused and bewildered. He

scarcely knew what he said, and the sudden loss of his poor old friend, the watch, stunned him.

'Let us get to church,' he murmured piteously in Nita's ear. 'Santo Spirito is the nearest church, I think. Come, come, quick, for heaven's sake.'

'Mass is over,' said Nita, coolly, 'and we can go to church well enough at home.'

'But you said——!'

'Never mind what I said. What I say now is that I must get home, or father will be there before me.'

'But you promised——!'

'No woman is bound by a mere promise,' replied Nita, who was putting on the coral before a little bit of mirror in the inner den of the shop.

'Is coral becoming to fair folks?' she asked doubtfully of the old Jew who had sold it to her. He rubbed his hands and shook his head with a smile.

'You should have chosen turquoises; turquoises suit red blondes like you, my dear.'

'But we have only such a little money!' said Anita, with a pouting discontent as she stuck one of the coral pins in her auburn braids. Rinaldo, heedless of the dealer's presence, and of the curious eyes of the people crowding round the doorway, seized her by the arm with unconscious violence.

'Will you come to the church or not? Have you brought me here on a fool's errand?'

Nita laughed, her pretty red lips, as bright as the coral, curling gaily up at the corners, and her light eyes glittering with amusement and anger.

'On a fool's errand? Eh! it is only fools who will trot about on those errands! High Mass is over by now, and I am in haste to be home. I will wear your corals—oh yes, that I will—at least, until somebody gives me something better!'

And she laughed saucily and long, encouraged by her aunt's approving titter, and the jeweller's cunning smile, and the grins on the faces of the passers-by who had paused before the door.

The face of Rinaldo grew red as fire, and then grey and pale under its sunny brown. The pavement and the river water, and the jewels and the ornaments, and the blue sky above them, were all blent in one swirl and eddy of light before his eyes, and the heat in his brain scorched him like hot iron.

'You have cheated me!' he shouted, his voice shrill as the scream of a wounded horse. 'You have cheated me! You have got all I had upon earth and you play me false!'

The shallow soul of the girl was startled into a sudden fear, but she was bold and cruel, and proud of her power. She set her hands on her hips, and stood in the doorway of the shop, and laughed impudently in his face.

'All you had! A fine store to marry upon! You are a pretty boy, 'Naldino, but you are a goose. Father is right. Trystings and kissings are nice sugared cakes, but in marriage one wants roast kid and silk gowns. When I do go to church, my lad, it won't be for a set of coral!'

Then she drew her veil closer about her head and nudged her aunt, and nodded to the old Jew salesman, and was about to elbow her way through the little crowd which was listening to her and egging her on because she was so pretty, and saucy, and amused them. But Rinaldo stood between her and them. He had thrown his hat on the stones, his eyes blazed like flame, his teeth chattered with rage, he breathed hardly and very loud.

'Look at her, ye townsfolk!' he shouted. 'A lass of the hills, as simple as a sheep, as coaxing as a cat, all wiles, and winningness, and softness! She has taken my all, and she promised to go before the priest with me; and now she has got what she wants, she jeers and flouts me! Body of Christ! the street-walker in your lanes is an honester soul than she! She shall never live to grin and to greet in another man's face, and fool him as she has fooled me. Ah! cursed red lips which are like a rose!'

And he struck her on the mouth violently, so that she fell backward on the floor of the jeweller's shop, and, leaping on her, he snatched the coral off her throat, her hair, her arms, and struck her with it in her eyes, on her cheeks, on her lips, in furious ceaseless blows, which made her face a bruised mass of bleeding flesh, smashed and shapeless like the broken coral toys.

The bystanders shrieked for help, but no one dared venture within, to touch or stop him. His passion spent itself in that one mad and brutal act; he gave a scornful kick with his foot to her prostrate body, and spurned it from his path, then he walked out of the shop, his head flung back, his nostrils dilated, his breast heaving in a tumult of rage and remorse.

No one dared to put a hand on him. He had done what it was his right to do, and the sympathies of the populace were with him. 'Women change a good youth into a mad devil full many a time,' said a greybeard amongst the crowd, as Rinaldo, looking neither to right nor left, thrust the people aside and passed on over the bridge.

When the guards came up, it was too late; he had mingled with the multitude pouring out from the churches, and was lost to sight in the dark and tortuous streets of the old 'Oltrarno. They could only lift up the prostrate form of the girl and carry it to the nearest hospital. Her life was in no danger, but her beauty was ruined for ever.

All that day Nonna Tessa watched for him at

home. When she had gone to let out her hens at sunrise, she had seen the disordered state of the faggots and fern, and had found the hole disturbed and the money vanished.

'The lad has taken it to throw away on the wench,' she said to herself.

Rinaldo had gone without a word to her, and gone down into the town. When the day had drawn to its close and the sun set, some gossips came up the hill breathless, and told her the story as they had heard it.

'They have come for Matteo,' they said, when the tale was done; 'he has gone down to the town like one mad. It seems your lad bought a power of goods, and then broke them on the girl's head; it is a bad job; he is in hiding. Who would ever have thought it of him, such a docile, good-humoured gentle youth!'

Nonna Tessa grew rigid as though she were made of stone, but she went on with her spinning.

'The boy is a good boy,' she said simply; 'if he have done wrong he hath been provoked.'

More than that the gossips could not extort

from her, and when they questioned her as to what money he could have had, she answered merely, that he had saved some; that he would never have taken what was not his own.

For the old are more loyal than are the young.

Night fell, and she hung a lantern in the open door as a sign that she was awake and awaiting him. She did not undress or go to bed, and the child slept on the floor, waking fitfully and crying out that people were hurting 'Naldino.

Long hours passed, sultry hours of a moonless summer night; there was no sound but from the owls on the wing, and now and then the scream of a mouse caught by one of them. The hills lay fold on fold in the dark, one with another, the air was dry, and scented with the aroma of the pines up above on the crest of Majaino.

Other persons came up the hillside bearing the same tale. Everyone loves to tell bad news.

The old woman listened in frozen calm. 'I will hear my boy's own story before I believe,' she said stubbornly, and they could not get anything else from her, and, tired, the other women went away to the house of Matteo, where, weeping and chattering and vieing with each other in the terrors and horrors of the versions they gave, all the lodgers and tenants were screaming and gesticulating together. Matteo stayed down in the town.

Nonna Tessa sat on at her door and span; but her hands shook and the flax shook in them: the child, aware that there was something wrong, but too young to understand what it was, sat quiet at her feet, playing sadly with blades of grass and little pebbles and the beetles which crept amongst them.

The old woman as the day wore away hung her soup-pot over a fire of sticks, and cut some slices from a stale loaf; but she fed the child, she could not eat herself. Her tongue clove to the roof of her mouth, her legs were cold as in winter and dragged heavily along; the suspense, the uncertainty tortured her, but she did not dare to leave the cottage and go out to try and hear the truth, for Rinaldo might come there in her absence.

'If he have done wrong he will come to me,' she thought, and in her innermost soul, though she would not have admitted it to any living creature, she had little doubt that the tale was true, since the money for the rent was gone.

Twilight fell and no one came near her any more. All the interest, all the sympathy, of the dwellers on the hillside were with the Procaccio and his daughter. The old woman folded her trembling hands in her lap, and tried to mutter her Aves, but the familiar words would not come to her; she could not think of them. She could only think of her boy.

'If I and the child had not burdened him, perhaps this would not have been,' she thought with self-torturing remorse.

If he should be dead? If he should have killed himself in despair and dread of what he had done?

She sat on the bench by the wall and strained her eyes into the gloom. A polecat stole across the path; the over-ripe figs dropped with a soft thud upon the grass; the great clouds coursed across the sky; all was still—as still as death. Perhaps, had he been unburdened and alone, he would have led his life, jocund and free, and been mated where he had wished. Her long and many years had been spent in toil, in sacrifice, in pain, in unselfish care of others, and what had they brought to her? Nothing.

'It has all been of no good,' she thought, while her chin drooped on her chest, and the fatigue of physical exertion dulled her anxious mind and lulled it into a momentary stupor of sleep.

She awoke abruptly, terrified and trembling from head to foot. 'Did you speak, lad?' she cried, as she stared into the darkness around her.

A human shadow came out of the shadows of the bushes, and ran across the piece of sward, and knelt down before her.

'I took the money, and I bought her corals, and she had promised to go before the priest with me, and she cheated me and flouted me, and I fell on her and no man will praise her beauty any more; I have sinned, I am vile; I have robbed you and the child. O granny, granny! curse me and let me die! I was ready to die; I had got down in the bed of the river, I had waded in waist deep, and the mud and the sand were sucking at me, drawing me down and down—and then all in a moment I saw your face, and I heard your voice, and I felt that I must just see you once more to say to you, " I am sorry, I am sorry for you." '

Then he laid his head on her knees and burst out sobbing as he had used to sob when a child, when he had done wrong, had broken a pitcher, or torn his shirt, or played truant from school on a summer day. As she had done then, she did now ; she laid her hands on his bowed head and touched his sunny curls tenderly.

'You are in a cruel strait, my lad,' she said gently. 'Passion has led you wide astray. The lass was not worth nor the gift nor the blow. But it was good of you to think of me—'

Her voice was choked in her throat ; he did not speak or move ; he knelt there with his head bowed down on her knees like a little chidden child. She sat still and mute, thinking, and her eyes peered through the darkness to try and see where her old home lay in the hollow under the olives.

'They will be after you, dear,' she said slowly at last. 'You must not stay here. They will take you like a netted quail. You must go.'

'Go! And leave you? It is because I cannot bear to leave you that I did not kill myself there in the river.'

'You must go,' she repeated. 'Wait. Let me think.'

She stood up; and he sat down in the dust at her feet, like a child; his back was bowed, his head hung down, his whole attitude was broken-hearted and full of despair; he had eaten nothing since the previous night; all the day he had skulked and hidden timidly in the lanes of the town and under the hedges of the outskirts. Nonna Tessa stood above him in the dark, her face set and drawn, her eyes staring.

'You must go,' she repeated; 'you must go.'

That was all that was clear to her; he must go before the hand of the law could seize him for what he had done. Suddenly, with hands strong as in youth, she dragged him up from the ground and pushed him indoors.

'Break your fast, my child; you are weak from hunger and shame,' she said, as she poured out some soup in an earthen pan and broke bread before him.

'I cannot; I choke!' he said faintly; but she persisted, and she fed him spoonful by spoonful, as she had done when he had been in his infancy, until, ashamed, he took the spoon from her and ate.

'I am a miserable brute!' he murmured as the tears rolled down his cheek.

'You did wrong,' she said gravely, 'but the woman tempted you.'

Then she went into the inner room, and busied herself putting together in a bundle the little linen and the few clothes he possessed, and she made ready a flask of poor wine which was kept for feast days, a goat's-milk cheese, and a loaf. These she brought out and laid on the table before him, and counted down beside them a few silver and bronze pieces.

'These I have had saved for years; I did not tell you, for I kept them for a worse day than any we have known. Take them and make your way into the Mugello; go to my brother Claudio, at the saw-mill of Ragona, beyond Camaldoli; it is forty years since he saw me, but he will not have forgotten; he will shelter you, and give you work; stay there till your name is forgotten.'

Rinaldo threw his hair out of his eyes and stared at her by the dim light of the lamp.

'And you? how will you live and the child?'

'How do the birds live with every man's hand against them? Think not of me but go.'

He thrust back the money with a passionate gesture.

'I have robbed you already. Not again, not again.'

She laid her hands on his shoulders, and looked long into his eyes.

'You did not rob me. You took what was your own. Besides you were mad and knew not what you did. Go, my lad, lose no more time. Will it be better for me and the child if you stand in the felon's dock? And Matteo will have no mercy.'

The little girl who was asleep on the floor awoke, and seeing him there sprang to her feet with a cry of joy.

''Naldino!' she murmured as she clung to his

knees. 'I saved some bilberries for you on a big leaf, and you never came home all day!'

Rinaldo lifted her up in his arms and his tears fell on her little brown head.

'Come with me, both of you,' he said with a sob. 'Then perhaps I shall have courage.'

'No, dear, we have been a clog to you all your days,' said Tessa. 'Let us do as we can. Go you, and the Madonna be with you.'

'I will not go alone,' said Rinaldo.

He sighed bitterly, and threw his arms upward in a wild despairing gesture.

'If I go alone I shall kill myself. Oh, how I loved her! And I have beaten the beauty out of her, and night and day, on earth and in hell, I shall only see her face!'

His grandmother looked at him and took up the lamp from the table.

'We will go together,' she said. 'It does not matter where my bones be laid.'

In half an hour they left the little house and closed the door and laid the key on the step. The old woman paused a moment and gazed at the opposite hills, dim and vague in the darkness and starlight. She was trying to see where her old home stood which she had loved so well.

A south-west wind was blowing, and it blew to her the smell of its pine trees, and of its briar roses. She made the sign of the cross and blessed the place.

'When I die, if you can, bring me back,' she said. It was her only hint of lament.

'Where are we going?' asked the little child, drowsily.

'God knows,' said Nonna Tessa.

Rinaldo said, 'Where we shall be together.'

Then the three shadows passed upward into the darkness of the higher trees, shunning the roads which others might traverse.

'When I am dead, bring me back hither,' said the old woman once more. And it seemed to her that she was dead already.

The hearth was cold, the door was shut, the house was empty. Life was over for her, as much as though the deal lid of her coffin had been nailed down upon her.

But her boy wanted her; she set her face bravely northward, and looked back no more.

And the three shadows went on together, along the side of the hill; and the darkness covered them, and their place knew them no more.

THE HALT

The Halt

SHE would not go to bed lest she should oversleep herself and fail to wake in time. Every morning of her life she did awake at cock-crow and arise, but she was afraid this night that she might lie too long.

'Will you not come?' she said to her husband for the hundredth time; and he replied:

'Guà! Not I. The lad is a good lad, but not worth a tramp of twenty miles across the hills, when grain is uncut and storms are nigh, as the astrologers do say.' And he would not move off his land; he was a peaceable, good soul, hard-working, and penurious and uncomplaining; but his blood was slow and his heart half asleep from over-toil and narrowness of means. He could not see why he should lose a day's work and take a long tramp to see a boy he had begotten pass by in a cloud of dust. Those crazes were for the women folk, he said, with the good-humoured pitying smile of his superior manhood.

' 'Tis silly of you to go, sposa,' he said to his helpmeet ; but she had set her soul on going. The troops were encamped fifty miles off in the Volterra country, and in their marchings and counter-marchings they would pass through a defile known as the Belva, which was within her reach, and there would halt at noonday and eat their noonday meal ; so at least was it said, and she was bent on going thither to see them if they came. For her boy was amongst them, her eldest born, her auburn-haired, blue-eyed, gentle, comely Daniello, whom she had not seen since he had gone away with other conscripts eighteen months before from the village in the valley which was his communal centre. Once or twice a few scrawled words on a dirty sheet of paper had come from the post to her, and she had carried it to the priest, and he had read it and told out of it that her boy was well and hoped it found her so likewise. That was all the news she had had in a year and a half of her eldest son, and then her man wondered that she wished to go over the hills to see the troops at their halting-place!

'A father's a poor creature,' she said with scorn.

She and he were very small peasants; their little farm was meagre and stony. Their master was a hard man; their lot was harsh, but they bore with it cheerfully; they had health and strength, and their children were docile, laborious, and healthy always, although they ate but rye bread with a little oil and a few beans, and drank nothing but brook water. The fine, clear mountain air fed them, as it fed the hill hare and the wild partridge. Their house was a stone cabin on the edge of a moor, and a few pines sheltered it from the north, and its few poor fields sloped southwards. All around them was a war-scarred, desolate-looking, treeless, volcanic country, where whole nations lay buried and little cities crouched in little hollows like a child's toys in a giant's palm.

Their lives were pinched and starved, and they had much to do to hold their bodies and souls together in bad years; but they were an affectionate people and cheerful of nature, and their mother was the most cheerful of all. 'If only they would not take away the lads,' she said; she would have asked nothing more of the Madonna or the State than this: only to leave the lads.

A pedlar coming on his rounds had told them that the troops would pass by quite near to her on their march only sixteen miles off as the falcon flew, and she knew that her boy's regiment would be with them. 'How will you tell him from the others in all that pother?' said her husband; and she had laughed. Not know her own son out of five hundred—five thousand—five million!

It is impossible for those who can bridge distance with all the resources of culture and science to understand the dead darkness, the utter blank, which absence is to the poor and the ignorant. It is like death; no message comes from it, no ray of light shines through its unbroken gloom. The boy had gone; they said he would return, but she knew not when nor why nor how. The State had got him; something impalpable, immutable, incomprehensible; she knew no more.

When Ruffo, the hawker, passing by on his bi-annual visit with his pack of needles, and pins, and tapes, and other necessaries, had said to her: 'The troops are down there; aye, a fine show; horse, foot, and gunners; I saw your 'Neillo in the camp; he told me to tell you he and his regiment would go through the Belva at noonday to-morrow and most like halt there. "Tell mother to come," says the lad. "Lord sakes, lad," says I, "'tis an endless twenty-mile tramp and more, and your mother is none so young as she was; and 'tis reaping time, as you know well." But 'Neillo, he only laughs, and he says, "Tell mother to come." So I tell ye. But 'tis not my fault if you go;' over her dark lean face a flash of great eagerness and joy had passed, but she had gone on with her work, which was stacking beans.

'I do not tell you to go,' said the pedlar. 'Just as like as not they won't march through the Belva. Those generals always change their minds at the last minute. But that was what the lad said to me. "Tell mother to come," says he. "We go through the Belva."'

'How looks he?' she asked.

'Aye, aye; a bit thin, but well; I am not saying he does not look well.'

She shot a quick glance at him from beneath her grey brows.

'He was never over-strong,' she said under her breath. 'When children have never enough in their bellies they cannot grow up strong men.'

'Lads would always be pecking if one let them,' he rejoined. 'He did not complain to me; not a word.'

''Neillo was never one to complain,' said the woman.

And she would not lie down lest she should by any chance oversleep herself, but kept walking to and fro plaiting her strands of straw whilst the children and the good-man slept.

There is but little night in the middle of the month of July, and when the moon is at the full there seems no night at all, but only a more ethereal and more luminous day.

At four o'clock she lifted the latch of the house-door and went out, leaving the bread and the weak cold coffee ready for them to break their fast. The eldest girl would heat up the coffee in its rude tin pot, and they would have a sup or two each to moisten their dry rye-crusts.

It was day already; the broken barren hills which stretched around her home were touched with soft roselight; a deep sense of coolness and of rest lay like a benediction on the noiseless scene; the stone slopes, so harsh and cheerless at other hours, were in this hour softened and spiritualised into beauty; clouds floated in their hollows, and white mists like inland seas stretched between the high hilltops.

She was a tall, gaunt woman, only thirty-eight years old by age, but twice that age in appearance. Her hair was grey and thick, her skin brown and deeply lined; her profile had the straight classic lines. She had been handsome in her youth, but that was all of beauty that remained to her;

her bosom was wrinkled and fallen, her teeth were few and rotten, her cheeks were hollow. Scorching summers, freezing winters, the soaking storms of spring, and the mountain winds of autumn had all played with her as with a loosened leaf, and buffeted her about and beat her out of womanhood. She toiled hard all through the year, hoeing, weeding, cutting grass, carrying wood and water, ploughing behind the little heifer up and down the steep and stony fields. The silence and the solitude around were so familiar to her that they had no terrors; she had lived all her life amongst these stony hills, this alternation of bare slate and granite with friable tufa and petrified lava mounds. She knew that to the west lay the sea and to the east were the fertile and radiant Tuscan plains; but with her own eyes she had never seen aught except her native hills, never known aught except the scanty nourishment for man and beast which they grudgingly yield, and the perpetual isolation to which those who dwell amidst them are condemned.

She had a piece of bread in her pocket, and she knew that there were water-springs here and there in the rocks; she had her sickle swinging at her side; she meant to cut grass if she found any, and bring it in a bundle on her shoulders on her return journey home. She was in the habit of never losing a moment nor neglecting a chance. She had put on her one better gown, a brown woollen skirt with a yellow bodice, and over it she had a great coarse cotton apron of a faded blue. She had nothing on her head, and her sleeves were rolled up to the elbow; she carried her shoes in her hand, not wishing to spoil them by so much walking, but meaning to wear them when she should enter the Belva gorge so as to do honour to her boy. She bought a pair once in ten years; strong leather things, with wooden soles, which were only worn on rare occasions. She had put also in her capacious pocket a little round cheese and a loaf of wheaten bread to give her son. She would willingly have brought wine also, but wine was never seen on those hilltops except in the priest's chalice at the little church where the stone pines stood in a hollow of the rocks.

She walked on at the level pace of one used to

cover ground quickly and evenly. The air was cool, the breeze blew from the sea, the lovely lights of sunrise chased the shadows of the dawn. Her mind was busy with her boy, travelling over all his short, uneventful life. She thought of him as he had lain at her breast a little conical bundle of swaddling-clothes, with only his small brown hands and his eager, red, wet mouth free. She thought of him at ten months old, escaping from her arms to totter across the stones before the door for the first time alone upon his feet. She remembered one day when he had fallen from a plum-tree and twisted his ancle, and lay in her lap sobbing and rubbing his curly head against her arm. Then there was the day he took his first communion, such a slim, bright-eyed, well-built little man, though small and thin ; for there was scanty food to divide amongst so many, and the children were always hungry. She had cut up her only good cotton gown to make him a shirt and breeches for that day ; it had been a day in midsummer ; the sun had shone on his auburn head as he went up over the rugged pavement of the church, so dark even at noon, except where the strong hot rays shot through the clefts of the narrow windows. He had been a good lad always, docile and active and chaste, kind to the little ones, obedient to his parents, and content with his lot. Then the State had caught him up out of her hand and she had ceased to know anything of him; a high blank wall had been built up between her and him; he had been taken far away, and she had had nothing left to do except to kneel down on the benches before the little picture of the Madonna and pray for him. Twenty-one years he had been hers, paid for by her pain, her labour, her privation, her sacrifice; and then all in a moment he had become nothing to her, he had been taken by the hand of the State. She had never understood it nor forgiven it. They might say what they would, it was cruel, it was wicked, it was accursed. He was hers, and they dragged him away and set the blankness of darkness between him and her.

But at last, perhaps, she would see him. He had bidden the pedlar ask her to come. He had not forgotten. If it were only to see him go by in the scorch and the sweat of the march, it was enough to live for, enough to walk to the end of the world for; and should there be a halt, a bivouac, as they said, she would clasp him in her arms and hear his voice, and see him eat of her bread and her cheese, and wipe the dust off his face as if he were a child once more. 'Tell mother to come to the Belva,' so he had said; dear lad, dear lad! he had not forgotten her, nor the way the country lay amongst the rocks about his home.

The light widened and brightened and became full day.

The air grew warm; the landscape, losing the rosy lights and silvery shadows of the earliest hours, became bare, bald, and sad, scored by heaps of shale thrown out where, ever since Etruscan days, men had delved for copper and disfigured the face of nature; the mines have been long unused, but the sears made by them remain. The path she followed was always the same, a scarce visible mark, passing over the short, scant grass which grew on the slate and gneiss of the rocks and the calcareous soil. Now and then there came in sight a flock of goats, a group of pine-trees, a church tower, or a disused posting-house; but these were far apart, and the whole country was cheerless, tedious, abandoned.

Her way lay southward and westward, by no regular road, but by tracks, scarcely seen, which were made and followed by the strings of mules carrying charcoal or lime which had passed over those mountain tops century after century since the days of Latin and Etruscan and Gaul.

She went many miles without meeting a soul. The habitations were very few, and the path she traversed was still only a mule-track scarcely traceable. When she at last did meet a human being, an old man on an ass with sacks before and behind him, she stopped and exchanged a few words for sake of saying that of which she was so proud: 'I am going to meet my son. He is passing through the Belva with his regiment. He sent for me.'

And the old man said:

'Oh, oh! That is fine pleasure for you. I was a soldier myself long ago—long ago. Good-day to you, good wife, and joy be with you.'

Then the little tinkling sound of his ass's hoofs

on the rocky ground died away in the distance, and she was once more alone in the midst of the dry, sear, stony hills, where only the horned toad and the squat tarantula had their lodgings.

It grew very hot, and the rocks seemed like heated copper as her bare feet smote them. Gnats buzzed and snakes basked in the heat. There was little or no vegetation, only here and there a starved pine or a stunted lentiscus. She was fatigued by the hard ground and the heat of the sun, but the farther she went the lighter grew her heart. 'Soon,' she said to herself, 'soon I shall see my boy face to face!'

The burning daylight poured down on her; there was no shade on these rocks, nor on the level friable soil which divided them. Mosquitoes were in clouds, and larger gnats in great numbers. But although footsore and weary, she was glad of heart. Yes, she said to herself, the old man was right; it was a fine pleasure for a woman to see her lad safe and sound.

When she came to a spot where a little spring issued from the rocks and flowed into a hollow, green with moss of its own creating, she drank from it and rested a short time, eating a crust.

When she passed a house, which was very seldom, and paused by its doorway to speak with the inmates, she said to them with a glow of pride:

'My son's regiment marches through the Belva to-day; he sent for me to go and see them pass; perhaps they will halt there.'

To have a son marching with his regiment seemed to her almost greater than to be a crowned queen, and more cruel than the saints' martyrdom.

In the distance still very far off she could see some dark lines and spots; she knew that they were the woods crowning the gorge of the Belva, the only trees in all that countryside. She quickened her pace as she saw them. The sun was high. Dear heaven! if, after all, the troops should pass through the gorge without halting there!

The pedlar had said that it was possible.

Her legs seemed to bend and quake underneath her at the thought. But she was a strong, tenacious woman, and she conquered her terror and continued on her way. It was two hours and more before she reached the outskirts of the woods and saw a little cluster of huts, flocks of goats, breadths of rough grassland, low undergrowth of chestnut and oak, tall groups of pine maritime and stone. The gorge of the Belva lay beneath.

It was now a breathless noontide. She began to descend under the welcome shade of the pines. The wild strawberry plants were in flower and gentians were growing thick; she looked at them curiously; there were no flowers where she lived.

A goat-herd lay half-asleep upon the moss, and awoke at her step.

'Have the regiments come into the gorge?' she asked him, her heart beating thickly against her ribs.

The man answered lazily, but half-awake:

'Aye; I heard their bugles a while ago. They halt there.'

'My son is amongst them,' she said with pride, and hurried past him and his flock.

It was such a great thing to have a son a soldier. Half an hour's descent through the oak and chestnut scrub brought her where she could see down into the gorge itself.

Yes, they were there; she could distinguish the white linen caps, the horses, the cannon; she could see masses moving to and fro, the sparkle of metal, the dull yellow white of canvas. Yes, they were there. She crossed herself and thanked God, kneeling for a moment on the carpet of fir needles, then rising and hurrying downward.

The descent was long and winding, and the trees hid the bottom of the ravine from her view; but when she reached it the regiments were still there, resting and breaking their fast. She went up to the first group of young soldiers whom she saw and said to them, 'I am his mother—'Neillo's mother. Will you take me to him, please? He sent for me.'

Her voice shook hoarsely with emotion; her fingers plucked at her apron. Before that unknown, confused, motley mass of men she trembled; how should she ever find her boy?

Her strength began to fail her. She went from man to man. The youths grinned in her face and turned their backs on her. They laughed, they joked, they teased, they bandied her about from one to another; she made the round of the camp, stumbling over the haversacks lying on the ground, staring stupidly at the strange scene.

There were big field-pieces unlimbered, artillery horses unharnessed and tethered, cooking-fires and eating-vessels, loosened knapsacks and dusty jackets; the men were for the most part in their shirt-sleeves, they were talking and shouting mirthfully, discipline being for the hour relaxed.

It was a busy, tumultuous, noisy kind of repose; and the cries and the din and the movement as she approached made her head spin and her ears sing. There seemed such numbers, such endless numbers, and they all looked alike with their cropped heads, their swathed legs, their puny stature. How was she to find her lad amongst that restless multitude?

But she was not daunted.

A soldier at last, more patient than the rest, or more pitiful, explained to her that this was the artillery, three field batteries, with a cavalry regiment; that her lad, whom he knew by name, was with the infantry in the rear column, which had halted a mile further down the glen. She thanked him and commended him to the Virgin's care, and went onward ; though her limbs were so stiff and their veins were so swollen that she walked with difficulty.

But she was full of joy and anticipation, because she had now heard for certain that her boy was there.

She spoke merrily to the men whom she passed ; light of heart and insensible to the pain of her swollen veins and the smart of her tired feet. 'Neillo was there ; that was enough.

'I have got a loaf and a cheese from home for my boy,' she said to a patrol who showed some suspicion of her bulging pocket ; and the patrol laughed, and she laughed too, and they let her pass.

Shrinking from interrogation and observation, yet always persevering, she pursued her quest, saying always, 'I am 'Neillo's mother. He wished me to come. I have walked all the way. Where is he, please ?'

The line regiments were some way off down the gorge, under the shade of some overhanging rocks.

Their short white-clothed figures were moving to and fro, crowding over camp-kettles, bringing water from a spring which a little way off trickled from the rocks; but there was not so much gaiety and chatter and activity as there had been amongst the gunners and the troopers. The officers were standing together under a solitary pine-tree, and their voices sounded low and grave, and they looked troubled. She came amongst them all timidly, yet with a bright expectation on her weary, hot face. She looked from one to another longingly, hopelessly, anxiously, but she could not see her 'Neillo.

At last she came to a group of young men who were very quiet and stood about, aimlessly, looking down on something on the ground. What they looked at were three lads like themselves lying on their backs in the shade under a large chestnut-tree. She came near to them timidly, with a vague, nameless fear chilling her heart.

'What is the matter with them?' she asked. 'Are they ill?'

The conscripts standing around answered in low tones:

'No, wife; they are dead. They fell down dead on the march. 'Twas thirty miles, and so hot.'

Then she drew nearer and nearer, and bent down over the prostrate figures, and drew the linen covering off each of their faces in turn; and thus at last she saw her son once more.

THE STABLE-BOY

The Stable=boy.

THE stable had once been a church. Not very long ago, indeed, it had still been a church, though service had not been said in it for more than a hundred years. When it had been utilised as a livery stable there had been no trouble taken to change its proportions. The pointed arches, the tall columns of dark granite, the narrow aisles, the leaden casements in the deep-set windows, had all been left unaltered. Wooden partitions had been set up between the pillars to make stalls for the horses, and straw had been thrown down on the obliterated mosaics of the pavement; that was all. It was situated in a narrow, old, dark street, with old houses with deep eaves, great sunken doorways, and curious stone corbels and cornices around it on every side. The street had once been full of martial movement and ecclesiastical splendour, and had a great monastery in it, which had been burned down during the siege by the Imperialists; its church had escaped the flames, but had sunk to a sadder fate. It was a livery stable, and the clang of pails, the stamp of hoofs, and the oaths of grooms were the only sounds heard where once the organ had pealed and the intoning resounded and the anthems of Palestrina and Corelli echoed. It was left to dirt, to gloom, to decay; the cobwebs hung thick as velvet in all the corners, the glass was opaque with long-accumulated dust; the pavement, with its marbles and mosaics, was slippery with dung and urine; here and there was a niche with an unmutilated statue, here and there was a fresco still traceable, a carving still visible; but although its lines were unchanged and its serried columns unbroken, it was a wreck of itself.

There are many of these old desecrated churches in Italy; some are workshops, some are warehouses, some are granaries, some, as this was, stables. And there is no sadder sight in the world : their quietude, their beauty, and their dignity protest in vain against their desecration. They are all old churches, built by true artists of the early centuries, 'masters of the living stone': churches which men painted and decorated and covered with emblem and symbol before which the rude knight and the rough free companion bared their heads and bent their knees. But neither their age nor their history spares them, there are so many of them in the streets and the worshippers have grown so few.

In this stable there were several horses and several vehicles, and coachmen and helpers went to and fro in it, and the ancient purpose and usage of it troubled none of them. The only one who ever thought of it was a little stable-boy, the butt and slave of everyone, who lived there night and day, having nowhere else to live, and who loved it in his dull way, as some canon or some abbot may have loved it in his finer way, during the days of its glory. Gino was the boy's name; he was fourteen years old; he had neither father nor mother, nor any relatives that he knew of, and it was a great thing for him to be a stable helper, with a franc a day and leave to sleep amongst the straw in the sacristy, which had been turned into a forage chamber. He was hardly treated and worked hard, for the drivers and stablemen were idle and rough, and put all they could upon him. But he was strong and willing, and did not complain. He was fond of the horses, and lived willingly amongst them, seldom leaving the dusky old street in which the stables were situated. In appearance he was small for his age, but robust. He had a round brown face with black eyes which had a great, unconscious pathos in them; he was never seen without his coarse apron and his stable cap. There were no feast-days or holy-days for him; all days were alike; the watering, the foddering, the harness-cleaning, the oats-sifting, the stall-cleaning, never varied. It was the same work every week, every month, every year. He did not complain. He even liked his work. He had been taken into the stables out of charity at eight years old, and they were all of home he knew. Besides, in them he had Stellina.

Stellina was his supreme comfort and companion, his one friend. She was a little black lupetto dog, with four white feet, and a small white point upon her chest, which had gained her the name of 'little star.' She had come a stray puppy to the stables four years before, and Gino had hidden her in the straw and fed her, and at last ventured to ask for, and by good fortune obtained, permission to keep her openly there. She was very quick and courageous in chasing rats, and this prowess found her favour in the eyes of the stablemen. Stellina, like Gino, never stirred out of the street. To her were all unknown the joys of meadow and garden, the scamper among the grass, the frolicking amongst the buttercups, the splashing in rainwater pools or river shallows, which are so dear to happier and freer dogs.

Their one world was the old church; its darksome aisles, its musty sacristy, and the sharp, uneven cobble stones paving the space in front of it. To Stellina as to her master it seemed a kingdom. They knew of nothing beyond, and what they had never known they did not miss, although instinct sometimes moved restlessly in both the boy and the dog in a vague, dim want of more space, more movement, more freedom. Yet they were both content with the busy, harmless, innocent lives under the old groined arches and the broken wings of the stone angels.

Stellina believed that the horses depended alone on her for defence and vigilance. With her erect furry ears sharply cocked she watched their coming and going, their grooming and feeding; barked when they neighed, and growled when they snorted. That the horses, and the men too, could not have existed an hour without her protection and surveillance Stellina was quite sure. When all the horses and men were away, which often happened, she and Gino conversed with one another sitting side by side in the straw caressing one another, but always keeping a weather eye open for any rat or mouse which might stir beneath the litter.

From time to time Stellina had puppies, and then she was prouder, happier, more vigilant than ever, with a snug nest made under one of the horses' mangers in a bale of hay. She was such a pretty dog, and so valiant against rodents, that her children easily found homes in the neighbourhood; but she was a fond mother and mourned for them long when they left her, and rejected all the consolations of her owner.

'Poor dear Stellina!' said Gino to her one day when she mourned thus, 'the next you have shall stay with you, or one of them at least; the master will not mind; he knows how good you are.'

So when her next puppies were born he renewed his promise that one at least of them should never be taken from her; they were three little white things and one black; their father was a white lupetto, who lived at a shop near, where they sold old iron and brass and copper utensils.

Gino was as happy in the possession of these treasures as Stellina was: out of his pence he bought her milk and tripe and white-bread, as much as she could eat. He had few idle moments, but those he had he passed squatted under the manger, looking at and talking to the mother and babes. He denied himself food, and drank nothing except the bad water of the stable well, that he might get them all they wanted. The men were good-natured, and did not tease him about his hobby, and the horse near whose hoofs Stellina had made her bed sniffed at them amiably, and took infinite care not to touch them with his iron shoe. Three of the puppies were already promised; and the fourth, the black one, he hoped to be able, somehow or other, to keep with its mother.

One day, when the puppies were two weeks old, he was alone in the stables. It was very warm weather, full midsummer. The horses and men were all out, only one old mare was dozing in her stall; the doors stood open to catch such evening cool as there might come into the air; the heavy curtains of dust and cobwebs hung before the casements sunk high in the masonry. Gino had been cleaning, brushing, splashing, sweeping; he was grey with dust and wet with heat; but he was well and happy, leaning against the lintel and looking into the street; tired in every limb, but satisfied with himself and his little world, and above all with Stellina, whom he had brushed and combed until she shone like a piece of black velvet. She never left her children for ten minutes; but they were sound asleep in the hay, and she had stolen out to her owner's side for a second, licking his hand and then sitting down on her little haunches just outside the door, looking up and down the street which was so familiar to her.

Gino, with a straw in his mouth and his shirt-sleeves rolled up, was half-asleep and half-dreaming, his eyelids closed and his lips parted; he had a smile on his face.

'Good Stellina! dear little Stellina!' he said sleepily, and then for an instant his fatigue overcame him and he lost consciousness, still leaning against the massive column of the door; he was not asleep two minutes, but his dream seemed long.

As a little child he had been in the country always, and in his sleep he revisited the green fields of his birth whenever he did dream at all. He thought he was running with the dog through the growing corn, under the maple and the vine boughs; there were tall red tulips in the corn, and a little runlet of water flowing under grass and watercress, and there were church bells ringing and birds singing, and it was all so green, so cool, so fresh. Stellina ran in the brook and splashed the drops in his face, and he took off his shoes and ran, too, in the brook, and it was so delicious and cold bubbling about his aching dusty feet.

He awoke with a start, and with a shrill shriek ringing in his ears.

In the yellow light of evening he saw Stellina's little body swinging in the air; a noose of cord was round her throat, and by it she was being drawn into space, the noose tightening as she was raised higher and higher, and the pressure on her gullet forcing her eyes from her head and her tongue from her jaws. She had given one scream as she was seized, then the rope had choked her into silence.

In an instant Gino knew what it was: the dog-snatchers had got her; the fatal cart, with its escort of guards and its brutal lasso-throwers, had come suddenly down the lane and had seized her as she sat before the stable gates. With a jerk she was flung into the cart and the lid shut down, the men laughing as they crammed her in and banged the lid. Scarcely awake, dull from fatigue and heat, and still dazed with his dream, Gino staggered forward and caught hold of the cart.

'Stop! stop!' he cried to them. 'Take her out! give her back! She has puppies in here. They will die; she will die. Let her out! let her out!'

But the guards pushed and dragged him off the cart to which he clung, and the dog-lifters swore at him, and one man, rougher than the rest, struck him in the chest and knocked him backward against the stable door; the cries of the dogs within the cart and of the street children running along with it adding to the confusion and the din. The boy was thrown down so that his head struck the stone gatepost; the cart with its myrmidons rolled on its way. He staggered to his feet, holloaing loudly: 'She will die! they will die! Let her out! let her out!'

He began to run on after the cart, which was turning round a corner, but an old woman of the quarter caught him by the arm. 'Tis no use, child; she said to him, 'they will not give her. They have no bowels of mercy, those brutes. Quiet yourself and let them alone, or they will haul you off to prison, and then where will your little dog be?'

'But the puppies will die! She will die!' he screamed. 'They are too little to be left, and her milk will burst and kill her!'

And he tore himself from the woman's hold and ran headlong after the cart, leaving the stables open and unwatched. He knew (what Florentine boy does not?) that the men would no more give her up than they would pity her or him; they were too hardened to their brutal work; but, hoping against hope, he ran on and on, blindly stumbling in his haste until he overtook the procession. The shrieks of the imprisoned dogs could be heard above the noise of the street.

'Give her to me! give her to me! She has puppies at home, and they will perish!' he cried again, keeping up step by step with the men. The tears rolled down his face; he was sick and gasping; he could hear Stellina's cries.

The guard who had thrown him down turned on him savagely. 'Get you gone, or I will take you to the Questura for obstructing the law!' he said with an oath.

'You will only do her more harm than good,' said a man in the crowd to the sobbing boy. 'Go home and look up your money, and in the morning buy her out if you can.'

'In the morning! She has never been out of the stables an hour, and how will her little ones bear the night starving?'

He sobbed aloud, wringing his hands.

The little crowd which moved along with them murmured and took his part. 'Give him the bitch if she is in milk,' said a woman's voice. But the creatures of the law were only angered by the expostulation; they did not net their victims only to lose them, and lose with each the blood-money paid for them. Obdurate and unfeeling, and swollen with the accursed official tyranny, they went on their way, the dog-stranglers foremost, the cart second, the guards last.

'You will not get her to-night were it ever so,' said some men to him. 'It is eight of the clock. Was she never caught before? Nay, nay, do not look so, lad. A dog is a dog, and there are scores of them.'

Then the little throng dispersed and went divers ways, and left him alone, its interest in him gone.

Mechanically, by sheer habit, he returned to the stable, frightened at his neglect of duty and bewildered by his grief. The little pups were bleating like new-born lambs, plaintively, in the straw. 'The pups, the pups!' he said over and over again, choking down his sobs. They must die without their mother; they could not lap or take any kind of food. He took them up one after another and tried to make them suck a wisp of hay or an old rag soaked in milk; but the little blind things could not understand; they only whimpered. He put them back, and covered them up, and, with the tears running down his cheeks, took his pitchfork and began to renew the fodder for the night and clear the dung away out of the stalls.

It had always been a terror upon him lest the lasso should seize Stellina; but she had been so home-staying and so prudent that the danger had never been realised by him to its full extent. Like a true Tuscan, he had always been sure that chance would favour him.

But this day the dog-snatchers had not even been commonly fair in their brutality. They had seized her on her own ground, on the very threshold of her home.

How she must suffer, cooped up in that narrow hole, without light or air, choked with a stifling collar and flung into a horrid den, if she had reached the slaughter-house, whither all captured dogs are carried; breaking her heart in the agonies of her maternal love and of her physical sufferings!

Gino worked on, not seeing the straw and the dung for his tears. The people had told him to get his money together to buy back Stellina; but he had no money; he never had any money; the scanty wage which he received was always forestalled for payments of his food and hers, and for such poor clothing as he was forced to wear. He had never known in his life what it was to have a franc to spare or to put by for future use. Get his money together! They might as well have said to the poor misused ass in the scavenger's cart,

'Get yourself gilded oats and jewelled harness!' He had nothing.

When the men came in he told them of his grief, and begged their help; but they were improvident and extravagant fellows, in debt themselves up to their necks, and fond of drink. One laughed at him; one pitied him, but, turning out his pockets, found only a halfpenny; a third told him with an oath not to talk rot, but harness quickly; and a fourth, meaning to be good-natured, said, 'Let her go, lad, and drown the whelps; you can get another bitch fast enough.'

That was all the memory they had of Stellina, who had jumped on them and frisked round them and made much of them, and killed rats for them five whole years.

No one slept in the stables except Gino, who, being a homeless boy, had always thought it a great blessing to have a bed of sacking spread on the straw or on the top of one of the corn-bins as he chose. He had usually but little time to sleep, as the horses and vehicles came in late and the morning work began at daybreak or before it. This night he did not even try to sleep, but could not have slept had he tried, for the piteous, plaintive piping of the baby dogs crying for their mother. They whined and wailed unceasingly, seeking their natural food and their natural warmth, and finding neither. He could do nothing to comfort them. He hugged them to his heart in vain. Hunger was torturing them, and they were too young to know anything except the first embryonic, semi-conscious pain. The boy was distracted by their ceaseless cries, which answered his own passionate grief for their absent mother. He felt them growing more and more weak, less and less warm, and he knew that if they could not eat they must die.

The deep tones of the Santo Spirito clock striking four of the morning told him that day was here though no light came as yet into the dusky aisles of the desecrated church. The horses were already stamping in their stalls and striking with their fore-hoofs against the woodwork of their boxes; he shivered with cold, as the little puppies did, in the hot musty air reeking with ammonia of the stables, and laid the poor little things each in their nest under the manger and began to do his morning work. But he did his work ill.

When the men came in they swore at him, and hustled him, and one gave him a kick on his shin. 'You lumbering dolt!' said this one, 'go and choke with your bitch. You are no use here.'

They had no pity on him.

There was a wedding in the town, for which all the horses and carriages were engaged, and they were all in a hurry, grooming, washing, and polishing with extra speed and care. Gino tried to do well, but he scarcely knew what he was about, and his head buzzed and span; he was thinking of Stellina in her captivity and pain. The puppies whimpered and whined. 'Drat those little beasts,' said the men; 'pitch them in a pail of water.'

The livery-stable keeper came in to see if the horses were being made smart for the bridal festivities; he heard the noise of the puppies and turned round impatiently to the spot whence it came.

'Take out those whelps,' he said to the stable boy. 'You make the place a kennel.'

'O sir!' said the lad with a sob, 'they were so happy, but the dog-cart took their mother last night, and they are dying of hunger.'

'They lassoed your black lupetta?'

'Yes, sir; yesterday, at eight o'clock in the evening.'

'Well, it cannot be helped. Drown the pups; you can't rear them. Here, you, Fortunio,' said his master to an ostler, 'if the boy is too soft-hearted to do it, chuck them in a pail and have done with them.'

Then he turned on his heel, whistling an air from the *Cavalleria Rusticana*.

The ostler Fortunio, nothing loth, went to the stall where the little animals were, and thrust his hand into the hay under the manger to drag them out of their nest; they were whimpering piteously. But Gino sprang before him and caught hold of them and hugged them to his breast.

'No one shall touch them,' he said fiercely. 'Let them be, let them be. Give me leave to go out, sir, and I will take them to the Macelli and ask them to let me put them with their mother. They surely will. Oh, they surely will!'

'They surely will not, you fool,' said his master, half touched, half irritated. 'But you may try if you like. Get you gone with your whimpering little blind beasts.'

Hugging them up in his apron, the boy waited not one moment, but stumbled out of the door, the tears still blinding his eyes, and ran down the street. He went out so little that he knew not where the slaughter-houses were, nor how to get to them; but he knew vaguely that they were out at the north-west of the town, where the country began, and took his uncertain way thither. Further on he asked the road, and, being told, ran on along the waterside, while the sun blazed on the pavements and on the front walls of the palaces.

It is a long way from the Oltramo, where the stables were, across the bridge and along the quays and boulevards to the Rifridi suburb, where the public slaughter-houses are situated; a long ugly, dusty way, lying through the hideous modern streets and vulgar squares, which have sprung up like wens and tumours between the Porta al Prato and the gates of San Gallo and of Santa Croce.

The boy went out of the former gate, and went onwards over stones and dust, to what is called the Ponte Rocco. All was dreary, noisome, full of strife and squalor. There were dirty tramway stations, heaps of refuse, stinking soap factories, mounds of cinder and peat, broken-down hedges, bald-faced houses, women and children filthy and ragged, dreariness and ugliness as far as the eyes could see, until they met the lovely lines of the mountains beyond. To such a pass has modern greed and modern waste (for the two go ever hand-in-hand) brought this once noble and royal road, which, bordered by stately walls and lovely gardens, led to the painted courts and cypress woods of the hunting-palace, where the Venus wrings the water from her hair.

The wailing of the puppies was feebler and fainter; one of them was quite still. He walked as fast as ever he could, feeling sick and weak himself, not having slept and not having eaten. The gates of the slaughter-house stood open, guards were idling about the dog-cart, and the lassoers were coming out for their morning's gyrations, poor bleating calves were being driven into sheds; the barking and howling of dogs, the bellowing of cattle, the plaintive voices of sheep, were all mingled together in one far-off, indistinct, terrible protest of unpitied woe. Gino went on unobserved until he entered the building. There he was roughly stopped and asked his business.

'You took the mother last night, and they are dying for need of her,' he said as he opened his apron and showed the puppies. 'Will you let me take them to her in the cell? They are such little things, only ten days old; they cannot see, and they will die, and she will die too on account of her milk.'

The men to whom he pleaded broke into loud unkind laughter.

'Do you think the Macelli is a foundling hospital? Get out, you and your whelps! If you bring the order from the Communal Palace and the money, you can take the bitch away. A franc and a half a day for her food; and twelve francs the tub; and two francs the fine. You know that.'

'But I have no money!' he cried, 'and the

pups are dying, and Stellina will die too! Take them to her—for pity's sake, take them to her! If you will not let me in——'

'What is that lad shrieking about?' said the hoarse savage voice of the superintendent. 'How dare you let him through the gates! What does he come for? Stop his bellowing.'

'O good sir! kind sir, do let me take her children to Stellina!' cried the boy, and tried to unfold his little tale; but the superintendent roughly bade him hold his tongue.

'Was the dog's tax paid?' he added sharply.

'No, sir, it never was; but she was so much use and so good; and she must die, and the puppies too, if you will not let them go to her,' said the boy, breaking down in his prayer, and sobbing as if his heart would break.

'Turn him out,' said the superintendent curtly to his men. 'We can have no maudlin, mewing beggars in these gates. Take him to the Questura if he resist. Stay. Write down his name and address. He must be summoned for contravention.'

'But they are dying!' cried Gino desperately.

The superintendent laughed, and his men grinned. Dogs died there every day. The only object of a dog's life was, in their view of it, to die, and yield skin for the glove or toy makers, and phosphates for the manufacturers of manure.

'Put the fool outside the gates,' said the superior officer.

They did so, first wringing out of him in his misery and bewilderment the declaration of who he was, whom he served, and where he lived. He could not tear himself away from the vicinity of Stellina.

'Bring the money and buy her out,' they had said to him. But for a poor lad, if he be honest, to get money is an impossibility; he might as well try to get blood out of a stone, water out of a brick. He had nothing in the world except the boots and clothes in which he stood.

He had not forgotten his work, but he could not bring himself to go away and go back. He went and sat down on some rough grass near the edge of the Mugnone water, and looked at the little things in his apron. They were all dead but one. Their tender and frail organisms had been unable to resist hunger and neglect. He kept hoping that he might see someone, do something, be able to help her in some way. He kept the little dead pups in his apron, and tried to warm the one still living inside his shirt against his flesh. But it was growing colder and colder, and though it felt about feebly with its lips seeking nourishment there was but little life left in it. He got up and walked to and fro, up and down, here and there, stupidly, longing for some word of help, of counsel, of assurance as to his dog's safety. She might be dead now of terror, of fever, of struggle against her fate. In this horrible place, where nothing came except for torture and death, there was no pity. With money, escape could be bought, but he could no more get money than he could root up the Baptistery or the Apennines.

While he held the last surviving puppy in his breast he felt its body and limbs twitch; he heard it wail feebly; he looked at it and saw that it also was dying. In another few minutes more it was dead. He laid it with its brothers in his apron, and folded the coarse canvas round them. He intended to take them home.

Half the day had dragged by; it was now three o'clock. The heat was great. There was a high wind, and it blew the dust and sand around him in circles.

At last he saw a man whom he knew; a carter of forage, by name Zanobi, who had come often to the stables, and had known Stellina. The boy went to him and told him his story; the carter was good-hearted and not without sympathy. Money he had none to give, but he did what he could.

'I have a cousin who works yonder,' he said with a gesture towards the slaughter-houses. 'After my day is done I will see him and ask what one could do to get Stellina out. Alas, I know it means money, and much money; but perhaps, as a favour, and if one promised to send her in the country—at any rate I will see him, and I dare say he will manage to show her to me. Cheer up; they must let two days and a half go by before they kill the dogs or give them to the doctors. Get you home to your stables or you will lose your place, and what good will that do? Go home now, promise me, child, and when I have heard anything I will come round in the evening and tell you what I know. But unless you will go to your stables I will do nothing; for what will you better Stellina by throwing yourself out of place?'

Then the man went on with his wagon-load of iron rails and rods, and Gino turned away and began to walk towards his home, knowing that the carter spoke truly. A little spark of hope had sprung up in his heart. Perhaps after all she might be saved; but the pups—for them there was no hope. He carried them still in his apron. He meant to bury them when no one was looking, under the manger where they had been born.

He returned home over the railway embankments and along the boulevards. It was a long way, and he went slowly, for he was terribly tired and his stomach had long been empty.

It was five in the afternoon when he reached the livery stable. The stable-man who had had to do his duty for him met him with a rain of blows from a stick and a volley of abuse. Gino did not resist, nor did he answer. He said nothing and put his apron with the little dead babes in it in a corner where no one saw. He drank thirstily of the bad water and resumed his work in silence. All the carriages and coachmen were out; the helper, tired of his long day shut up there alone, flung a bit of wood at his head, bade him look sharp or he would get more, and went away. When he was quite sure that he was gone Gino dug a hole under the manger in the earth under the pavement, and laid some hay in it, and then buried the puppies. When the place was closed and the litter strewn over it, no one could tell that the ground had been ever disturbed.

'If she come back she will understand they are there,' he said to himself.

The rest of the day wore away. The men and the horses came in, hot, tired, and out of temper, after the long day with the nuptial party in the country. There were loud wrangling, banging, swearing, quarrelling; the boy was unnoticed except that he received now a cuff on the head, now a kick on the shins. No one asked him anything of Stellina; all were in haste to unharness and get away to their suppers. Gino did not speak; he did his work when he was wanted, but his head swam and his heart ached; still he clung to his one hope of hearing news from the carter.

When the horses were in their stalls and the carriages rolled into the chancel, which served as coach-house, and the drivers and helpers were on the point of going to their evening meal, their employer came in. He had been drinking, he was heated; he had lost at lotto, and he was in that humour in which a naturally good-natured man is for the time being a savage tyrant, and vents his ill-humour on the first thing he sees. He caught sight of the boy and attacked him.

'Oh, you there! I hear you have been out all day. I gave you leave to go out for an hour and you take a day! A fine payment for all my charity! What are you rubbing down that horse for? You are not here to rub down horses; a brat like you. Claudio asked you? Let Claudio do his own work. Where is he? Gone out? Gone out ten minutes after he brings in his carriage? You and he may leave these stables to-morrow. To-morrow, before noon, you take your week's wage and go. You are a young scoundrel.'

Gino trembled and grew white, but he said nothing. He thought, 'If Stellina come out I will work somewhere, somehow for her. We might get together into the country.'

Yet he felt stunned; he could not imagine that he should live anywhere except in these stables of the old church.

His employer scolded, swore, and found fault for many minutes more, venting his ill-humour on men and beasts; then went away leaving terror and dismay behind him. Gino alone of them all did not speak.

'Cheer up, little chap; I will get you a place,' said an old driver who was always kind to him in a rough way. 'You know you did wrong staying out all day. The master can't abide idlers.'

Gino did not defend himself.

An hour later he was alone as usual at night in the stable. There was no light except that which came from one old lantern swinging from the high groined roof. The doors were open to the street.

In the gloom he saw a man's figure, and the yellow rays of the lantern fell on the face of his friend the carter Zanobi.

'Stellina!' cried the boy, as he sprang forward breathless. The carter came across the threshold and sat down on a pail which was turned upside down.

'Do not fret, my poor lad,' he said slowly. 'I am rare sorry to bring you no better news.'

'She is dead!' cried Gino.

'They killed her,' said Zanobi bitterly. 'Her milk and her grief drove her wild, and they were afraid of her, and got the vet to declare she was mad, and they killed her at nine o'clock in the morning, poor little brave soul! No bowels of mercy in them, even for her as a mother! And I saw her pretty black skin even now a-drying on a nail. Lord save us, child, do you not take on so!'

Gino had fallen speechless under the old mare's body as she stood munching in her stall.

The carter dashed water on his head and face, and shook him roughly, and he soon rallied, or seemed to rally, and said little except to ask again and again the details of her death. Zanobi went away as the clock struck ten of the night, glad that the shock had passed off without evil effects. 'He was fond of the dog, but it was only a dog, and he will not fret much. I will buy one for him somewhere to-morrow,' thought the good rude man as he went away in the moonlight between the tall ancient houses.

Gino was left alone. He sat still some time, his chin resting on his hands; at last he got up and drank thirstily, stroked the old mare upon her nose, and barred the stable-door.

By the light of the lamp he cleaned his boots and the metal clasp of his waist-belt, and laid them together on the lid of a corn-bin, with an old dirty mass-book which had been given him in his childhood.

Then he took his fork and upturned the hay which covered the stone under which the dead puppies lay; he raised the stone and took them out and kissed them; they were all which was left of Stellina. He put them in his apron and slung them round his throat. He paused a little while looking at the darkness which hid the aisles of the church from his sight; close at hand the rays of the lantern shone on the ribbed roof, the mutilated angels, the wooden gates of the stalls; there was no sound but of the breathing of the horses, and the hot black space was full of their scent.

Gino crossed himself; then he fastened one of the stable halters fast to a beam, passed its noose round his neck, and mounted a wooden stool on which he had sat hundreds of evenings when his work was done, with Stellina's little form between his knees.

Then he kicked the stool from under his bare feet.

When the men came in the morning, and, finding the doors closed, with none to open them, had them forced by smiths, they saw Gino hanging there dead, the dead puppies tied around his neck.

Life had been too hard for the little stable-boy.

LA ROSSICCIA

La Rossiccia.

'PER rossiccia, rossiccia 'l è ; ma 'l è belloccia.'

'For red, yes, she is red, but she is a big beauty.'

So said a man leaning on his spade amongst the flax-fields, and following with his eyes the form of a young and handsome woman who stepped with a lithe step over the clods of fresh-turned earth. He was an old man, bent and black with long years of toil under hot suns; but he was not so old that he could not tell a good-looking lass when he saw one.

She was always called La Rossiccia on account of that ruddy, auburn hair which the dead Venetian painters loved, and which she possessed; and she had with it the milk-white skin which usually is its corollary; she had a straight profile, a beautiful throat, and a figure fit for a statue of Artemis; she was famous for that goddess-like form on all her countryside, and the men and youths all said as the old labourer had done, 'Rossiccia 'l è, ma 'l è belloccia.' She was only a poor girl, very poor, daughter of a bargeman who had gone to and fro on the broad waters of the Po, carrying charcoal and timber, and doing rough work from morn till eve till he could do it no longer, and lay bedridden. The house she lived in was hardly more than a hut, built up with stones and wattles on the edge of a great plain covered with flax, through which the sluggish waters of a canal passed, giving out fever heats in summer and chilly mists in winter. Far away in the distance were the towers and domes and bridges of a once great city, Ferrara, but they were so far away that they were mere specks in the golden haze of the horizon, and within the walls of Ferrara she had never been.

She was by name Caterina Fallaschi, but she

was known to the few people who made up her little world as Rossiccia; she had been called so ever since her babyhood, when her auburn curls had shone in the sun as she danced in the marsh pools or ran through the dust of the highway, which was barely trodden now by man or or beast, though in the old posting days it had been a well-known road for travellers and the carriers of the mail.

The little group of sun-baked, mist-soaked cottages stood together amongst the rank grass on the left bank of the canal, and the sluggish, muddy waters and the white deserted road went by them, going to forms of life of which the occupants of these cabins knew nothing, and never would know aught. All around them were the flat fields, intersected by ditches, with here and there a few pollarded willows and lopped mulberries, and above them all the beautiful sky; the same blue serene sky as the painters of the Lombard schools put above their Madonnas and behind their angels. For many months of the year it was blue as the flax flowering under it; and when it was covered with silvery mist or black with stormcloud it was always beautiful; not so intense in colour as the sky farther south, but etherial, exquisite, spiritual. It lent something of its own loveliness to the monotonous plain, the stagnant water, the dull road; it brought its own grace and glory even to the squalid huts, until the house-leek on their thatch looked gold and the bulrushes by their water steps seemed the spears of fairy armies. There was only one blot upon it to which it could lend no enchantment, of which its light and air could not soften the harsh and offending lines. It was the ugly whitewashed fort which stood in the midst of the flax-fields, angular, ominous, sombre, suspicious, the modern edifice which was called the Polveriera, and which was a blot upon the landscape, speaking ever of the brutal machinery of modern war.

These broad, level lands which unrolled themselves to the far edge of the mountains had seen many centuries of carnage, from the hordes of the Huns and the Goths to the battalions and squadrons of Napoleon, from the children of Etruria flying before the march of the Legions, to the conscripts of France rallying at the voice of Desaix as the sun set on

Marengo. The black toads who lived under the reeds had seen the young soldiers, blackened and burned with the smoke of Arcola, marching with weary feet along the dusty highway where nothing now passed except mule carts and bullock wagons; and against the plastered walls of the posting-house there had leaned the matchlocks and there had swung the torches of free lances and of reiters as the armies of the emperors poured over the Lombard plains generation after generation, when the plough and harrow passed over the sites of ruined cities, and smoking hamlets marked the passage of the conquerors. But of all which it had witnessed nothing had been so ugly, so mean, and yet so deadly as this round white fort rising naked, ominous, out of the fields around with immeasurable powers of destruction shut within its enceinte, yet without ignoble and unlovely, with all the meanness and the ugliness of modern architecture.

On these plains, which had seen the splendour of Francis, the brilliancy of Pescara, which had drunk the hero's blood of Bayard, and of Gaston de Foix, which had been the battlefield of Europe through so many ages, ever since the fires of Altala had lit up its morning skies, this powder magazine, common and ugly as a factory, set bare and angular amongst the frogs and flax, was an epitome of that dreariness and deadliness which lie like a curse on modern war as on modern peace.

It held force enough within it to blow up into nothingness a million of men; but in its outer aspect it was ignoble, common, trivial, emblem of the time which had created it. It had been built but a few years, and the people of the plains hated it, dreaded it, looked askance at it as they perforce passed beneath its shadow in their boats or with their mules. It stood a perpetual menace, a standing terror amidst the slow and quiet waters and the peaceful fields. The building of it had scarred and spoiled the earth around, and left mounds of rubble and bare earth, where nettles alone flourished. When it had been completed, and the ordnance wagons and their heavy caissons had come slowly through the darkness of winter days to bring it the explosives which were to be stored in it, the escort of troopers passing slowly on either side of the long lines of wagons, a weight of fear and of ever-present peril fell on the souls of the dwellers near. It was an infernal thing set ever in their sight. For scores of miles along those level lands the ugly white thing could be seen, its iron conducting-rods disfiguring the sky and the landscape, its lines of telegraph wires stretching far and wide until they were lost in space.

But habit familiarises with all forms of horror; and in a year or two after the building of it the people of the district thought little of it except to look anxiously towards it in hours when electric storms were driving their clouds in masses over the plains and lightnings ran in fury from the distant alps to the unseen seas. They knew that if the lightning struck it they and theirs for miles around would be hurled up to the high heavens in lifeless, shattered, smoking fragments; the boatmen and bargees knew it, the labourers and carters knew it, the millers knew it whose mill-wheels turned in the sullen waters, the beggars knew it who sat in the shade or the sun; but familiarity breeds indifference, if not contempt, and they lived within reach of the imprisoned powder-devils as the vintagers live and laugh on the slopes beneath Vesuvius and under the woods of Etna. Only these people of the plains rarely laughed, because the pellagra was constantly amongst them eating away their skins and poisoning their blood, and ague and marsh fever often laid them low, and they worked for other men's profit, and they had little joy in their lives, and small hope. The soldiers who came to guard the powder magazine brought with them, moreover, into the district around a little money and the zest of something novel. There were no more than the strict number needful for the care and defence of the building, and those few hated the service in it and their exile from Ferrara or Mantua. But when any of them were off guard they sauntered to the old post-house or to the water-mills and gossiped and drank and played some game or another, and found favour invariably in the eyes of the women. They were but ugly fellows in ugly uniforms, with shaven heads and of puny stature; wholly unlike their forefathers, who had worn their long rapiers, their bright-coloured doublets, their loose love-locks, their plumed hats so gallantly in those old days of free-companions and musketeers, of Marignan and of Pavia, of which the waters rippling amongst the reeds and the church steeples rising amongst the mulberries seemed still to tell so many tales. But they were men, and better than nothing as they brought with them some little change, some little stimulant into the sickly, poverty-stricken hamlets amongst the flax. Yet the toilers of the soil loved them not; the soldiers were strangers, and the Italian dreads and dislikes strangers; and the fact that they were welcomed by their women made them disliked by the women's husbands and brothers and lovers. The soldiers were, moreover, in accordance with the policy and practice of the State, generally sent from southern provinces, and therefore foreigners in the sight of the dwellers of the plains. They were called the accursed Sicilians, Sicilian being a generic name used to denote all who came from the lands where oranges and citrons were common orchard trees, and the evil eye was held in honour.

The sight of the soldiers offended Rossiccia more

than anyone; when they bathed in the canal, or ran races along the road, or sauntered in their shirt-sleeves out of the sullen-looking gates of the depôt, they were odious to her sight; other women might chat with them, kiss with them, drink with them; she would do none of these things. They were foreigners, and they were slaves.

'Poor lads! they cannot help themselves,' said her father.

'They could go over seas,' she answered.

Many like them did go; to get to some land as far away as possible, where there is no conscription, is the dream of the Italian peasant; his dream takes him oftentimes where he dies miserably and prematurely in the sands of Panama, in the swamps of the Amazons, in the floods and frosts of the West, in the opium-hells of New York.

The soldiers hated the place no less than they were hated in it. The strict discipline, the dreary inaction, the rare relaxation, and the severe rules which the safety of the fort demanded made life bitter and irksome to these young men, who a little while ago had been shepherds wandering with their flocks, or cattle-keepers wild and free amongst the myrtle and lentiscus, or loafers in sunny southern streets, or charcoal-burners in the deep green cork-woods, or labourers upon the rich volcanic soil. The exactions and constraints of barrack-life are always odious, but in a powder-magazine their burden is, of necessity, much heavier, their ligatures much more tightly drawn. No man can play truant or infringe a rule, for he knows well that his life and his comrades' lives will pay the forfeit for any negligence, if a spark from a pipe be shaken out or a match be let drop from a careless hand. Ague and fever lurked in all the flax and hemp fields, and floated over the swamps in which, for sake of isolation, the powder depôt had been built; the soldiers cooped up in it—most of them in their second year of service—grew lean and yellow and hollow-eyed. The night sentries suffered most, for when the moon rose death rose with it. There was only one person in the district whom the miasma never hurt; it was Rossiccia. Her health was so perfect, her frame so vigorous, that the deadly vapours swept around her and over her harmlessly though she took no heed of them and no precaution against them, but lightly smote with bare feet the poisonous soil, and sang joyously as she met the fever-laden languors of the wind. She had the force and the invulnerability of the 'huntress of the moon,' and from her earliest years she had been proof against all disease, as though her mortal form were nourished by a goddess's blood.

Her father was a sallow, sickly man, lying half his days on his back on his grass mattress. Her brothers were weakly youths, though they laboured like the rest amongst the flax and hemp. Her mother had died years before, in the early childhood of Rossiccia. Whence had sprung this miracle of admirable and vigorous life? No one could say. Some gossips recollected that the mother, when young and good-looking, had spent one carnival time in Ferrara, and had come back pregnant, and that there had been talk of a noble of that town, and that there had been for a while easier means and better food in their cabin, and that when the child had been born the mother had shown her to the neighbours, and had said, 'Rare race runs in her veins; and see her satin skin!' But her putative father had never shown either anger or jealousy, and had accepted the child with the rest, only he had never liked her. Rossiccia knew these suspicions of her origin, as people do know that which intimately concerns them, yet which is never directly told to them in actual words; and she flattered and amused herself with many dreams of glory, and her proud fancies made her cleaner and more orderly, more careful and coquettish in the putting on of her poor clothes, than were the wretched women around her, whose skin never touched water from one Easter to another, and who huddled on their rags without a thought of comeliness or cleanliness. She waited for something; she knew not what; some favour of fortune, some change, some miracle.

At sixteen she had married one of the labourers, without love, from that instinct towards sexual union common to her class. She had been very poor; he had treated her ill. She had had a child and buried it, and the man had died of fever—all before two years more had passed over her head. She had gone back to live with her family, saying to herself, '*Nessun me piglierà più*' ('Nobody shall get me again'). Her only associations with what is called love were discomfort, quarrels, physical pains. With her own people she was poor, indeed, but unmolested: she was of use to them, and they were grateful, in a rough, dumb, semi-conscious way: as the oxen in the carts were when she gave them water and wiped the dust from their hot eyes.

In the liberty and comparative contentment which followed her return to her father she returned to work at the flax-bleaching; foul-smelling, unhealthy work: for they have not patience to let it be done by the rains and the suns, as of old, but steep the cut stalks in acids and whiten them overmuch and over-quickly, so that the strands soon rot and the linen woven therefrom soon grows poor and ragged. But neither the evil smells nor the evil exhalations hurt her; and she made her daily dole somewhere or other out of the flax, either by field work or factory. When the flax was in flower, blue as the sky, the ugly land, level though it was, grew beautiful, and the wonder of its transformation sometimes touched her as she worked amongst it: a little bright flower, gay as a forget-me-not, turning to so many things, filling the housewives' presses, covering the bridal couch, sheltering the bed in labour, filling looms and warehouses and shops, clothing gentlefolks, putting food in poor men's mouths. She was sorry when the blossoms faded and the stalks were cut down. Something of her heart seemed to go out with the dry, dull brown bundles which the acid ate. But all these were foolish wandering fancies, which she told to no one. The flax helped her to her daily bread; that was all the outward concern she had with it.

The women of her little world were very envious of her. They knew very well that in their own poor squalid world she was supreme. The black-browed, yellow-skinned soldiers from the fort crowded about her like wasps about a ripe peach, and the boatmen and towing-men upon the canal went to mass at the half-ruined lime-washed church only on the chance of seeing her dip her fingers in the holy-water basin or kneel down to say her Aves on the damp red bricks. Rossiccia only threw them a few ungracious words, or laughed at them rudely, showing her white teeth; but her indifference was more attractive than the willingness of others. And in that ague-stricken, fever-haunted community her health alone was an amazing and irresistible charm. She was like a green and lusty vine, springing lithely when all the rest of the vineyard was tainted and sear.

She had courage, too; that rarest quality on Italian soil. They had seen her once, when the waters flooded the fields, wading and swimming to rescue the old and feeble who had been surprised by the flood; and once again, when a goaded ox had charged down amongst a group of children, she had seized him by his lowered horns and held him firm and turned him backwards, the great creature obedient to her commands. She had no fear in her, except one; and of that she was ashamed and never spoke. It was a vague, shapeless, but painful fear of the Polveriera. It had been built in her childhood, and she had watched its rising with dislike and terror. It was associated in her mind with the groans of the poor oxen and mules lashed brutally as they had brought the materials for its building, and it had destroyed a piece of waste land which had been covered with grasses and reeds and bryony and bearberry; a place precious to children and sacred to their play through many generations. She had watched the wild shrubs uprooted, the sods upturned, the brambles and briars burned, the spades and mattocks plunged into the wounded earth, and the whole spot ruined, that the foundations of the powder-fort might be laid. Her play-place had been as sacred to her as the waters of the Alphæus and the woods and lawns of Olympus were to a child of Greece.

In her dumb shut soul there stirred, half-consciously, that same sympathy with desecrated and violated nature which from the great soul of Leconte de Lisle pours forth in articulate and conscious splendour of invective in the imprecations of *La Fôret Vierge*. She knew not and could not have said what moved her, but it was the same sentiment, though in her immature and embryonic, fated never to know birth. She was unlike the people round her. She had more daring and more tenderness. When the children put living lizards on the hot charcoal, or sewed their mouths up to see the vain efforts of the little creatures in their torture, she rescued the poor harmless things; or, if she came too late to do so, made their tormentors feel the weight of her strong hand. 'Guai! c' è la Rossiccia!' the cowardly urchins shouted to one another when they saw her approach, if they were busy with any cruel sport. They were horribly afraid of her, though when they were sick, or hurt, or in trouble she would do more for them than their own mothers would do; and diphtheria, and scrofula, and fever were often amongst them, giving them as their last cradle a yard of the damp and dangerous earth where the rank grass and the black crosses were so thick.

She had watched the erection and completion of the edifice with hatred of it in her soul, and she had seen the files of grim wagons bringing it the deadly provisions it needed as she might have watched a dragon fed with human flesh. The other children had capered for joy as the whips had cracked, and the wheels of the ordnance wagons had creaked and jolted; but she had turned her back on them sullenly, thinking of the red bear-berry fruit and the wild white roses she had been used to gather where there now stood that ugly, naked, frowning tower of death which none could pass near unchallenged. So in her womanhood the artillerymen who were stationed in the fort found no favour in her sight; and she always wished that the tower were not there, two miles off her own dwelling, with its close-packed powers of death lying unseen behind its walls. It was a scar on the landscape, a blot on the horizon, and when the sun set behind it and its whitewash changed in the shadows into grey, it lost its common sordid look and seemed to grow sinister and gigantic, menacing even the sky.

Once or twice, to cure herself of her fancies, she went close up to its base, answering the challenge of the sentries; not a bough or briar or blade of grass grew nigh; the ground around had all been flattened and battened down, so that no seed could multiply upon it. There was not a single trace of the leafy life which once had flourished there and sheltered the hare and the lizard and the low-nesting birds. There were only the sullen casements, the ugly sentry-boxes, the iron-clamped doors, the bare walls where the plaster was peeling from the damp and the sun. She went away from it hating it more, thinking of the time when here on its site she had filled her little brown hands with berries and seen the green locust cling to the wild oleander blooms.

Some vague sad sense of the perpetual destruction of all beauty and all peace which is for ever at work under the pressure of an artificially created necessity came to her, ignorant and isolated creature though she was. Some perception of the hideous insanity with which these engines of war are perpetually multiplied and accumulated and every year made more and more intricate, deadly, and universal, seemed borne in upon her with the sight of that ugly magazine of war standing nude and straight and angular where once the finches nested and the asphodel bloomed. Men had not always used that foul gunpowder, she knew. In the village church (once a great and stately one) where she went on every holy-day and feast-day there were frescoed walls, faded and mildewed, but still easy to see, where the knights rode at each other lance in rest, and the bowmen met the charges of the pikes, and the angelic hosts hovered above in gay panoply, smiting the paynim with the sun-rays for their spears; time had been, she knew, when a stout heart and a supple blade and a strong arm had been all the weapons a man needed in warfare, when the race had been really to the swift and the battle to the strong.

'Were they ever like these?' she asked the sacristan one day, pointing to the fresco which had been begun by Vittore Pisano, and continued by some unknown but vigorous hand.

'Ay, ay,' he answered, 'they made war just so; all fair and open, and the good saints striking for the right.'

'It was better so,' said Rossiccia gravely and with regret.

'For sure it was better so,' said the sacristan; 'nowadays they mix the devil's doses in factories and kill you so that no man sees or knows whence your death comes. Someone sets a tube a-smoking miles off you behind a bank or a hedge, and you and all round you fall dead men. You don't even see your enemy oftentimes; 'tis only a puff of smoke and a screech; and the saints keep themselves safe behind the clouds.'

One day, when she was near the fort, one of the officers came out of it and overtook her.

'I have seen you here more than once,' he said, with severity and suspicion. 'What brings you here? You have no errand?'

'No,' she answered him, curtly.

'Why do you come, then? At evening, too! The sentinels should arrest you.'

'Arrest me if you like.'

'Why do you come? Tell me.'

'It is no business of yours.'

'Is it not! I would have you know, woman, that I am second in command here.'

'You may be first in command here. But you are not in command of me.'

'If you speak in that fashion I will put you under arrest. You are found on forbidden ground, and will give no account of yourself.'

She laughed, showing her white small teeth. 'What good will that do you? You would have to let me go.'

'I can have you searched.'

She folded her arms on her bosom and looked at him.

'On what plea?'

The young man was embarrassed. He was aware that he had no right to insist, and he was dazzled by her great sparkling eyes and the whiteness of her throat.

'No one is allowed to be nearer the powder depôt than yonder stone,' he said, pointing to a block of granite. 'That is well known to the whole district. And if you violate the rule for no wrong purpose, but merely from ignorance or in wilfulness, you would not make this mystery of your coming.'

'I make no mystery,' she answered, puzzled by the word, which was strange to her. 'But I come and go when I please, and the place is my birthplace, and I shall not ask leave of strangers and men from foreign towns.'

'Foreign towns! I am of Palermo.'

'You are a foreigner,' said Rossiccia, with the obstinacy of the peasant and the contempt of the Lombard for the men of the south.

'There is only one Italy,' said the soldier, with increasing anger.

Rossiccia laughed.

'The bundle of sticks is a faggot however tight you bind it together; it is never the trunk of a tree.'

He looked at her in astonishment.

'Where did you get your ideas? Who taught them to you?'

'I have thought about things; no one has taught me,' she answered, and then she turned round and walked away slowly. He hesitated; he was deeply angry, and a little disquieted and suspicious, but he let her go unmolested. She was a woman of the village; he knew that it would be easy to learn all about her.

He was annoyed by her insolence, but he was moved by her beauty and her noble stature. He saw by her clothes and her bare feet that she was only one of the poor people of the little hamlet of

Trestella, but she had the carriage and the glance which an artist would have given to Tullia or Flavia. He was a young man, and easily excited by such charms. Life in the Polveriera was tedious, monotonous, and wearisome. There was constant anxiety in it, yet no action. There was no diversion except a game of cards or dice. There was little or no liberty, and it was hardly better in many ways than a prison. He was a lieutenant of artillery, and for the time being in command there; he was an illegitimate son of a noble family; he had been educated well, but scantily provided for; he was well made in form and feature; lithe, slender, dark, graceful as any panther; even the uncouth uniform and the close-cropped hair could not make him otherwise than picturesque; and when he stripped to the waist in the close heat of the casemates, or plunged naked into the canal water to bathe and swim, he was beautiful with the old classic beauty, which is not dead, but only disguised under the shapeless clumsiness of modern costume and custom. He was by name Odone Palmestris, the latter being the name of his mother, who had been a singer in

T

the theatres of the south; nature had made him an artist, pressure from others and indifference on his own part had made him remain a soldier when his term of forced service had come to an end. He was now twenty-six, and was favoured in the service through the influence of his father, who was attached to him, and had always seen him from time to time. At heart he was disinclined to submit to discipline, but he was ambitious, and saw no other way to become known than through the army. For some trifling act of insubordination he had been punished by being sent to the powder fort in the marshes; a post tiresome, dull, arduous, and of heavy responsibility. All his ardent, passionate, chafing, and galled life was put to torture there; in the long, slow, hot days and nights his spirit wore itself out as an imprisoned animal wears off its hair against the bars of its hated cage. He had solicited a change of duty, and had written to his father begging him to support his prayer with the authorities; but as yet there had come no answer to his request, and every week dragged drearily along, each seeming emptier and longer than the others. In such a moment and in such a mood the appearance near the fort of such a woman as Rossiccia awakened his imagination, and attracted his attention as in other and fuller hours it might have failed to do. Her answers had irritated him, and he thought of her often in the long dull night after he had gone on his round of inspection, and changed the sentries and seen the lights extinguished.

'Eh! 'l è la Rossiccia; la Rossiccia 'l è,' said the people to him when he inquired for a tall, fair woman with auburn hair and a silver dagger run through it, and they showed him the low rush-thatched cabin a little outside the village where she dwelt.

It vexed him to be ignored and flouted by a woman so poor, so illiterate, yet so indifferent; and, as always happens, irritation increased the influence which she exercised over him. A score of times he swore to himself to think no more of the red-haired jade; and the mere sight of her afar off, walking through the flax fields with her distaff, spinning as she went, or going down to the water-side with a bronze pitcher balanced on her head, overwhelmed all his resolutions and stimulated a caprice into a passion. He bitterly repented that he had blamed her for coming near the fort; and he would have forfeited his grade and epaulettes to have persuaded her to return. She never did so. She knew that nothing could give her back the wild oleander shrubs and the white briar roses of her old playground.

One morning he saw her beating linen where a little space of water was shut off by logs of wood for washing purposes. The other women were beating and splashing and shouting and laughing clamorously, but she alone worked in silence, her fine arms shining like marble in the sun against the yellow water and the moss-grown logs. He approached the group and bandied light words with the other people, but she took no heed of him; she did not look off her work.

'He is well to look at,' murmured one of the women to her; but Rossiccia answered with contempt:

'These soldiers all strut like the red partridges in pairing-time, but they are nothing but slaves when all is said.'

'Men are slaves to a beautiful woman, whether they are soldiers or civilians,' said Odone as he lingered amongst the osiers grey and yellow in the heat.

Rossiccia appeared as though she did not hear, and beat her linen more rudely and loudly: it was not linen, indeed, it was only the hempen cloth of which her own shifts and her men's shirts were made.

He seated himself on a stone and watched her. He had unbuttoned his tunic, and, though his limbs were disfigured by the military uniform, he was a graceful and picturesque figure as he leaned his head on his hand and smoked, jesting with the others but looking only at her.

Rossiccia took no notice of him, but finished her labour, threw the wet shirts she had wrung out in a lightly-twisted mass on her shoulder and went homeward.

'A sullen wench,' said Palmestris angrily to one of the other women.

'Nay, she is good-natured,' the woman answered, 'but she hates the sight of soldiers; 'tis to her as the red dog is to the white one.'

'Why?' he asked, interested and curious.

'Eh, for no reason I know of,' she replied. 'But yon fort was built on a bit of waste land which she was fond of as a child, and the sight of all you who dwell in it is to her like a week of rain when the flax flowers.'

'She cannot hate it more than we do,' said the young man with a laugh and a sigh. 'If she suppose that we can enjoy ourselves, she must think a rat happy in a wire trap.'

'Is it as bad as that?' said the woman. 'At least you get your victuals free and certain.'

To her this seemed the one supreme felicity of life; a few beans, a little maize-flour, a few drops of oil were all she got, and those were often wanting, and sometimes she had to make her bread with husks and grass seeds.

Odone did not hear her: he was following with his eyes the now distant figure of Rossiccia, tall and dark against the pale grey lights of the hot vapours which rose in visible mist from the flax fields.

'She has no *damo*?' he asked wonderingly. 'A

woman without a lover is as strange and stupid a thing as an unfertilised vine.'

'''Tis open for you,' said the woman with a grin. 'Try; and you will taste that little lance she wears in her hair.'

'You tempt me,' he answered.

He was tempted without her suggestion. The insolence and the indifference of Rossiccia stimulated the admiration which her physical strength and beauty had aroused in him. She seemed to look down on him, as if he were some mere insect which crept on the masonry of the powder magazine. He was above her and beyond her in every way: in blood, in knowledge, in culture, in circumstances. She could not scrawl her own name or read a line. He had passed difficult examinations with credit, and expected in time to pass into the staff. He had studied for pleasure as well as for necessity, and his natural talent was refined by culture. But he felt that he was nothing in her sight except a mere vassal of the government.

One night as the sun set in August he met her on the bank by the water-side, on the narrow towing-path which the horses used. She had a rope passed over her shoulders and was doing horse's work, pulling a boat up stream. Her feet were bare as they trod heavily the hot dusty grass; her throat was bare, he saw the blue veins in it throb and swell under the pressure of the rope, and her breasts under her thin cotton bodice rise and fall in the stress of the labour like two waves. The boat she towed was constantly checked in its course by the reeds and water-weeds growing in the half-stagnant water; the one man in it aided its progress as well as he could with a long pole, which he used alternately to part the tangle of the weeds and to keep the boat off the bank. Odone stood in her way as she came, and kept his place purposely.

'That is not work for a woman,' he said.

'Yes, it is,' said Rossiccia curtly. 'Women are beasts of burden.'

'Why do you do it?' he asked.

'That is no affair of yours. One makes pence as one can. Stand aside!'

He kept his place.

'Ho, you!' he cried to the man in the boat. 'Come up and take the tow-rope, and give me the pole. It is a fine sight to see you leaning your lazy length down there!'

The man looked up and laughed.

'She is a strong wench. She wants nobody to take up cudgels for her.'

'Will you come out of that boat?' said Odone, imperiously.

'Not I,' said the man; and he put his pipe in his mouth.

Odone, without any words, leaped from the bank into the boat, struck the pipe out of the other's lips, caught him by the waist, and tossed him, with no gentle hand, up on to the towing-path. The man fell heavily on the dusty grass.

'Give him the rope,' Odone cried to her, as the other got sullenly and sulkily upon his feet.

Rossiccia stood still, with her brown eyes wide open.

Then, despite herself, she laughed.

'You are an impudent meddler! What is it to you what others do? Say, Renato, are you hurt?'

she asked of the crestfallen boatman, who was swearing every foul oath in his repertory.

'Give him the rope,' said Odone.

'That I shall not do. He has hired me,' she answered; and she bent her back and strained her shoulders, and drew the boat slowly through the reeds. Odone was forced to use the pole to keep it from grinding against the bank; but when he had disengaged it he sprang ashore and seized the rope as it passed over her shoulders.

'I have said that you shall not do it!' he swore, with a furious oath. His hands touched her skin, and bruised it.

'Eh? You are no master of mine! How dare you—how dare you?' she said, with equal violence trying to force the rope out of his hands. The struggle was fierce, and the whole strength and volition of each of them were put into it. The boatman Renato, who had risen on to his feet and was behind the soldier, seeing how wholly engrossed he was in his conflict with the woman, whipped out of his waistband the narrow sharp knife, called a cook's knife, which almost all men of the populace carry, and, coming close up to Odone, struck at him with it under the shoulder-blade. But Rossiccia, who saw the movement, intercepted it; she let go the rope with one hand, and caught the knife by the blade before it could pierce her adversary's tunic. In the brief collision, the knife cut her badly ere Odone was aware that she was touched. The other man seeing her blood flow, flung his knife into the water and fled, thinking that he had stabbed one or other of them. Odone and she, sobered and subdued, stood apart from each other, breathing heavily, the rope still lying upon her shoulders.

'You are wounded!' he cried with emotion as he saw the red gash on her palm: he was wholly unaware of Renato's attempt. 'Did I do it with the rope?' he cried, in poignant affliction at what he thought was the consequence of his own violence. 'Oh, forgive me!—for pity's sake forgive me! I was mad; I knew not what I did!'

'What come you meddling here for?' she said roughly, whilst the pain of the cut flesh made her colour come and go despite herself. 'Let me alone, or I shall do you a mischief. I am not patient.

Because you keep guard over a cask of powder, you deem yourself a fine gentleman who can lay the law down to everybody——'

She stopped, breathless from the struggle with him, and sick, despite herself, from the smart and pain of the wound, round which she had hastily wrapped her skirt.

He looked in her face with so strange an expression in his own that it disturbed and daunted her.

'You say I am mad,' he said abruptly. 'Well, I may be; but it is you who have made me so. Ever since that day I saw you by the fort I have been bewitched; and to see you doing mule's work for that lazy rascal made me beside myself. I love you—dear God! how I love you!'

'Madonna mia!' exclaimed Rossiccia, and there were scorn, incredulity, and impatience in her tone: no emotion, no pleasure, no gratitude. 'You will make no fool of me!' she added sternly. 'I know that ranting, rancid stuff, and I am never duped by it. Get you gone! You have done harm enough for one day.'

She tried to pass him whilst the rope lay between them like a grey snake and the abandoned boat floated motionless amongst the weeds. But he saw the blood from her hand soaking through the cotton stuff which enwrapped it, and heeded not her rude, unfeeling words, but fell on his knees on the lonely path and clasped her skirts.

'I have hurt you in the flesh,' he murmured, 'but you have wounded me in the heart and stricken my very soul. I do not dupe you. I do not lie to you. I only love you, as God lives.'

Something in the vibration of his voice made her eyes look down on his unwillingly, involuntarily drawn to his gaze by some magnetic force. Suddenly all her face grew hot; she believed, she understood, almost she was conquered.

But she pushed him backward with her unwounded hand and disengaged herself from his hold.

'If it be true I do not want to hear, I do not choose to hear; men are nothing to me, and soldiers are less than men. Let me go.'

With a quick, unforeseen movement she ran

down the bank and springing into the abandoned boat, ferried herself over to the opposite bank.

He had always borne himself well both as a soldier and a man. Her gibe was an injustice as well as an absurdity, and, thrown at him in a moment when his passions were at a white heat, it shocked, stung, chilled, embittered him.

'I am a fool, and neglect my duty for a thankless fury,' he said in his teeth; and without looking back, he walked away towards the fort, which was three miles off across the plains.

When it was dusk that day Rossiccia returned to the spot where the boat had been left, and sat down in the reeds and waited. She had bound her hand up, but it was more and more painful as the flesh stiffened, and it enraged her because it would prevent her from working until it should heal. She waited to see the man who had done it; she divined that he would come at dark to look for his boat and take it away. No one was likely to steal it; it was well known on the water, and could not be appropriated without the risk of recognition.

She reckoned rightly: the boat was there with

its load of rank grass. She sat down above it on the dusty bank and let her hot feet dangle in the water: the frogs were croaking, the night-crickets were humming; big water-beetles boomed through the air; the lights at the night nets of the fishermen glowed here and there on the surface of the water; all was dark and still, for there was no moon.

She waited some time; the bats flew round her now and then, brushing her hair with their wings. At last she heard a cautious step of unshod feet treading the stones in the shallow bed of the stream; she could see the outline of a figure by the faint luminance of the stars. 'Is that you, Renato?' she cried, as she slipped down from the bank and stood erect between him and his boat rocking amongst the sedges.

He slunk back, afraid; but she held him by the shoulder with her unwounded arm.

'I saw what you tried to do,' she said contemptuously. 'You tried to stab from behind. You are a knave.'

'I was in my right,' said the man with excitement and no shame. 'The brute had insulted me—thrown me; why did you interfere? If you got hurt you deserved it. Why did you stop my knife?'

'You were a knave,' she repeated; 'you did not dare to fight.'

'Only fools fight,' said Renato. 'What is steel for, save to help one on the sly? And you made me throw my good little knife into the water—a good little knife which cost me three francs in the cutlers' quarter in Ferrara itself!'

'I did wrong; I ought to have kept it to slit your throat,' she replied, still holding him by the shoulder.

'What harm did I do you? You say you hate those soldiers, and this one is a viper from the south.'

Rossiccia was silent.

A sudden suspicion occurred to the mind of the other, who was old, sly, and malicious.

'Did you tell him?' he asked.

'Not I. You are one of us, and he is what he is.'

'And you will not tell?'

'No, I will not; so long as you keep the peace to him.'

'Why do you say that? Is he your *damo*, then?'

'I have no *damo*. But right is right.'

'Right is right, and first of all rights one pays an offence off as one can. What do you wait for here?'

'Only to tell you that. Keep your peace with him and I will keep my silence.'

Renato laughed a little impudently.

'You may say what you like, and there are plenty of cutlers' stalls, or a box of matches mayhap would serve him out best.'

'Well, I have warned you to leave him alone,' said Rossiccia sternly, little believing in his threats, for he was known to be of small courage. He was an ugly little old man born in the village, and thought of poor repute in it, though she, having known him from her childhood, was glad to do any work for him when he asked her. She left him and went home, ill at ease. Renato was not a good enemy, and that secret thrust which she had seen, haunted her like the remembrance of a nightmare.

It served the suit of Odone better than all his

own eloquence. When the moon rode high that night, a shield of gold in the star-studded heavens, she lying sleepless on her rude bed of dried rushes, heard a voice with the accent of the south in it, singing beneath her open shutter a love-lay of Sicily.

> Esci dalla finestra, core ingrato,
> Core di sasso, ed anima crudele.
> Non mi fate morire appassionato ;
> Ditemi di venir, caro il mio bene.
> Se mi dice di sì, il mio core brilla ;
> Se mi dice di no, muore di doglia.

The words were simple, but the melody to which they were sung was rich and passionate and fervid with all the fires of the land of lava.

Rossiccia kept her face buried amongst the dry rushes, and made no sign ; but her heart softened, and her mouth smiled in the dark.

A little later on, the song changed to one of triumph ; the Sicilian, despised, derided and rejected, became her master. She was conquered and took pride in her own subjection, as women do, and the proudest women most abjectly.

On her side it was one of those great passions

which, at their onset resisted and contemned, become the sole ruler of the life in which they are aroused; and on his, although begotten of the senses, it had some higher sentiment in it than mere physical admiration.

He had suffered and thought and studied, and his passions and his affections were strong; the stronger because they had been starved in his youth. He felt that in this woman, though to others she was only a peasant with unshod feet and empty brain, and lips locked by ignorance, and a temper violent from excess of feeling, there was something which made her akin to the better side of his nature.

He had little liberty, but what he had he gave to her; they met by the solitary banks of the stream or where the maize grew as tall as they, or at night he came under her window and she undid the bolts of the door noiselessly whilst her people slept. But it was very seldom that he got leave of absence; the number was few at the fort, and the responsibility was great.

The difficulty and the rarity of their meeting gave it a zest and sweetness such as are never known to security. All day long she went about her rude tasks with a joyous bird singing, as it were, for ever in her breast; and he, grave, taciturn, and solitary, to his fellows, thought only of her as he paced the rounds of the dreary and dangerous place to which he was confined.

They loved each other greatly, and too well to part or to obey the dictation of circumstance.

'After all, who has any authority over us? And we wrong no one,' they said to each other.

There was no jealous wife on his side, no suspicious husband on hers, no conjugal jealousies to be set up in arms between them and bar their meeting. They hurt no one by their surrender to their passion. They continued to meet as constantly as they could, and as secretly. Mystery is the very heart of the rose of love; pulled open in the light of day, the love, like the rose, is spoilt and drops. The obligation to keep their meeting secret lent to their attachment that glamour and that charm which can never accompany sentiments laid bare to others. Something from it has fled, never to return, when a third knows the joy of two.

He was but as a splinter of wood in the great grinding wheel of modern military service, and she was of no more account on earth than a speck of dust or a blade of grass in the towing-path; but they loved each other with the old Italian passion; the passion of Paolo and Francesca, of Romeo and Juliet, of Ginevra and Rondinelli, which still is alive as a devouring flame in the land, and which ever and again sends the stiletto or the dagger straight through breast and bone. *Per l'amore* is the cause of crime written against the names of half the toilers in the gangs of the galley-slaves of central and southern Italy. *Far' l'amore* is still to gentle and to simple the supreme pursuit, perfection, and perfume of life. Jealousy, cruel as the grave, and caprice, inconstant as the breeze, may be its companions; but it is lord of life and of death.

To meet, to be all in all to each other, to pass through the rest of the hateful hours only that the rising moon might show them heaven in each other's eyes, this was all for which either lived as completely as the Angelica and Medoro of the amorous poet whose ink was held for him by a Cupid when he dwelt within the walls of that Ferrara which lay red in the setting sun beyond the fields of flax. The sear, chill, shallow, selfish, modern temper may have slain Eros elsewhere, and torn his wings in strips to stretch them under the lens of the object-glass, but in Italy he still lives, child of the stars and the moonbeams, companion of the nightingales, sweet singer to the river-reeds, and if his soft hand close up on a blade of steel, he is only lovelier because also terrible.

One night when he was bidding her farewell, Odone said to her, 'To-morrow and for five to-morrows I cannot leave the fort at night, nay, scarce by day; my captain goes at daybreak on leave to Sardinia, and I am left in command. It will be utterly impossible for me to forsake my post. But we cannot live six days and nights asunder. Will you come to me there?'

'I hate the fort: it is cruel, it is dangerous; it is frightful to look at and to think of, dear!' she answered, with her old hatred and fear of it rising up in her, and finding no words strong enough to speak her abhorrence of it.

'Nay, I have loved it ever since I saw you under its pale walls,' he replied. 'You would make it beautiful if you came to it.'

'But no woman can come to it; nor can any stranger.'

'That is the rule, no doubt; but there might be a way. Say, love, to please me, would you have courage to come thither, if I found the way? It is a gruesome spot.'

'Go yonder!'

The blood left her cheeks at the mere thought. She was a woman, strong in body and in will; but she was of quick imagination, and the place was horrible to her, in fact and in fancy.

'If there were no other way for us to meet?' he asked, his lips touching, as he spoke, the whiteness of her throat.

She waited a moment, drawing her breath swiftly and painfully.

'Nay, to hell itself would I go, for that!' she answered at length, with the intensity of a great unspeakable emotion in the words. 'But you talk idly, beloved one,' she added. 'A woman cannot come thither; and could I come, it would disgrace you in your soldiers' eyes.'

'Were it known—yes; but if you would come as a lad, better still, as a conscript, it need be never known; you would be seen as my friend, or as one on business sent; and I could give you the clothes and tell you the password. See, dear, it would be quite easy. I am left in command; I can open the gates and close them. No one of the men will see anything strange. There will be no risk whatever, and we shall have sweet hours, if all too few; and in greater surety still than here.'

'Surety! In that place?'

'Ah! you are afraid of the place itself? Well, I can understand that it has terrors; that it seems like sleeping on the very roof of hell, like kissing the live mouth of a cannon as it belches, but——'

'I am not afraid in that way,' she said quickly. 'What! afraid for myself when *you* lie there alone so many a night? Dear soul, you should not think such shame of me.'

'I hardly did think it, my golden-eyed lioness. But if not that, what kind of fear, then?'

'I have always feared it. It grew up there, a sickly-looking, hideous, cruel thing of brick and stone and iron, where the yellow broom and the dog-roses and the St. Joseph's nosegays used to grow; and it is full of evil stuff to lay low gallant lads and the lovers and brothers and fathers of women. And I have heard my uncles tell of war; and it is the foul fiend of war which lives shut up there—yes; so I am afraid.'

He laughed in that familiarity with peril which breeds contempt of it.

'It is a foul fiend safe in irons, unless we of our own will let him out,' he said, carelessly. 'And, in truth, it is not as a fiend that we view the powder: explosives are as much in need for defence as for attack; these plains have been oftentimes ravaged by many a foe, and may be so again; then the death which sleeps under our hand will leap up like a waking lion and roar out, "Thus far shalt thou go, and no farther."'

'I know,' she answered impatiently, as her eyes looked across to the shadow of the fort, now dark against the moon, round, dark, sinister, like those numberless, nameless towers which rise without history or tradition under the cork woods and by the rocky coasts of Sardinia. It was impossible for her to put into words the dread she felt, which was altogether alien to either timidity or suspicion.

'Then, if you are not afraid you will come?' he urged with a man's narrow limitation to the personal.

'I said not so,' she answered with embarrassment. 'For you to come to me, that is as it should be: as it hath ever been betwixt men and women; but for me to seek you——'

'But I cannot leave, in common honour!' he cried passionately. 'Any personal risk would I run of court-martial, of dismissal, of anything; but to leave a post of danger which is confided to me—that I cannot do without shame. If aught happened and I were absent, what would men say of such a cur?'

'Then we will wait. Six days and six nights are long; the priests say that they did suffice for the making of the world; but we shall live through them.'

'Then, if you think so, you have no love for me!' he cried, with the eternal rebuke of the lover, who captiously asks for proof upon proof of that which he knows as certainly as he knows that the earth is under his feet. 'Think of me alone yonder, all alone; for the comradeship which once was welcome is only irksome, tedious, intolerable now;--six days and six nights without a word, a glance, a touch!--it is a foretaste of death. Is not life short enough, that we should give away twelve times twelve hours to silence—to solitude—to separation? When we lie dying shall we not say, "All that time we might have been happy, and we were not!" You are cruel! What is it I ask of you? You do things more unwomanly when you throw the towing-rope above your breast. Well, I love you better than you love me. I will do what is shameful, disloyal, treacherous; I will leave the fort when the moon is high, and come hither as I have come to-night; and if any ill happen whilst I am away, I can but kill myself upon your body; you will know that I loved you then!'

His face was pale as marble in his passion; his eyes flashed and glanced; the passion of his words vibrated through her, as some chords of music will thrill through the imprisoned souls of animals. She caught his hands to her bosom, and kissed them many times.

'No, no! I will come,' she said to him. 'After all, it matters nothing for me, if you wish it so. Tell me how; tell me when. You must never do what would shame you for me.'

That day he brought her a conscript's suit; the ugly, coarse, poor linen clothes which are given to the soldiers in summer, with the rude gaiters, the leathern belt, and the peaked cap of the service. She hid them under the sacking and dry rushes of her bed, and tried them on when night had fallen and the little house was still. She had only a small cracked piece of a mirror and the cotton-wick of an oil-lamp wherewith to view herself; but she smiled as she saw how straight and comely her limbs looked, and how tall and fine she stood in this boy's jerkin and breeches, with her hair tucked up in a great coil upon her head, so that the cap hid it from sight. She, who had never heard of Rosalind, looked Rosalind to the life, even though her clothes were so rude and mean.

It was a dark night, for the young moon had set

and clouds obscured the stars. The heat was great, so great that darkness seemed rather to increase than to dispel it. She who was used to go barefoot and clad according to season, could scarcely make her way with the weight of the gaiters and boots, and she did not dare remove them, lest such removal might betray her sex. The familiar paths, the plains known to her from her infancy, the outlines so engraven on her mind by long association that she could trace them in the dark, seemed no longer the same, because her own personality seemed the same no more. She got over the parched and dusty soil clumsily, slowly, with a gait wholly unlike her usual fleet and careless tread ; but although she felt as if some leaden hand plucked her back every step as she went, she drew nearer and nearer to the fort, made visible by a little light which he had promised her to set by one of the loopholes, and which sparkled starlike in the darkness.

As she approached it her eyes, grown used to the dark, could trace the ugly pale building on its solitary mound. It was a dread trysting-place, a grim bower for love ; but she pressed onward with a sensation which she could not have analysed, half fear, half triumph over fear. She went straight up to the bolted iron gates; the sentry, with a sharp rattle of his musket, summoned the shadow, which alone he saw, to stand and give the password. She gave it, and added as her lover had bade her, that she had come there to see the officer left in command. 'Pass in,' said the sentry, satisfied; the soldier at the gates asked her more questions and held up a lanthorn to look at her, but he saw only another young soldier like himself, as he thought, and after a while she got through the doors and within the building. Odone met her as he would have met a brother or a comrade; drew her within his own chamber and closed the door.

At dawn he unbarred the gates himself and she went homeward. No one who saw her amongst the sleepy and sullen men kept on watch-duty thought for a moment that she was other than what she looked; a conscript, a little taller, brighter, more elastic in movement than are most of the wretched youths dragged from their homes under the colours. She went over the ground backward to her village as silently as a vapour wreath moved over the river-bed. None of her own people knew of her absence; their maize paste and bread was ready as usual for them on their bare breakfast-board; and when her father's querulous, piping voice demanded his pipe and drop of coffee, both were there. With such complete security and immunity had the midnight tryst been kept, that, when night came again and the church-bells tolled the hour over the marshes, she put on her boy's clothes as a matter of course, and took her way again towards the fort.

This second night was radiant from the stars, so that the moon was little missed, but her passage over the marsh and the flat fields was more open to sight, were any there to see. The country was so lonely that she met no one; but, unseen by her, the man Renato, who was cutting reeds—stolen reeds—half-way to his waist in stagnant water, looked by chance at this figure of a young soldier flitting through the shadows, and looked again and again more curiously and closely, and said to himself:

'May an apoplexy take me! If that lad were not a lad and a soldier, I should say he was Rossiccia's self; that is the turn of her head, though the hair looks cropped; that is the skim of her foot, only it is clogged by the leather.'

His curiosity and malice being aroused, he wandered along through the osiers and willows, keeping her in sight for half a mile or so, until he saw her strike straight across the flat fields towards the place of the powder fort. He was stupid, but he was cunning; he grinned as he dragged himself through the sedges: 'Two turtle-doves nesting on a cask of gunpowder, pretty dears, pretty dears!' He grinned again, and stood still with his sickle in his hand, gnawing the black stump of his pipe.

If it had been a man of their own plains he would have seen no harm in it; but a stranger, a Sicilian, a man from over-seas, where fire-mountains burned all the year round, and the men, made of fire too, slit your throat did you but brush their ploughshare with your heel!—that was different, that was against every law of the soil writ and unwritten.

Whom could he tell? Her father? he was a

bedridden gaby. Her brothers? they were children who looked to her for the bread they ate. Her neighbours? 'twas no business of theirs; they would wag their heads and laugh.

No matter: they should not sleep in peace much longer, he promised himself, as he worked amongst the dusky willow rods, watching ever and again the lights hung out by the fishermen against their nets for fear the fishers should perceive his pile of cut reeds and rods. The ignorant mind is slow to take in an idea, still slower to trace out a plan; but it is tenacious of its resentment, and holds fast to its gratification of grudge and reprisal.

Thus his little, narrow, malignant brain worked on as well as it was able at one thought: the lovers who were there within those gates of hell. Not that he had any amorous jealousy or envy; he was too hungry and too poor a creature to cherish passion, but he hated the man who had flung him up out of his own boat on to the sand like a dead mole, and he would have liked to come between that scornful foreigner and his good luck. For it was rare good luck to have the Rossiccia for a *ganza*; though he

X

himself was too concerned with picking and stealing and scraping halfpence together to have much sense or sight left in him for women, he knew that she was good to look at, and to love, white-skinned, strong-limbed, full-breasted wench that she was, drawing a barge along as easily as other women would draw a child's go-cart. Had he not seen her do it? Had she not done it for him? And now she was a fine foreign soldier's mistress, and went to her popinjay amongst his casks and kegs of death! An angry sense of envy, which was only not jealousy because he was too old and too indifferent from long absorption in the sorriest means of existence, stirred in him as he splashed amongst the reeds and looked across at the round pale tower of the powder-magazine. The form of Rossiccia was no longer visible between the building and the water.

He chewed his pipe-stem moodily and thought ugly thoughts; and as a little shrew swam by him, stoned it because he was willing to hurt something.

It pleased him to think that if he could only get inside that building, a few sparks from his pipe would send these lovers into the blackness and emptiness of that vast vault which over-arched the stars. But he could not get in, he knew that: neither he nor his pipe could ever pass those ceaselessly marching sentries who paced beneath the walls. He bent down again and began to cut more reeds: it did not matter to him where he cut them, none of the osier-beds were his, he took them as he took the quail or the teal, when and wherever he found them. If he could have driven his knife into the stranger who had affronted him, and seen his blood flow, he would have been immediately appeased, and would have borne no ill-will later on; but, having been baulked of his just revenge by Rossiccia's intervention, his hatred had grown and deepened and strengthened, and added to it was the sense of injustice which rankles in one who has been denied his right. He pondered long with such dull wits as he possessed, sharpened by envy and malice and natural cunning; and, first stacking his stolen osiers in his boat and taking them down stream to his cabin on the bank, unperceived, he cleaned the river mud off himself and procured a lift on a market cart going at dawn to the city with a load of water-melons and pumpkins.

He had taken a few coins which he had kept hidden in a hole in the thatch, and shook them in his closed hand in his pocket, as he jolted on amongst the smooth and the wrinkled globes of the green fruits.

'It will buy a fine big box of matches,' he thought with a chuckle. 'Or a nice black slow-worm with a fiery eye in her head. Or a good little knife like the one that rusts in the mud.'

He felt proud of his omnipotence. He was only an ugly old man, with only a few pence, and a hut made of rushes and wattles, but his powers for evil made him feel like a king. As the waggon rolled through the slumbrous, grass-grown streets of Ferrara he looked at the opening shops with a cruel smile of contentment and coming vengeance.

He lingered all day in the town, unable to decide what he would buy. But at the last he chose a rough provincial thing, a long taper-like slow-match and a blasting fusee in connection with it; a match which would creep, creep, creep gingerly and securely for half an hour, until it would reach the fuse and scatter ruin round it. It was sold to him in one of the low dens of the town by a maker of fireworks of a common sort, who asked no questions and might be safely trusted to forget the sale. Cleopatra never clasped her asp more fondly than he hugged the ugly coil which he carried away from the shop.

'My good little knife, my good little knife!' he said to himself as he drifted out of Ferrara on one of the barges; 'she will be sorry she made me put it in the water!'

He had been a stonemason in his early manhood, and he had watched the building of the powder-magazine with a shrewd eye, noting where the work was scamped, and soft or porous stone used and ill-baked bricks. He knew its weak points, and knew that if a man on moonless nights could conceal himself often enough and long enough to have time for the operation, he could easily penetrate through the masonry at the rear of the building. The idea pleased him, and he dwelt on it fondly. He liked to think of all those men pluming themselves on their safety whilst he, when the moon was young, should be working away in the rank grass and coarse sand to send them all to perdition.

Eh! the Sicilian had tossed him up on to the bank like a dead cat and had said never a word in excuse, and she, the jade whom he had always admired and praised, had treated him like the sod of earth beneath her foot. Where would they be when, some moonless night, he should sit in the sedges and watch the column of smoke tower into the air, and feel the whole solid ground shake and crack?

Eh! it was a fine thing to have been a working-mason, and to have known the tricks of the trade, and to have a few pence to spend in powder! He was so elate at his own capacity and cunning that he hugged the fuse to his breast and kissed it before he put it safely away in a covered corner of his belt.

The absent commander prolonged his absence in Sardinia, loth to return to the fort in the flax-fields, and Odone commanding in his stead remained tied to his dangerous duty. The canicular heats were at their greatest, and many of the soldiers were ill with fever or dysentery, or the vague nameless nausea and weakness brought on by life on these lands in summer time. The earth around the powder depôt was less healthy than when the bilberry and bearberry had sucked up the moisture of the soil; and the miasma mists were heavy and poisonous where the sluggish waters crept beneath the duckweed and vallisneria.

His days were overfilled and anxious and arduous; he had no one to share the burden of responsibility with him; the young man under him in command was laid low with the marsh fever, and he could not quit the fort for an hour.

Only when the sun set and the welcome coolness of night descended on the plains, did he throw off his heavy load of care, and surrender himself to the consolations of a love which had had as yet no time to wane or pall, but which by mystery and difficulty and rarity retained the first ecstatic charm of its earliest hours.

Whether the men knew or guessed aught he could not be sure, but if they did they were discreet and sympathetic; there was no one who cared or dared to wonder at the frequent visits of the strange young soldier, when the heavens were full of stars, and the owls hooting above the grey thickets of the willow-rods.

They were as much alone in those hours before the dawn as though they had been uncompanioned in a virgin world. The old man Renato, who alone knew of their trysts, said nothing; he was intent on his own work; chuckling to himself as he drilled and chipped, unseen, unheard, and in the dark, to think what fiery splendour would celebrate their union, ere the moon should again have leisure to grow large.

One night when morning was quite near Rossiccia was awake whilst her lover slept. He had taken some touch of fever himself; he was weak and chilly and over-tired; the insidious poison of the soil had crept into his veins, and stolen from his sinews their elasticity and force.

He slept the heavy dreaming sleep of incipient illness, and she watched him, leaning her elbow on his pillow and her cheek upon her hand, listening for his every breath and praying over him all the dim imperfect prayers she knew.

The low light of a safety-lamp burned by the narrow camp-bed. The small high window was open to the air. The heat was great. The only sound in the stillness was the croaking of frogs in the distant water and the monotonous tread of the sentinel pacing without under the wall. All was so still that she could hear the beating of her own heart, and his, as though the same life moved them both. She did not stir a finger lest she should awaken him, but she knew that it was near daybreak, and that soon she must arise and go, lest in the light of day she should be seen and recognised.

She was about to try and rise without disturbing him when her anxious ear was caught by a slight crackling noise, very faint, such as might be caused by the moving of an insect amongst dry grasses; but there was no grass here in this barren labyrinth of brick and stone, and such a sound could mean but one thing—that thing against which all the senses of the dwellers in it were for ever on the stretch and strain by night and day.

Her first impulse was to awaken Odone.

But as she looked at him by the rays of the lamp, the extreme fatigue and the deep slumber expressed in his attitude and on his features so appealed to her for repose, that she resisted her impulse, and turned the rays of the lamp from him. Besides, she thought, what was there that she could not go and see as well as he? She took the keys, which lay beside him, and the lanthorn, and went softly out into the passage. She could hear the tread of the patrol on the stone floor of the corridor, and the step of the sentinel on the ground without below the walls. They were pacing to and fro with even steps, evidently dreaming of no danger nigh. It might be her fancy that there was any harm near; the little sound might be the rattle of a mouse between the masonry, so she told herself; but she took her lanthorn and the keys and stole on tiptoe to the great doors of the adjacent powder-rooms. Strong as she was, it cost her a mighty effort to turn them in the wards and then to turn the hinges in their sockets. The impenetrable darkness of the great vaulted windowless chambers alone met her view; close by, the outlines of barrels of melinite and other explosives were visible in the rays of the lanthorn; there was no sound at all.

She had been dreaming, she thought; she began to draw the doors towards her again, afraid lest the patrol should pass and find her there. But at that moment her ear was caught again by the tiny crackle as of a moving insect It came from the left-hand side of the chamber. She set down her lanthorn without the door and went in amongst the dread merchandise of death, her bare feet falling noiseless on the stone.

Far away against the right-hand wall she saw a little spark, no bigger than the light of a fire-fly when one sparkled amongst the flax. But a mortal terror gripped her heart, as with a hand of steel. She knew what such a spark in such a place meant for every living thing within the walls and without them for many a mile. Not an instant of time did she lose in hesitation, nor did a sound escape from her lips; a superhuman power entered into her veins, her limbs, her whole being. With a lightning flash of knowledge she realised that the man whom she loved, the soldiers under his command, the villagers whom she had lived with from babyhood, her father lying helpless in his bed, one and all, depended on her and her alone to save them from a sudden and ghastly end, by violence and fire, let loose upon them in the hush and peace of night. Without a second's pause, she sprang on to the barrel nearest her and leaped from it to another, and another, and another, heedless of the imprisoned terror which her feet touched, and in a few swift bounds she reached the place where the spark glittered: the small red, cruel dot of fire made by a slow-match. She stooped and saw the fuse, long, black, sinuous, made of the common blasting powder which the man Renato had bought in the gunner's shop in Ferrara. She caught 'the wicked worm of death' in her hands, clutching the burning spot, and held it high above her head: then slowly, lest a spark might fall, retraced her steps through the dark, walking on the heads of the barrels. The match quickened with the motion, the flame brightened; it burned her hands, the heat bit and gnawed through the flesh of her fingers; in any moment it might reach the powder in the fuse and blast her into space, and bury her in the ruins of the building which she tried to save. But she did not loosen her hold nor falter on her way; the fire caught the linen sleeve of the conscript's shirt which she wore, and hissed up her wrists, and in little rings and tongues of flame circled and licked her arms; but she continued to bear it erect above her head and out of the doors of the powder-room into the naked safety of the stone corridor, and there cast it down into a tank of cold water, which was kept there ever-filled in case of peril, and the fiery snake sank harmless in the flood, hissing and spitting on the liquid surface of the hostile element.

It was barely in time: her charred and tortured hands had lost all power to hold anything, their sinews and muscles glowed like red-hot wires, the hempen sleeves were burning to her elbows.

She staggered down the passage-way to her lover's room, trying to hide her burning clothes from him as he arose, startled out of his sleep, only half awake, and but half conscious.

'Dear love, it is nothing,' she said faintly. 'Be not afraid; the match is out. Only go you, if you can, and close the doors; I could not. And if they find them open they will blame you.'

By sunset on the morrow she was dead: her beautiful arms were like two blackened branches of a burnt tree. But she died leaning upon her lover's breast, the soldiers and the people of the village weeping round her bed; and that fiery death in the full height of a perfect passion was a lovelier portion than life, lonely, obscure, abandoned and forgotten, could have been. She had broken off the perfect flower of life in its full bud. So best.

OUIDA'S NOVELS.

Crown 8vo. cloth extra, 3s. 6d. each; post 8vo. illustrated boards, 2s. each.

Held in Bondage.	*Ariadne.*
Tricotrin.	*Friendship.*
Strathmore.	*Moths.*
Chandos.	*Pipistrello.*
Cecil Castlemaine's Gage.	*A Village Commune.*
Idalia.	*In Maremma.*
Under Two Flags.	*Bimbi.*
Puck.	*Wanda.*
Folle Farine.	*Frescoes.*
A Dog of Flanders.	*Princess Napraxine.*
Pascarel.	*Othmar.*
Two Little Wooden Shoes.	*Guilderoy.*
Signa.	*Ruffino.*
In a Winter City.	

Syrlin. Crown 8vo. cloth extra, 3s. 6d.
Santa Barbara, &c. Square 8vo. cloth extra, 6s.

Wisdom, Wit, and Pathos, selected from the Works of OUIDA by F. SYDNEY MORRIS. Post 8vo. cloth extra, 5s. Cheap Edition, illustrated boards, 2s.

London: CHATTO & WINDUS, Piccadilly.

June, 1891.

A List of Books
PUBLISHED BY
CHATTO & WINDUS,
214, Piccadilly, London, W.

Sold by all Booksellers, or sent post-free for the published price by the Publishers.

ABOUT.—THE FELLAH: An Egyptian Novel. By EDMOND ABOUT. Translated by Sir RANDAL ROBERTS. Post 8vo, illustrated boards, **2s.**

ADAMS (W. DAVENPORT), WORKS BY.
A DICTIONARY OF THE DRAMA. Being a comprehensive Guide to the Plays, Playwrights, Players, and Playhouses of the United Kingdom and America. Crown 8vo, half-bound, **12s. 6d.** [*Preparing.*
QUIPS AND QUIDDITIES. Selected by W. D. ADAMS. Post 8vo, cloth limp, **2s. 6d.**

ADAMS (W. H. D.).—WITCH, WARLOCK, AND MAGICIAN: Historical Sketches of Magic and Witchcraft in England and Scotland. By W. H. DAVENPORT ADAMS. Demy 8vo, cloth extra, **12s.**

AGONY COLUMN (THE) OF "THE TIMES," from 1800 to 1870. Edited, with an Introduction, by ALICE CLAY. Post 8vo, cloth limp, **2s. 6d.**

AIDE (HAMILTON), WORKS BY. Post 8vo, illustrated boards, **2s.** each.
CARR OF CARRLYON. | CONFIDENCES.

ALBERT.—BROOKE FINCHLEY'S DAUGHTER. By MARY ALBERT. Post 8vo, picture boards, **2s.**; cloth limp, **2s. 6d.**

ALEXANDER (MRS.), NOVELS BY. Post 8vo, illustrated boards, **2s.** each.
MAID, WIFE, OR WIDOW? | VALERIE'S FATE.

ALLEN (GRANT), WORKS BY. Crown 8vo, cloth extra, **6s.** each.
THE EVOLUTIONIST AT LARGE. | COLIN CLOUT'S CALENDAR.
VIGNETTES FROM NATURE.
Crown 8vo, cloth extra, **6s.** each; post 8vo, illustrated boards, **2s.** each.
STRANGE STORIES. With a Frontispiece by GEORGE DU MAURIER.
THE BECKONING HAND. With a Frontispiece by TOWNLEY GREEN.
Crown 8vo, cloth extra, **3s. 6d.** each; post 8vo, illustrated boards, **2s.** each.
PHILISTIA. | FOR MAIMIE'S SAKE. | THIS MORTAL COIL.
BABYLON. | IN ALL SHADES. | THE TENTS OF SHEM.
| THE DEVIL'S DIE. |
THE GREAT TABOO. Crown 8vo, cloth extra, **3s. 6d.**
DUMARESQ'S DAUGHTER. Three Vols., crown 8vo. [*Shortly.*

AMERICAN LITERATURE, A LIBRARY OF, from the Earliest Settlement to the Present Time. Compiled and Edited by EDMUND CLARENCE STEDMAN and ELLEN MACKAY HUTCHINSON. Eleven Vols., royal 8vo, cloth extra. A few copies are for sale by Messrs. CHATTO & WINDUS (published in New York by C. L. WEBSTER & Co.), price **£6 12s.** the set.

ARCHITECTURAL STYLES, A HANDBOOK OF. By A. ROSENGARTEN. Translated by W. COLLETT-SANDARS. With 639 Illusts. Cr. 8vo, cl. ex., **7s. 6d.**

ART (THE) OF AMUSING: A Collection of Graceful Arts, GAMES, Tricks, Puzzles, and Charades. By FRANK BELLEW. 300 Illusts. Cr. 8vo, cl. ex., **4s. 6d.**

ARNOLD (EDWIN LESTER), WORKS BY.
THE WONDERFUL ADVENTURES OF PHRA THE PHŒNICIAN. With Introduction by Sir EDWIN ARNOLD, and 12 Illusts. by H. M. PAGET. Cr. 8vo, cl., **3s. 6d.**
BIRD LIFE IN ENGLAND. Crown 8vo, cloth extra, **6s.**

ARTEMUS WARD'S WORKS: The Works of CHARLES FARRER BROWNE, better known as ARTEMUS WARD. With Portrait and Facsimile. Crown 8vo, cloth extra, **7s. 6d.**—Also a POPULAR EDITION, post 8vo, picture boards, **2s.**
THE GENIAL SHOWMAN: Life and Adventures of ARTEMUS WARD. By EDWARD P. HINGSTON. With a Frontispiece. Crown 8vo, cloth extra. **3s. 6d.**

ASHTON (JOHN), WORKS BY. Crown 8vo, cloth extra, **7s. 6d.** each.
HISTORY OF THE CHAP-BOOKS OF THE 18th CENTURY. With 334 Illusts.
SOCIAL LIFE IN THE REIGN OF QUEEN ANNE. With 85 Illustrations.
HUMOUR, WIT, AND SATIRE OF SEVENTEENTH CENTURY. With 82 Illnsts.
ENGLISH CARICATURE AND SATIRE ON NAPOLEON THE FIRST. 115 Illusts.
MODERN STREET BALLADS. With 57 Illustrations.

BACTERIA.—A SYNOPSIS OF THE BACTERIA AND YEAST FUNGI AND ALLIED SPECIES. By W. B. GROVE, B.A. With 87 Illustrations. Crown 8vo, cloth extra, **3s. 6d.**

BARDSLEY (REV. C. W.), WORKS BY.
ENGLISH SURNAMES: Their Sources and Significations. Cr. 8vo. cloth, **7s. 6d.**
CURIOSITIES OF PURITAN NOMENCLATURE. Crown 8vo, cloth extra, **6s.**

BARING GOULD (S., Author of "John Herring," &c.**), NOVELS BY.**
Crown 8vo, cloth extra, **3s. 6d.** each; post 8vo, illustrated boards, **2s.** each.
RED SPIDER. | EVE.

BARRETT (FRANK, Author of "Lady Biddy Fane,"**) NOVELS BY.**
Post 8vo, illustrated boards, **2s.** each; cloth, **2s. 6d.** each.
FETTERED FOR LIFE. | BETWEEN LIFE AND DEATH.

BEACONSFIELD, LORD: A Biography. By T. P. O'CONNOR, M.P. Sixth Edition, with an Introduction. Crown 8vo, cloth extra, **5s.**

BEAUCHAMP.—GRANTLEY GRANGE: A Novel. By SHELSLEY BEAUCHAMP. Post 8vo, illustrated boards, **2s.**

BEAUTIFUL PICTURES BY BRITISH ARTISTS: A Gathering of Favourites from our Picture Galleries, beautifully engraved on Steel. With Notices of the Artists by SYDNEY ARMYTAGE, M.A. Imperial 4to, cloth extra, gilt edges, **21s.**

BECHSTEIN.—AS PRETTY AS SEVEN, and other German Stories. Collected by LUDWIG BECHSTEIN. With Additional Tales by the Brothers GRIMM, and 98 Illustrations by RICHTER. Square 8vo, cloth extra, **6s. 6d.**; gilt edges, **7s. 6d.**

BEERBOHM.—WANDERINGS IN PATAGONIA; or, Life among the Ostrich Hunters. By JULIUS BEERBOHM. With Illusts. Cr. 8vo, cl. extra, **3s. 6d.**

BESANT (WALTER), NOVELS BY.
Cr. 8vo, cl. ex., **3s. 6d.** each; post 8vo, illust. bds., **2s.** each; cl. limp, **2s. 6d.** each.
ALL SORTS AND CONDITIONS OF MEN. With Illustrations by FRED. BARNARD.
THE CAPTAINS' ROOM, &c. With Frontispiece by E. J. WHEELER.
ALL IN A GARDEN FAIR. With 6 Illustrations by HARRY FURNISS.
DOROTHY FORSTER. With Frontispiece by CHARLES GREEN.
UNCLE JACK, and other Stories. | CHILDREN OF GIBEON.
THE WORLD WENT VERY WELL THEN. With 12 Illustrations by A. FORESTIER.
HERR PAULUS: His Rise, his Greatness, and his Fall.
FOR FAITH AND FREEDOM. With Illustrations by A. FORESTIER and F. WADDY.

Crown 8vo, cloth extra, **3s. 6d.** each.
TO CALL HER MINE, &c. With 9 Illustrations by A. FORESTIER.
THE BELL OF ST. PAUL'S.
ARMOREL OF LYONESSE: A Romance of To-day. With 12 Illusts. by F. BARNARD.
THE HOLY ROSE, &c. With Frontispiece by F. BARNARD.

ST. KATHERINE'S BY THE TOWER. With 12 full-page Illustrations by C. GREEN. Three Vols., crown 8vo.
FIFTY YEARS AGO. With 137 Plates and Woodcuts. Demy 8vo, cloth extra, **16s.**
THE EULOGY OF RICHARD JEFFERIES. With Portrait. Cr. 8vo, cl. extra, **6s.**
THE ART OF FICTION. Demy 8vo, **1s.**

BESANT (WALTER) AND JAMES RICE, NOVELS BY.
Cr. 8vo, cl. ex., 3s. 6d. each; post 8vo, illust. bds., 2s. each; cl. limp, 2s. 6d. each.

READY-MONEY MORTIBOY.
MY LITTLE GIRL.
WITH HARP AND CROWN.
THIS SON OF VULCAN.
THE GOLDEN BUTTERFLY.
THE MONKS OF THELEMA.
BY CELIA'S ARBOUR.
THE CHAPLAIN OF THE FLEET.
THE SEAMY SIDE.
THE CASE OF MR. LUCRAFT, &c.
'TWAS IN TRAFALGAR'S BAY, &c.
THE TEN YEARS' TENANT, &c.

*** There is also a LIBRARY EDITION of the above Twelve Volumes, handsomely set in new type, on a large crown 8vo page, and bound in cloth extra, 6s. each.

BENNETT (W. C., LL.D.), WORKS BY. Post 8vo, cloth limp, 2s. each.
A BALLAD HISTORY OF ENGLAND. | SONGS FOR SAILORS.

BEWICK (THOMAS) AND HIS PUPILS. By AUSTIN DOBSON. With 95 Illustrations. Square 8vo, cloth extra, 6s.

BLACKBURN'S (HENRY) ART HANDBOOKS.
ACADEMY NOTES, separate years, from 1875-1887, 1889, and 1890, each 1s.
ACADEMY NOTES, 1891. With Illustrations 1s.
ACADEMY NOTES, 1875-79. Complete in One Vol., with 600 Illusts. Cloth limp, 6s.
ACADEMY NOTES, 1880-84. Complete in One Vol., with 700 Illusts. Cloth limp, 6s.
GROSVENOR NOTES, 1877. 6d.
GROSVENOR NOTES, separate years, from 1878 to 1890, each 1s.
GROSVENOR NOTES, Vol. I., 1877-82. With 300 Illusts. Demy 8vo, cloth limp, 6s.
GROSVENOR NOTES, Vol II., 1883-87. With 300 Illusts. Demy 8vo, cloth limp, 6s.
THE NEW GALLERY, 1888-1890. With numerous Illustrations, each 1s.
THE NEW GALLERY, 1891. With Illustrations. 1s.
ENGLISH PICTURES AT THE NATIONAL GALLERY. 114 Illustrations. 1s.
OLD MASTERS AT THE NATIONAL GALLERY. 128 Illustrations. 1s. 6d.
ILLUSTRATED CATALOGUE TO THE NATIONAL GALLERY. 242 Illusts. cl., 3s.
THE PARIS SALON, 1891. With Facsimile Sketches. 3s.
THE PARIS SOCIETY OF FINE ARTS, 1891. With Sketches. 3s. 6d.

BLAKE (WILLIAM): India-proof Etchings from his Works by WILLIAM BELL SCOTT. With descriptive Text. Folio, half-bound boards. 21s.

BLIND.—THE ASCENT OF MAN: A Poem. By MATHILDE BLIND. Crown 8vo, printed on hand-made paper, cloth extra. 5s.

BOURNE (H. R. FOX), WORKS BY.
ENGLISH MERCHANTS: Memoirs in Illustration of the Progress of British Commerce. With numerous Illustrations. Crown 8vo, cloth extra, 7s. 6d.
ENGLISH NEWSPAPERS: The History of Journalism. Two Vols., demy 8vo, cl., 25s.
THE OTHER SIDE OF THE EMIN PASHA RELIEF EXPEDITION. Crown 8vo, cloth extra, 6s.

BOWERS' (G.) HUNTING SKETCHES. Oblong 4to, hf.-bd. bds., 21s. each.
CANTERS IN CRAMPSHIRE. | LEAVES FROM A HUNTING JOURNAL.

BOYLE (FREDERICK), WORKS BY. Post 8vo, illustrated boards, 2s. each.
CHRONICLES OF NO-MAN'S LAND. | CAMP NOTES.
SAVAGE LIFE. Crown 8vo, cloth extra, 3s. 6d.; post 8vo, picture boards, 2s.

BRAND'S OBSERVATIONS ON POPULAR ANTIQUITIES; chiefly illustrating the Origin of our Vulgar Customs, Ceremonies, and Superstitions. With the Additions of Sir HENRY ELLIS, and Illustrations. Cr. 8vo, cloth extra, 7s. 6d.

BREWER (REV. DR.), WORKS BY.
THE READER'S HANDBOOK OF ALLUSIONS, REFERENCES, PLOTS, AND STORIES. Fifteenth Thousand. Crown 8vo, cloth extra, 7s. 6d.
AUTHORS AND THEIR WORKS, WITH THE DATES: Being the Appendices to "The Reader's Handbook," separately printed. Crown 8vo, cloth limp, 2s.
A DICTIONARY OF MIRACLES. Crown 8vo, cloth extra, 7s. 6d.

BREWSTER (SIR DAVID), WORKS BY. Post 8vo, cl. ex., 4s. 6d. each.
MORE WORLDS THAN ONE: Creed of Philosopher and Hope of Christian. Plates.
THE MARTYRS OF SCIENCE: GALILEO, TYCHO BRAHE, and KEPLER. With Portraits.
LETTERS ON NATURAL MAGIC. With numerous Illustrations.

BOOKS PUBLISHED BY

BRET HARTE, WORKS BY.
LIBRARY EDITION, Complete in Six Volumes, crown 8\
BRET HARTE'S COLLECTED WORKS. Arranged and I
Vol. I. COMPLETE POETICAL AND DRAMATIC WORKS.
Vol. II. LUCK OF ROARING CAMP—BOHEMIAN PAPERS—
Vol. III. TALES OF THE ARGONAUTS—EASTERN SKETCH
Vol. IV. GABRIEL CONROY.
Vol. V. STORIES—CONDENSED NOVELS, &c.
Vol. VI. TALES OF THE PACIFIC SLOPE.

THE SELECT WORKS OF BRET HARTE, in Prose and
Essay by J. M. BELLEW. Portrait of Author, and 50 Illus
BRET HARTE'S POETICAL WORKS. Hand-made paper a
THE QUEEN OF THE PIRATE ISLE. With 28 o
GREENAWAY, reproduced in Colours by EDMUND EVAN
   Crown 8vo, cloth extra, 3s. 6d. eacl
A WAIF OF THE PLAINS. With 60 Illustrations by S
A WARD OF THE GOLDEN GATE. With 59 Illustrati
A SAPPHO OF GREEN SPRINGS, &c. With Two Illus
COLONEL STARBOTTLE'S CLIENT, &c. With Front. b
   Post 8vo, illustrated boards, 2s. eacl
GABRIEL CONROY. | THE LUCK OF
AN HEIRESS OF RED DOG, &c | CALIFORNIAN
   Post 8vo, illustrated boards, 2s. each; cloth limp,
FLIP. | MARUJA. | A PHY
   Fcap. 8vo picture cover, 1s. each
THE TWINS OF TABLE MOUNTAIN. | JEFF BRIGG

BRILLAT-SAVARIN.—GASTRONOMY AS A FIN
SAVARIN. Translated by R. E. ANDERSON. M.A. Post 8v

BRYDGES.—UNCLE SAM AT HOME. By HA
8vo, illustrated boards. 2s.; cloth limp. 2s. 6d.

BUCHANAN'S (ROBERT) WORKS. Crown 8vo, c
SELECTED POEMS OF ROBERT BUCHANAN. With F
THE EARTHQUAKE; or, Six Days and a Sabbath.
THE CITY OF DREAM: An Epic Poem. With Two Il
THE OUTCAST: A Rhyme for the Time. With 12 F
   numerous Vignettes. Crown 8vo, cloth extra, 8s.
ROBERT BUCHANAN'S COMPLETE POETICAL WOR
   trait. Crown 8vo, cloth extra, 7s. 6d.
   Crown 8vo, cloth extra, 3s. 6d. each; post 8vo, illustra
THE SHADOW OF THE SWORD. | LOVE ME FO
A CHILD OF NATURE. Frontispiece. | ANNAN WATE
GOD AND THE MAN. With 11 Illus- | THE NEW AE
   trations by FRED. BARNARD. | MATT: A Story
THE MARTYRDOM OF MADELINE. | THE MASTER
   With Frontispiece by A. W. COOPER | THE HEIR OF

BURTON (CAPTAIN).—THE BOOK OF THI
History of the Sword and its Use in all Countries, from
RICHARD F. BURTON. With over 400 Illustrations. Squa

BURTON (ROBERT).
THE ANATOMY OF MELANCHOLY: A New Edition
   Classical Extracts. Demy 8vo, cloth extra, 7s. 6d.
MELANCHOLY ANATOMISED Being an Abridgment, fo
   ANATOMY OF MELANCHOLY. Post 8vo, cloth limp. 2s.

CAINE (T. HALL), NOVELS BY. Crown 8vo, c
   post 8vo, illustrated boards, 2s. each; cloth limp, 2s. 6
SHADOW OF A CRIME. | A SON OF HAGAR. | T

CAMERON (COMMANDER).—THE CRUISE
PRINCE" PRIVATEER. By V. LOVETT CAMERON, R.N
tions by P. MACNAB. Crown 8vo, cloth extra, 5s.; post 8v

CAMERON (MRS. H. LOVETT), NOVELS BY.
Crown 8vo, cloth extra, 3s. 6d. each; post 8vo, illustra
JULIET'S GUARDIAN. | DECEIVERS I

CARLYLE (THOMAS) ON THE CHOICE OF BOOKS. With Life by R. H. SHEPHERD, and Three Illustrations. Post 8vo, cloth extra, 1s. 6d.
THE CORRESPONDENCE OF THOMAS CARLYLE AND RALPH WALDO EMERSON, 1834 to 1872. Edited by CHARLES ELIOT NORTON. With Portraits. Two Vols., crown 8vo. cloth extra, 24s.

CARLYLE (JANE WELSH), LIFE OF. By Mrs. ALEXANDER IRELAND. With Portrait and Facsimile Letter. Small demy 8vo, cloth extra, 7s. 6d.

CHAPMAN'S (GEORGE) WORKS. Vol. I. contains the Plays complete, including the doubtful ones. Vol. II., the Poems and Minor Translations, with an Introductory Essay by ALGERNON CHARLES SWINBURNE. Vol. III., the Translations of the Iliad and Odyssey. Three Vols., crown 8vo. cloth extra, 6s. each.

CHATTO AND JACKSON.—A TREATISE ON WOOD ENGRAVING, Historical and Practical. By WILLIAM ANDREW CHATTO and JOHN JACKSON. With an Additional Chapter by HENRY G. BOHN, and 450 fine Illusts. Large 4to. hf.-bd., 28s.

CHAUCER FOR CHILDREN: A Golden Key. By Mrs. H. R. HAWEIS. With 8 Coloured Plates and 30 Woodcuts. Small 4to, cloth extra, 6s.
CHAUCER FOR SCHOOLS. By Mrs H. R. HAWEIS. Demy 8vo. cloth limp. 2s. 6d.

CLARE.—FOR THE LOVE OF A LASS: A Tale of Tynedale. By AUSTIN CLARE. Post 8vo, picture boards, 2s.; cloth limp, 2s. 6d.

CLIVE (MRS. ARCHER), NOVELS BY. Post 8vo, illust. boards, 2s. each.
PAUL FERROLL. | WHY PAUL FERROLL KILLED HIS WIFE.

CLODD (EDW., F.R.A.S.).—MYTHS AND DREAMS. Cr. 8vo, cl. ex., 5s.

COBBAN.—THE CURE OF SOULS: A Story. By J. MACLAREN COBBAN. Post 8vo, illustrated boards, 2s.

COLEMAN (JOHN), WORKS BY.
PLAYERS AND PLAYWRIGHTS I HAVE KNOWN. Two Vols., 8vo, cloth, 24s.
CURLY: An Actor's Story. With 21 Illusts. by J. C. DOLLMAN. Cr. 8vo, cl., 1s. 6d.

COLLINS (C. ALLSTON).—THE BAR SINISTER. Post 8vo, 2s.

COLLINS (MORTIMER AND FRANCES), NOVELS BY.
Crown 8vo, cloth extra, 3s. 6d. each; post 8vo, illustrated boards, 2s. each.
SWEET ANNE PAGE. | FROM MIDNIGHT TO MIDNIGHT. | TRANSMIGRATION.
BLACKSMITH AND SCHOLAR. | YOU PLAY ME FALSE. | VILLAGE COMEDY.
Post 8vo, illustrated boards, 2s. each.
A FIGHT WITH FORTUNE. | SWEET AND TWENTY. | FRANCES.

COLLINS (WILKIE), NOVELS BY.
Cr. 8vo. cl. ex., 3s. 6d. each; post 8vo, illust. bds., 2s. each; cl. limp, 2s. 6d. each.
ANTONINA. With a Frontispiece by Sir JOHN GILBERT, R.A.
BASIL. Illustrated by Sir JOHN GILBERT, R.A., and J. MAHONEY.
HIDE AND SEEK. Illustrated by Sir JOHN GILBERT, R.A., and J. MAHONEY.
AFTER DARK. With Illustrations by A. B. HOUGHTON.
THE DEAD SECRET. With a Frontispiece by Sir JOHN GILBERT, R.A.
QUEEN OF HEARTS. With a Frontispiece by Sir JOHN GILBERT, R.A.
THE WOMAN IN WHITE. With Illusts. by Sir J. GILBERT, R.A., and F. A. FRASER.
NO NAME. With Illustrations by Sir J. E. MILLAIS, R.A., and A. W. COOPER.
MY MISCELLANIES. With a Steel-plate Portrait of WILKIE COLLINS.
ARMADALE. With Illustrations by G. H. THOMAS.
THE MOONSTONE. With Illustrations by G. DU MAURIER and F. A. FRASER.
MAN AND WIFE. With Illustrations by WILLIAM SMALL.
POOR MISS FINCH. Illustrated by G. DU MAURIER and EDWARD HUGHES.
MISS OR MRS.? With Illusts. by S. L. FILDES, R.A., and HENRY WOODS, A.R.A.
THE NEW MAGDALEN. Illustrated by G. DU MAURIER and C. S. REINHARDT.
THE FROZEN DEEP. Illustrated by G. DU MAURIER and J. MAHONEY.
THE LAW AND THE LADY. Illusts. by S. L. FILDES, R.A., and SYDNEY HALL.
THE TWO DESTINIES.
THE HAUNTED HOTEL. Illustrated by ARTHUR HOPKINS.
THE FALLEN LEAVES. | HEART AND SCIENCE. | THE EVIL GENIUS.
JEZEBEL'S DAUGHTER. | "I SAY NO." | LITTLE NOVELS.
THE BLACK ROBE. | A ROGUE'S LIFE. | THE LEGACY OF CAIN.
BLIND LOVE. With Preface by WALTER BESANT, and Illusts. by A. FORESTIER.

COLLINS (CHURTON).—A MONOGRAPH ON DEAN SWIFT. By J. CHURTON COLLINS. Crown 8vo, cloth extra, 8s. [*Shortly.*]

BOOKS PUBLISHED BY

COLMAN'S HUMOROUS WORKS: "Broad Grins," "My Nightgown and Slippers," and other Humorous Works of GEORGE COLMAN. With Life by G. B. BUCKSTONE, and Frontispiece by HOGARTH. Crown 8vo, cloth extra, 7s. 6d.

COLQUHOUN.—EVERY INCH A SOLDIER: A Novel. By M. J. COLQUHOUN. Post 8vo, illustrated boards, 2s.

CONVALESCENT COOKERY: A Family Handbook. By CATHERINE RYAN. Crown 8vo, 1s.; cloth limp, 1s. 6d.

CONWAY (MONCURE D.), WORKS BY.
DEMONOLOGY AND DEVIL-LORE. With 65 Illustrations. Third Edition. Two Vols., demy 8vo, cloth extra, 28s.
A NECKLACE OF STORIES. 25 Illusts. by W. J. HENNESSY. Sq. 8vo, cloth, 6s.
PINE AND PALM: A Novel. Two Vols., crown 8vo, cloth extra, 21s.
GEORGE WASHINGTON'S RULES OF CIVILITY Traced to their Sources and Restored. Fcap. 8vo, Japanese vellum, 2s. 6d.

COOK (DUTTON), NOVELS BY.
PAUL FOSTER'S DAUGHTER. Cr. 8vo, cl. ex., 3s. 6d.; post 8vo, illust. boards, 2s.
LEO. Post 8vo, illustrated boards, 2s.

CORNWALL.—POPULAR ROMANCES OF THE WEST OF ENGLAND; or, The Drolls, Traditions, and Superstitions of Old Cornwall. Collected by ROBERT HUNT, F.R.S. Two Steel-plates by GEO. CRUIKSHANK. Cr. 8vo. cl., 7s. 6d.

CRADDOCK.—THE PROPHET OF THE GREAT SMOKY MOUNTAINS. By CHARLES EGBERT CRADDOCK. Post 8vo, illust. bds., 2s.; cl. limp, 2s. 6d.

CRUIKSHANK'S COMIC ALMANACK. Complete in Two SERIES: The FIRST from 1835 to 1843; the SECOND from 1844 to 1853. A Gathering of the BEST HUMOUR of THACKERAY, HOOD, MAYHEW, ALBERT SMITH, A'BECKETT, ROBERT BROUGH, &c. With numerous Steel Engravings and Woodcuts by CRUIKSHANK, HINE, LANDELLS, &c. Two Vols , crown 8vo, cloth gilt, 7s. 6d. each.
THE LIFE OF GEORGE CRUIKSHANK. By BLANCHARD JERROLD. With 84 Illustrations and a Bibliography. Crown 8vo, cloth extra, 7s. 6d.

CUMMING (C. F. GORDON), WORKS BY. Demy 8vo, cl. ex., 8s. 6d. each.
IN THE HEBRIDES. With Autotype Facsimile and 23 Illustrations.
IN THE HIMALAYAS AND ON THE INDIAN PLAINS. With 42 Illustrations.
VIA CORNWALL TO EGYPT. With Photogravure Frontis. Demy 8vo. cl., 7s. 6d.

CUSSANS.—A HANDBOOK OF HERALDRY; with Instructions for Tracing Pedigrees and Deciphering Ancient MSS., &c. By JOHN E. CUSSANS. With 408 Woodcuts, Two Coloured and Two Plain Plates. Crown 8vo, cloth extra. 7s. 6d.

CYPLES (W.)—HEARTS of GOLD. Cr. 8vo, cl., 3s. 6d.; post 8vo, bds., 2s.

DANIEL.—MERRIE ENGLAND IN THE OLDEN TIME. By GEORGE DANIEL. With Illustrations by ROBERT CRUIKSHANK. Crown 8vo, cloth extra, 3s. 6d.

DAUDET.—THE EVANGELIST; or, Port Salvation. By ALPHONSE DAUDET. Crown 8vo, cloth extra, 3s. 6d.; post 8vo, illustrated boards, 2s.

DAVENANT.—HINTS FOR PARENTS ON THE CHOICE OF A PROFESSION FOR THEIR SONS. By F. DAVENANT, M.A. Post 8vo. 1s.; cl., 1s. 6d.

DAVIES (DR. N. E. YORKE-), WORKS BY.
Crown 8vo, 1s. each; cloth limp, 1s. 6d. each.
ONE THOUSAND MEDICAL MAXIMS AND SURGICAL HINTS.
NURSERY HINTS: A Mother's Guide in Health and Disease.
FOODS FOR THE FAT: A Treatise on Corpulency, and a Dietary for its Cure.
AIDS TO LONG LIFE. Crown 8vo, 2s.; cloth limp, 2s. 6d.

DAVIES' (SIR JOHN) COMPLETE POETICAL WORKS, including Psalms I. to L. in Verse, and other hitherto Unpublished MSS., for the first time Collected and Edited, with Memorial-Introduction and Notes, by the Rev. A. B. GROSART, D.D. Two Vols., crown 8vo, cloth boards, 12s.

DAWSON.—THE FOUNTAIN OF YOUTH: A Novel of Adventure. By ERASMUS DAWSON, M.B. Edited by PAUL DEVON. With Two Illustrations by HUME NISBET. Crown 8vo, cloth extra, 3s. 6d.

DE MAISTRE.—A JOURNEY ROUND MY ROOM. By XAVIER DE MAISTRE. Translated by HENRY ATTWELL. Post 8vo, cloth limp, 2s. 6d.

DE MILLE.—A CASTLE IN SPAIN. By JAMES DE MILLE. With a Frontispiece. Crown 8vo, cloth extra, 3s. 6d.; post 8vo, illustrated boards, 2s.

DERBY (THE).—THE BLUE RIBBON OF THE TURF: A Chronicle of the RACE FOR THE DERBY, from Diomed to Donovan. With Notes on the Winning Horses, the Men who trained them, Jockeys who rode them, and Gentlemen to whom they belonged; also Notices of the Betting and Betting Men of the period, and Brief Accounts of THE OAKS. By LOUIS HENRY CURZON. Cr. 8vo, cloth extra, 6s.

DERWENT (LEITH), NOVELS BY. Cr. 8vo, cl., 3s. 6d. ea.; post 8vo, bds., 2s. ea.
OUR LADY OF TEARS. | CIRCE'S LOVERS.

DICKENS (CHARLES), NOVELS BY. Post 8vo, illustrated boards, 2s. each.
SKETCHES BY BOZ. | NICHOLAS NICKLEBY.
THE PICKWICK PAPERS. | OLIVER TWIST.
THE SPEECHES OF CHARLES DICKENS, 1841-1870. With a New Bibliography. Edited by RICHARD HERNE SHEPHERD. Crown 8vo, cloth extra, 6s.—Also a SMALLER EDITION, in the *Mayfair Library*, post 8vo, cloth limp, 2s. 6d.
ABOUT ENGLAND WITH DICKENS. By ALFRED RIMMER. With 57 Illustrations by C. A. VANDERHOOF, ALFRED RIMMER, and others. Sq. 8vo, cloth extra, 7s. 6d.

DICTIONARIES.
A DICTIONARY OF MIRACLES: Imitative, Realistic, and Dogmatic. By the Rev. E. C. BREWER, LL.D. Crown 8vo, cloth extra, 7s. 6d.
THE READER'S HANDBOOK OF ALLUSIONS, REFERENCES, PLOTS, AND STORIES. By the Rev. E. C. BREWER, LL.D. With an ENGLISH BIBLIOGRAPHY. Fifteenth Thousand. Crown 8vo, cloth extra, 7s. 6d.
AUTHORS AND THEIR WORKS, WITH THE DATES. Cr. 8vo, cloth limp, 2s.
FAMILIAR SHORT SAYINGS OF GREAT MEN. With Historical and Explanatory Notes. By SAMUEL A. BENT, A.M. Crown 8vo, cloth extra, 7s. 6d.
SLANG DICTIONARY: Etymological, Historical, and Anecdotal. Cr. 8vo, cl., 6s. 6d.
WOMEN OF THE DAY: A Biographical Dictionary. By F. HAYS. Cr. 8vo, cl., 5s.
WORDS, FACTS, AND PHRASES: A Dictionary of Curious, Quaint, and Out-of-the-Way Matters. By ELIEZER EDWARDS. Crown 8vo, cloth extra, 7s. 6d.

DIDEROT.—THE PARADOX OF ACTING. Translated, with Annotations, from Diderot's "Le Paradoxe sur le Comédien," by WALTER HERRIES POLLOCK. With a Preface by HENRY IRVING. Crown 8vo, parchment, 4s. 6d.

DOBSON (AUSTIN), WORKS BY.
THOMAS BEWICK & HIS PUPILS. With 95 Illustrations. Square 8vo, cloth, 6s.
FOUR FRENCHWOMEN: MADEMOISELLE DE CORDAY; MADAME ROLAND; THE PRINCESS DE LAMBALLE; MADAME DE GENLIS. Fcap. 8vo, hf.-roxburghe, 2s. 6d.

DOBSON (W. T.), WORKS BY. Post 8vo, cloth limp, 2s. 6d. each.
LITERARY FRIVOLITIES, FANCIES, FOLLIES, AND FROLICS.
POETICAL INGENUITIES AND ECCENTRICITIES.

DONOVAN (DICK), DETECTIVE STORIES BY.
Post 8vo, illustrated boards, 2s. each; cloth limp, 2s. 6d. each.
THE MAN-HUNTER. | TRACKED AND TAKEN.
CAUGHT AT LAST! | WHO POISONED HETTY DUNCAN?
A DETECTIVE'S TRIUMPHS. [*Preparing*
THE MAN FROM MANCHESTER. With 23 Illustrations. Crown 8vo, cloth, 6s.; post 8vo, illustrated boards, 2s.

DOYLE (A. CONAN, Author of "Micah Clarke"), **NOVELS BY.**
THE FIRM OF GIRDLESTONE. Crown 8vo, cloth extra, 6s.
STRANGE SECRETS. Told by CONAN DOYLE, PERCY FITZGERALD, FLORENCE MARRYAT, &c. Cr. 8vo, cl. ex., Eight Illusts., 6s.; post 8vo, illust. bds., 2s.

DRAMATISTS, THE OLD. With Vignette Portraits. Cr. 8vo, cl. ex., 6s. per Vol.
BEN JONSON'S WORKS. With Notes Critical and Explanatory, and a Biographical Memoir by WM. GIFFORD. Edited by Col. CUNNINGHAM. Three Vols.
CHAPMAN'S WORKS. Complete in Three Vols. Vol. I. contains the Plays complete; Vol. II., Poems and Minor Translations, with an Introductory Essay by A. C. SWINBURNE; Vol. III., Translations of the Iliad and Odyssey.
MARLOWE'S WORKS. Edited, with Notes, by Col. CUNNINGHAM. One Vol.
MASSINGER'S PLAYS. From GIFFORD's Text. Edit. by Col. CUNNINGHAM. One Vol.

DUNCAN (SARA JEANNETTE), WORKS BY.
A SOCIAL DEPARTURE: How Orthodocia and I Went round the World by Ourselves. With 111 Illustrations by F. H. TOWNSEND. Crown 8vo, cloth, 7s. 6d.
AN AMERICAN GIRL IN LONDON. With 80 Illustrations by F. H. TOWNSEND. Crown 8vo, cloth extra, 7s. 6d. [*Preparing*.

DYER.—THE FOLK-LORE OF PLANTS. By Rev. T. F. THISELTON DYER, M.A. Crown 8vo, cloth extra, 6s.

EARLY ENGLISH POETS. Edited, with Introductions and Annotations, by Rev. A. B. GROSART, D.D. Crown 8vo, cloth boards, 6s. per Volume.
FLETCHER'S (GILES) COMPLETE POEMS. One Vol.
DAVIES' (SIR JOHN) COMPLETE POETICAL WORKS. Two Vols.
HERRICK'S (ROBERT) COMPLETE COLLECTED POEMS. Three Vols.
SIDNEY'S (SIR PHILIP) COMPLETE POETICAL WORKS. Three Vols.

EDGCUMBE.—ZEPHYRUS: A Holiday in Brazil and on the River Plate. By E. R. PEARCE EDGCUMBE. With 41 Illustrations. Crown 8vo, cloth extra, 5s.

EDWARDES (MRS. ANNIE), NOVELS BY:
A POINT OF HONOUR. Post 8vo, illustrated boards, 2s.
ARCHIE LOVELL. Crown 8vo, cloth extra, 3s. 6d.; post 8vo, illust. boards, 2s.

EDWARDS (ELIEZER).—WORDS, FACTS, AND PHRASES: A Dictionary of Curious, Quaint, and Out-of-the-Way Matters. By ELIEZER EDWARDS. Crown 8vo, cloth extra, 7s. 6d.

EDWARDS (M. BETHAM-), NOVELS BY.
KITTY. Post 8vo, illustrated boards, 2s.; cloth limp, 2s. 6d.
FELICIA. Post 8vo, illustrated boards, 2s.

EGGLESTON (EDWARD).—ROXY: A Novel. Post 8vo, illust. bds., 2s.

EMANUEL.—ON DIAMONDS AND PRECIOUS STONES: Their History, Value, and Properties; with Simple Tests for ascertaining their Reality. By HARRY EMANUEL, F.R.G.S. With Illustrations, tinted and plain. Cr. 8vo, cl. ex., 6s.

ENGLISHMAN'S HOUSE, THE: A Practical Guide to all interested in Selecting or Building a House; with Estimates of Cost, Quantities, &c. By C. J. RICHARDSON. With Coloured Frontispiece and 600 Illusts. Crown 8vo, cloth, 7s. 6d.

EWALD (ALEX. CHARLES, F.S.A.), WORKS BY.
THE LIFE AND TIMES OF PRINCE CHARLES STUART, Count of Albany (THE YOUNG PRETENDER). With a Portrait. Crown 8vo, cloth extra, 7s. 6d.
STORIES FROM THE STATE PAPERS. With an Autotype. Crown 8vo, cloth, 6s.

EYES, OUR: How to Preserve Them from Infancy to Old Age. By JOHN BROWNING, F.R.A.S. With 70 Illusts. Eighteenth Thousand. Crown 8vo, 1s.

FAMILIAR SHORT SAYINGS OF GREAT MEN. By SAMUEL ARTHUR BENT, A.M. Fifth Edition, Revised and Enlarged. Crown 8vo, cloth extra, 7s. 6d.

FARADAY (MICHAEL), WORKS BY. Post 8vo, cloth extra, 4s. 6d. each.
THE CHEMICAL HISTORY OF A CANDLE: Lectures delivered before a Juvenile Audience. Edited by WILLIAM CROOKES, F.C.S. With numerous Illustrations.
ON THE VARIOUS FORCES OF NATURE, AND THEIR RELATIONS TO EACH OTHER. Edited by WILLIAM CROOKES, F.C.S. With Illustrations.

FARRER (J. ANSON), WORKS BY.
MILITARY MANNERS AND CUSTOMS. Crown 8vo, cloth extra, 6s.
WAR: Three Essays, reprinted from "Military Manners." Cr. 8vo, 1s.; cl., 1s. 6d.

FICTION.—A CATALOGUE OF NEARLY SIX HUNDRED WORKS OF FICTION published by CHATTO & WINDUS, with a Short Critical Notice of each (40 pages, demy 8vo), will be sent free upon application.

FIN-BEC.—THE CUPBOARD PAPERS: Observations on the Art of Living and Dining. By FIN-BEC. Post 8vo, cloth limp, 2s. 6d.

FIREWORKS, THE COMPLETE ART OF MAKING; or, The Pyrotechnist's Treasury. By THOMAS KENTISH. With 267 Illustrations. Cr. 8vo, cl., 5s.

FITZGERALD (PERCY, M.A., F.S.A.), WORKS BY.
THE WORLD BEHIND THE SCENES. Crown 8vo, cloth extra, 3s. 6d.
LITTLE ESSAYS: Passages from Letters of CHARLES LAMB. Post 8vo, cl., 2s. 6d.
A DAY'S TOUR: Journey through France and Belgium. With Sketches. Cr. 4to. 1s.
FATAL ZERO. Crown 8vo, cloth extra, 3s. 6d.; post 8vo, illustrated boards, 2s.

Post 8vo, illustrated boards, 2s. each.
BELLA DONNA. | LADY OF BRANTOME. | THE SECOND MRS. TILLOTSON.
POLLY. | NEVER FORGOTTEN. | SEVENTY-FIVE BROOKE STREET.

LIFE OF JAMES BOSWELL (of Auchinleck). With an Account of his Sayings, Doings, and Writings; and Four Portraits. Two Vols., demy 8vo, cloth extra. 24s. [*Preparing.*

FLETCHER'S (GILES, B.D.) COMPLETE POEMS: Christ's Victorie in Heaven, Christ's Victorie on Earth, Christ's Triumph over Death, and Minor Poems. With Notes by Rev. A. B. GROSART, D.D. Crown 8vo. cloth boards, 6s.

FLUDYER (HARRY) AT CAMBRIDGE: A Series of Family Letters. Post 8vo, picture cover, 1s.; cloth limp, 1s. 6d.

FONBLANQUE (ALBANY).—FILTHY LUCRE. Post 8vo, illust. bds., 2s.

FRANCILLON (R. E.), NOVELS BY.
Crown 8vo, cloth extra, 3s. 6d. each; post 8vo, illustrated boards, 2s. each.
ONE BY ONE. | QUEEN COPHETUA. | A REAL QUEEN. | KING OR KNAVE?
OLYMPIA. Post 8vo. illust. bds., 2s. | ESTHER'S GLOVE. Fcap. 8vo, pict. cover. 1s.
ROMANCES OF THE LAW. Crown 8vo. cloth, 6s.; post 8vo. illust boards, 2s.

FREDERIC (HAROLD), NOVELS BY.
SETH'S BROTHER'S WIFE. Post 8vo, illustrated boards, 2s.
THE LAWTON GIRL. With Frontispiece by F. BARNARD. Cr. 8vo, cloth ex., 6s.; post 8vo, illustrated boards, 2s.

FRENCH LITERATURE, A HISTORY OF. By HENRY VAN LAUN. Three Vols., demy 8vo, cloth boards. 7s. 6d. each.

FRENZENY.—FIFTY YEARS ON THE TRAIL: Adventures of JOHN Y. NELSON, Scout, Guide, and Interpreter. By HARRINGTON O'REILLY. With 100 Illustrations by PAUL FRENZENY. Crown 8vo. cloth extra, 3s. 6d.

FRERE.—PANDURANG HARI; or, Memoirs of a Hindoo. With Preface by Sir BARTLE FRERE. Crown 8vo. cloth, 3s. 6d.; post 8vo. illust. bds., 2s.

FRISWELL (HAIN).—ONE OF TWO: A Novel. Post 8vo, illust. bds., 2s.

FROST (THOMAS), WORKS BY. Crown 8vo, cloth extra, 3s. 6d. each.
CIRCUS LIFE AND CIRCUS CELEBRITIES. | LIVES OF THE CONJURERS.
THE OLD SHOWMEN AND THE OLD LONDON FAIRS.

FRY'S (HERBERT) ROYAL GUIDE TO THE LONDON CHARITIES. Showing their Name, Date of Foundation, Objects, Income, Officials, &c. Edited by JOHN LANE. Published Annually. Crown 8vo, cloth. 1s. 6d.

GARDENING BOOKS. Post 8vo. 1s. each; cloth limp, 1s. 6d. each.
A YEAR'S WORK IN GARDEN AND GREENHOUSE: Practical Advice as to the Management of the Flower, Fruit, and Frame Garden. By GEORGE GLENNY.
OUR KITCHEN GARDEN: Plants, and How we Cook Them. By TOM JERROLD.
HOUSEHOLD HORTICULTURE. By TOM and JANE JERROLD. Illustrated.
THE GARDEN THAT PAID THE RENT. By TOM JERROLD.

MY GARDEN WILD, AND WHAT I GREW THERE. By FRANCIS G. HEATH. Crown 8vo, cloth extra, gilt edges, 6s.

GARRETT.—THE CAPEL GIRLS: A Novel. By EDWARD GARRETT. Crown 8vo, cloth extra 3s. 6d.; post 8vo, illustrated boards. 2s.

GENTLEMAN'S MAGAZINE, THE. 1s. Monthly. In addition to the Articles upon subjects in Literature, Science, and Art, for which this Magazine has so high a reputation, "TABLE TALK" by SYLVANUS URBAN appears monthly.
** *Bound Volumes for recent years kept in stock, 8s. 6d. each. Cases for binding, 2s.*

GENTLEMAN'S ANNUAL, THE. Published Annually in November, 1s.

GERMAN POPULAR STORIES. Collected by the Brothers GRIMM and Translated by EDGAR TAYLOR. With Introduction by JOHN RUSKIN, and 22 Steel Plates by GEORGE CRUIKSHANK. Square 8vo. cloth. **6s. 6d.**; gilt edges. **7s. 6d.**

GIBBON (CHARLES), NOVELS BY.
Crown 8vo, cloth extra, **3s. 6d.** each; post 8vo, illustrated boards, **2s.** each.
ROBIN GRAY. | LOVING A DREAM. | OF HIGH DEGREE.
THE FLOWER OF THE FOREST. | IN HONOUR BOUND.
THE GOLDEN SHAFT.

Post 8vo, illustrated boards, **2s.** each.
THE DEAD HEART. | IN LOVE AND WAR.
FOR LACK OF GOLD. | A HEART'S PROBLEM.
WHAT WILL THE WORLD SAY? | BY MEAD AND STREAM.
FOR THE KING. | THE BRAES OF YARROW.
QUEEN OF THE MEADOW. | FANCY FREE. | A HARD KNOT.
IN PASTURES GREEN. | HEART'S DELIGHT. | BLOOD-MONEY.

GIBNEY (SOMERVILLE).—SENTENCED! Cr. 8vo, **1s.**; cl., **1s. 6d.**

GILBERT (WILLIAM), NOVELS BY. Post 8vo, illustrated boards, **2s.** each.
DR. AUSTIN'S GUESTS. | JAMES DUKE, COSTERMONGER.
THE WIZARD OF THE MOUNTAIN. |

GILBERT (W. S.), ORIGINAL PLAYS BY. In Two Series, each complete in itself, price **2s. 6d.** each.
The FIRST SERIES contains: The Wicked World—Pygmalion and Galatea—Charity—The Princess—The Palace of Truth—Trial by Jury.
The SECOND SERIES: Broken Hearts—Engaged—Sweethearts—Gretchen—Dan'l Druce—Tom Cobb—H.M.S. "Pinafore"—The Sorcerer—Pirates of Penzance.

EIGHT ORIGINAL COMIC OPERAS written by W. S. GILBERT. Containing: The Sorcerer—H.M.S. "Pinafore"—Pirates of Penzance—Iolanthe—Patience—Princess Ida—The Mikado—Trial by Jury. Demy 8vo, cloth limp, **2s. 6d.**

THE "GILBERT AND SULLIVAN" BIRTHDAY BOOK: Quotations for Every Day in the Year, Selected from Plays by W. S. GILBERT set to Music by Sir A. SULLIVAN. Compiled by ALEX. WATSON. Royal 16mo. Jap. leather, **2s. 6d.**

GLANVILLE (ERNEST), NOVELS BY.
THE LOST HEIRESS: A Tale of Love, Battle and Adventure. With 2 Illusts. by HUME NISBET. Cr. 8vo, cloth extra, **3s. 6d.**
THE FOSSICKER. With a Frontispiece. Crown 8vo, cloth extra, 3s. 6d.

GLENNY.—A YEAR'S WORK IN GARDEN AND GREENHOUSE: Practical Advice to Amateur Gardeners as to the Management of the Flower, Fruit, and Frame Garden. By GEORGE GLENNY. Post 8vo, **1s.**; cloth limp, **1s. 6d.**

GODWIN.—LIVES OF THE NECROMANCERS. By WILLIAM GODWIN. Post 8vo, cloth limp, **2s.**

GOLDEN TREASURY OF THOUGHT, THE: An Encyclopædia of QUOTATIONS. Edited by THEODORE TAYLOR. Crown 8vo. cloth gilt, **7s. 6d.**

GOWING.—FIVE THOUSAND MILES IN A SLEDGE: A Midwinter Journey Across Siberia. By LIONEL F. GOWING. With 30 Illustrations by C. J. UREN, and a Map by E. WELLER. Large crown 8vo. cloth extra. **8s.**

GRAHAM.—THE PROFESSOR'S WIFE: A Story. By LEONARD GRAHAM. Fcap. 8vo, picture cover, **1s.**

GREEKS AND ROMANS, THE LIFE OF THE, described from Antique Monuments. By ERNST GUHL and W. KONER. Edited by Dr. F. HUEFFER. With 545 Illustrations. Large crown 8vo. cloth extra. **7s. 6d.**

GREENWOOD (JAMES), WORKS BY. Cr. 8vo. cloth extra, **3s. 6d.** each.
THE WILDS OF LONDON. | LOW-LIFE DEEPS.

GREVILLE (HENRY), NOVELS BY:
NIKANOR. Translated by ELIZA E. CHASE. With 8 Illusts. Cr. 8vo, cl. extra, **6s.**
A NOBLE WOMAN. Translated by ALBERT D. VANDAM. Crown 8vo, cloth extra, **5s.**; post 8vo, illustrated boards, **2s.**

HABBERTON (JOHN, Author of "Helen's Babies"), **NOVELS BY.**
Post 8vo, illustrated boards **2s.** each; cloth limp, **2s. 6d.** each.
BRUETON'S BAYOU. | COUNTRY LUCK.

HAIR, THE: Its Treatment in Health, Weakness, and Disease. Translated from the German of Dr. J. PINCUS. Crown 8vo, 1s.; cloth limp, 1s. 6d.

HAKE (DR. THOMAS GORDON), POEMS BY. Cr. 8vo, cl. ex., 6s. each.
NEW SYMBOLS. | LEGENDS OF THE MORROW. | THE SERPENT PLAY.
MAIDEN ECSTASY. Small 4to, cloth extra, 8s.

HALL.—SKETCHES OF IRISH CHARACTER. By Mrs. S. C. HALL. With numerous Illustrations on Steel and Wood by MACLISE, GILBERT, HARVEY, and GEORGE CRUIKSHANK. Medium 8vo, cloth extra, 7s. 6d.

HALLIDAY (ANDR.).—EVERY-DAY PAPERS. Post 8vo, bds., 2s.

HANDWRITING, THE PHILOSOPHY OF. With over 100 Facsimiles and Explanatory Text. By DON FELIX DE SALAMANCA. Post 8vo, cloth limp, 2s. 6d.

HANKY-PANKY: A Collection of Very Easy Tricks, Very Difficult Tricks, White Magic, Sleight of Hand, &c. Edited by W. H. CREMER. With 200 Illustrations. Crown 8vo, cloth extra, 4s. 6d.

HARDY (LADY DUFFUS).—PAUL WYNTER'S SACRIFICE. By Lady DUFFUS HARDY. Post 8vo, illustrated boards, 2s.

HARDY (THOMAS).—UNDER THE GREENWOOD TREE. By THOMAS HARDY, Author of "Far from the Madding Crowd." Post 8vo, illust. bds., 2s.

HARWOOD.—THE TENTH EARL. By J. BERWICK HARWOOD. Post 8vo, illustrated boards, 2s.

HAWEIS (MRS. H. R.), WORKS BY. Square 8vo, cloth extra, 6s. each.
THE ART OF BEAUTY. With Coloured Frontispiece and 91 Illustrations.
THE ART OF DECORATION. With Coloured Frontispiece and 74 Illustrations.
CHAUCER FOR CHILDREN. With 8 Coloured Plates and 30 Woodcuts.
THE ART OF DRESS. With 32 Illustrations. Post 8vo, 1s.; cloth, 1s. 6d.
CHAUCER FOR SCHOOLS. Demy 8vo, cloth limp, 2s. 6d.

HAWEIS (Rev. H. R., M.A.).—AMERICAN HUMORISTS: WASHINGTON IRVING, OLIVER WENDELL HOLMES, JAMES RUSSELL LOWELL, ARTEMUS WARD, MARK TWAIN, and BRET HARTE. Third Edition. Crown 8vo, cloth extra, 6s.

HAWLEY SMART.—WITHOUT LOVE OR LICENCE: A Novel. By HAWLEY SMART. Crown 8vo, cloth extra, 3s. 6d.

HAWTHORNE.—OUR OLD HOME. By NATHANIEL HAWTHORNE. Annotated with Passages from the Author's Note-book, and Illustrated with 31 Photogravures. Two Vols., crown 8vo, buckram, gilt top, 15s.

HAWTHORNE (JULIAN), NOVELS BY.
Crown 8vo, cloth extra, 3s. 6d. each; post 8vo, illustrated boards, 2s. each.
GARTH. | ELLICE QUENTIN. | BEATRIX RANDOLPH. | DUST.
SEBASTIAN STROME. | DAVID POINDEXTER.
FORTUNE'S FOOL. | THE SPECTRE OF THE CAMERA.
Post 8vo, illustrated boards, 2s. each.
MISS CADOGNA. | LOVE—OR A NAME.
MRS. GAINSBOROUGH'S DIAMONDS. Fcap. 8vo, illustrated cover, 1s.
A DREAM AND A FORGETTING. Post 8vo, cloth limp, 1s. 6d.

HAYS.—WOMEN OF THE DAY: A Biographical Dictionary of Notable Contemporaries. By FRANCES HAYS. Crown 8vo, cloth extra, 5s.

HEATH.—MY GARDEN WILD, AND WHAT I GREW THERE. By FRANCIS GEORGE HEATH. Crown 8vo, cloth extra, gilt edges, 6s.

HELPS (SIR ARTHUR), WORKS BY. Post 8vo, cloth limp, 2s. 6d. each.
ANIMALS AND THEIR MASTERS. | SOCIAL PRESSURE.
IVAN DE BIRON: A Novel. Cr. 8vo, cl. extra, 3s. 6d.; post 8vo, illust. bds., 2s.

HENDERSON.—AGATHA PAGE: A Novel. By ISAAC HENDERSON. Crown 8vo, cloth extra, 3s. 6d.

HERMAN.—A LEADING LADY. By HENRY HERMAN, joint-Author of "The Bishops' Bible." Post 8vo, cloth extra, 2s. 6d.

HERRICK'S (ROBERT) HESPERIDES, NOBLE NUMBERS, AND COMPLETE COLLECTED POEMS. With Memorial-Introduction and Notes by the Rev. A. B. GROSART, D.D.; Steel Portrait, &c. Three Vols., crown 8vo, cl. bds., 18s.

HERTZKA.—FREELAND: A Social Anticipation. By Dr. THEODOR HERTZKA. Translated by ARTHUR RANSOM. Crown 8vo, cloth extra, 6s.

HESSE-WARTEGG.—TUNIS: The Land and the People. By Chevalier ERNST VON HESSE-WARTEGG. With 22 Illustrations. Cr. 8vo, cloth extra, 3s. 6d.

HINDLEY (CHARLES), WORKS BY.
TAVERN ANECDOTES AND SAYINGS: Including the Origin of Signs, and Reminiscences connected with Taverns, Coffee Houses, Clubs, &c. With Illustrations. Crown 8vo, cloth extra, 3s. 6d.
THE LIFE AND ADVENTURES OF A CHEAP JACK. By ONE OF THE FRATERNITY. Edited by CHARLES HINDLEY. Crown 8vo, cloth extra, 3s. 6d.

HOEY.—THE LOVER'S CREED. By Mrs. CASHEL HOEY. Post 8vo, illustrated boards, 2s.

HOLLINGSHEAD (JOHN).—NIAGARA SPRAY. Crown 8vo, 1s.

HOLMES.—THE SCIENCE OF VOICE PRODUCTION AND VOICE PRESERVATION: A Popular Manual for the Use of Speakers and Singers. By GORDON HOLMES, M.D. With Illustrations. Crown 8vo, 1s.; cloth, 1s. 6d.

HOLMES (OLIVER WENDELL), WORKS BY.
THE AUTOCRAT OF THE BREAKFAST-TABLE. Illustrated by J. GORDON THOMSON. Post 8vo, cloth limp, 2s. 6d.—Another Edition, in smaller type, with an Introduction by G. A. SALA. Post 8vo, cloth limp, 2s.
THE PROFESSOR AT THE BREAKFAST-TABLE. Post 8vo, cloth limp, 2s.

HOOD'S (THOMAS) CHOICE WORKS, in Prose and Verse. With Life of the Author, Portrait, and 200 Illustrations. Crown 8vo, cloth extra, 7s. 6d.
HOOD'S WHIMS AND ODDITIES. With 85 Illustrations. Post 8vo, printed on laid paper and half-bound, 2s.

HOOD (TOM).—FROM NOWHERE TO THE NORTH POLE: A Noah's Arkæological Narrative. By TOM HOOD. With 25 Illustrations by W. BRUNTON and E. C. BARNES. Square 8vo, cloth extra, gilt edges, 6s.

HOOK'S (THEODORE) CHOICE HUMOROUS WORKS; including his Ludicrous Adventures, Bons Mots, Puns, and Hoaxes. With Life of the Author, Portraits, Facsimiles, and Illustrations. Crown 8vo, cloth extra, 7s. 6d.

HOOPER.—THE HOUSE OF RABY: A Novel. By Mrs. GEORGE HOOPER. Post 8vo, illustrated boards, 2s.

HOPKINS.—"'TWIXT LOVE AND DUTY:" A Novel. By TIGHE HOPKINS. Post 8vo, illustrated boards, 2s.

HORNE. — ORION: An Epic Poem. By RICHARD HENGIST HORNE. With Photographic Portrait by SUMMERS. Tenth Edition. Cr. 8vo, cloth extra, 7s.

HORSE (THE) AND HIS RIDER: An Anecdotic Medley. By "THORMANBY." Crown 8vo, cloth extra, 6s.

HUNT.—ESSAYS BY LEIGH HUNT: A TALE FOR A CHIMNEY CORNER, and other Pieces. Edited, with an Introduction, by EDMUND OLLIER. Post 8vo, printed on laid paper and half-bd., 2s. Also in sm. sq. 8vo, cl. extra, at same price.

HUNT (MRS. ALFRED), NOVELS BY.
Crown 8vo, cloth extra, 3s. 6d. each; post 8vo, illustrated boards, 2s. each.
THE LEADEN CASKET. | SELF-CONDEMNED. | THAT OTHER PERSON.
THORNICROFT'S MODEL. Post 8vo, illustrated boards, 2s.

HYDROPHOBIA: An Account of M. PASTEUR'S System. Containing a Translation of all his Communications on the Subject, the Technique of his Method, and Statistics. By RENAUD SUZOR. M.B. Crown 8vo, cloth extra, 6s.

INGELOW (JEAN).—FATED TO BE FREE. With 24 Illustrations by G. J. PINWELL. Cr. 8vo, cloth extra, 3s. 6d.; post 8vo, illustrated boards, 2s.

INDOOR PAUPERS. By ONE OF THEM. Crown 8vo, 1s.; cloth, 1s. 6d.

IRISH WIT AND HUMOUR, SONGS OF. Collected and Edited by A. Perceval Graves. Post 8vo, cloth limp, **2s. 6d.**

JAMES.—A ROMANCE OF THE QUEEN'S HOUNDS. By Charles James. Post 8vo, picture cover, **1s.**; cloth limp, **1s. 6d.**

JANVIER.—PRACTICAL KERAMICS FOR STUDENTS. By Catherine A. Janvier. Crown 8vo, cloth extra, **6s.**

JAY (HARRIETT), NOVELS BY. Post 8vo, illustrated boards, **2s.** each.
THE DARK COLLEEN. | THE QUEEN OF CONNAUGHT.

JEFFERIES (RICHARD), WORKS BY. Post 8vo, cloth limp, **2s. 6d.** each.
NATURE NEAR LONDON. | THE LIFE OF THE FIELDS. | THE OPEN AIR.
THE EULOGY OF RICHARD JEFFERIES. By Walter Besant. Second Edition. With a Photograph Portrait. Crown 8vo, cloth extra, **6s.**

JENNINGS (H. J.), WORKS BY.
CURIOSITIES OF CRITICISM. Post 8vo, cloth limp, **2s. 6d.**
LORD TENNYSON: A Biographical Sketch. With a Photograph. Cr. 8vo, cl., **6s.**

JEROME.—STAGELAND: Curious Habits and Customs of its Inhabitants. By Jerome K. Jerome. With 64 Illustrations by J. Bernard Partridge. Sixteenth Thousand. Fcap. 4to, cloth extra, **3s. 6d.**

JERROLD.—THE BARBER'S CHAIR; & THE HEDGEHOG LETTERS. By Douglas Jerrold. Post 8vo, printed on laid paper and half-bound, **2s.**

JERROLD (TOM), WORKS BY. Post 8vo, **1s.** each; cloth limp, **1s. 6d.** each.
THE GARDEN THAT PAID THE RENT.
HOUSEHOLD HORTICULTURE. A Gossip about Flowers. Illustrated.
OUR KITCHEN GARDEN: The Plants we Grow, and How we Cook Them.

JESSE.—SCENES AND OCCUPATIONS OF A COUNTRY LIFE. By Edward Jesse. Post 8vo, cloth limp, **2s.**

JONES (WILLIAM, F.S.A.), WORKS BY. Cr. 8vo, cl. extra, **7s. 6d.** each.
FINGER-RING LORE: Historical, Legendary, and Anecdotal. With nearly 300 Illustrations. Second Edition, Revised and Enlarged.
CREDULITIES, PAST AND PRESENT. Including the Sea and Seamen, Miners, Talismans, Word and Letter Divination, Exorcising and Blessing of Animals, Birds, Eggs, Luck, &c. With an Etched Frontispiece.
CROWNS AND CORONATIONS: A History of Regalia. With 100 Illustrations.

JONSON'S (BEN) WORKS. With Notes Critical and Explanatory and a Biographical Memoir by William Gifford. Edited by Colonel Cunningham. Three Vols., crown 8vo, cloth extra, **6s.** each.

JOSEPHUS, THE COMPLETE WORKS OF. Translated by Whiston. Containing "The Antiquities of the Jews" and "The Wars of the Jews." With 52 Illustrations and Maps. Two Vols., demy 8vo, half-bound, **12s. 6d.**

KEMPT.—PENCIL AND PALETTE: Chapters on Art and Artists. By Robert Kempt. Post 8vo, cloth limp, **2s. 6d.**

KERSHAW.—COLONIAL FACTS AND FICTIONS: Humorous Sketches. By Mark Kershaw. Post 8vo, illustrated boards, **2s.**; cloth, **2s. 6d.**

KEYSER.—CUT BY THE MESS: A Novel. By Arthur Keyser. Crown 8vo, picture cover, **1s.**; cloth limp, **1s. 6d.**

KING (R. ASHE), NOVELS BY. Cr. 8vo, cl., **3s. 6d.** ea.; post 8vo, bds., **2s.** ea.
A DRAWN GAME. | "THE WEARING OF THE GREEN."
PASSION'S SLAVE. Post 8vo, illustrated boards, **2s.**
BELL BARRY. 2 vols., crown 8vo.

KINGSLEY (HENRY), NOVELS BY.
OAKSHOTT CASTLE. Post 8vo, illustrated boards, **2s.**
NUMBER SEVENTEEN. Crown 8vo, cloth extra, **3s. 6d.**

KNIGHTS (THE) OF THE LION: A Romance of the Thirteenth Century. Edited, with an Introduction, by the Marquess of Lorne, K.T. Cr. 8vo, cl. ex., **6s.**

14   BOOKS PUBLISHED BY

KNIGHT.—THE PATIENT'S VADE MECUM: How to Get Most Benefit from Medical Advice. By WILLIAM KNIGHT, M.R.C.S., and EDWARD KNIGHT, L.R.C.P. Crown 8vo, **1s.**; cloth limp, **1s. 6d.**

LAMB'S (CHARLES) COMPLETE WORKS, in Prose and Verse. Edited, with Notes and Introduction, by R. H. SHEPHERD. With Two Portraits and Facsimile of a page of the "Essay on Roast Pig." Cr. 8vo, cl. ex., **7s. 6d.**
THE ESSAYS OF ELIA. Post 8vo, printed on laid paper and half-bound, **2s.**
LITTLE ESSAYS: Sketches and Characters by CHARLES LAMB, selected from his Letters by PERCY FITZGERALD. Post 8vo, cloth limp, **2s. 6d.**

LANDOR.—CITATION AND EXAMINATION OF WILLIAM SHAKSPEARE, &c., before Sir THOMAS LUCY, touching Deer-stealing, 19th September, 1582. To which is added, **A CONFERENCE OF MASTER EDMUND SPENSER** with the Earl of Essex, touching the State of Ireland, 1595. By WALTER SAVAGE LANDOR. Fcap. 8vo, half-Roxburghe, **2s. 6d.**

LANE.—THE THOUSAND AND ONE NIGHTS, commonly called in England **THE ARABIAN NIGHTS' ENTERTAINMENTS.** Translated from the Arabic, with Notes, by EDWARD WILLIAM LANE. Illustrated by many hundred Engravings from Designs by HARVEY. Edited by EDWARD STANLEY POOLE. With a Preface by STANLEY LANE-POOLE. Three Vols., demy 8vo, cloth extra, **7s. 6d.** each.

LARWOOD (JACOB), WORKS BY.
THE STORY OF THE LONDON PARKS. With Illusts. Cr. 8vo, cl. extra, **3s. 6d.**
ANECDOTES OF THE CLERGY: The Antiquities, Humours, and Eccentricities of the Cloth. Post 8vo, printed on laid paper and half-bound, **2s.**

Post 8vo, cloth limp, **2s. 6d.** each.
FORENSIC ANECDOTES. | **THEATRICAL ANECDOTES.**

LEIGH (HENRY S.), WORKS BY.
CAROLS OF COCKAYNE. Printed on hand-made paper, bound in buckram, **5s.**
JEUX D'ESPRIT. Edited by HENRY S. LEIGH. Post 8vo, cloth limp, **2s. 6d.**

LEYS (JOHN).—THE LINDSAYS: A Romance. Post 8vo, illust. bds., **2s.**

LIFE IN LONDON; or, The History of JERRY HAWTHORN and CORINTHIAN TOM. With CRUIKSHANK'S Coloured Illustrations. Crown 8vo, cloth extra, **7s. 6d.** [*New Edition preparing.*

LINSKILL.—IN EXCHANGE FOR A SOUL. By MARY LINSKILL. Post 8vo, illustrated boards, **2s.**

LINTON (E. LYNN), WORKS BY. Post 8vo, cloth limp, **2s. 6d.** each.
WITCH STORIES. | **OURSELVES:** ESSAYS ON WOMEN.

Crown 8vo, cloth extra, **3s. 6d.** each; post 8vo, illustrated boards, **2s.** each.
SOWING THE WIND. | **UNDER WHICH LORD?**
PATRICIA KEMBALL. | **"MY LOVE!"** | **IONE.**
ATONEMENT OF LEAM DUNDAS. | **PASTON CAREW, Millionaire & Miser.**
THE WORLD WELL LOST.

Post 8vo, illustrated boards, **2s.** each.
THE REBEL OF THE FAMILY. | **WITH A SILKEN THREAD.**

LONGFELLOW'S POETICAL WORKS. With numerous Illustrations on Steel and Wood. Crown 8vo, cloth extra, **7s. 6d.**

LUCY.—GIDEON FLEYCE: A Novel. By HENRY W. LUCY. Crown 8vo, cloth extra, **3s. 6d.**; post 8vo, illustrated boards, **2s.**

LUSIAD (THE) OF CAMOENS. Translated into English Spenserian Verse by ROBERT FFRENCH DUFF. With 14 Plates. Demy 8vo, cloth boards, **18s.**

MACALPINE (AVERY), NOVELS BY.
TERESA ITASCA, and other Stories. Crown 8vo, bound in canvas, **2s. 6d.**
BROKEN WINGS. With 6 Illusts. by W. J. HENNESSY. Crown 8vo, cloth extra, **6s.**

MACCOLL (HUGH), NOVELS BY.
MR. STRANGER'S SEALED PACKET. Second Edition. Crown 8vo, cl. extra, **5s.**
EDNOR WHITLOCK. Crown 8vo, cloth extra, **6s.**

McCARTHY (JUSTIN, M.P.), WORKS BY.

A HISTORY OF OUR OWN TIMES, from the Accession of Queen Victoria to the General Election of 1880. Four Vols. demy 8vo, cloth extra, 12s. each.—Also a POPULAR EDITION, in Four Vols., crown 8vo, cloth extra, 6s. each.—And a JUBILEE EDITION, with an Appendix of Events to the end of 1886, in Two Vols., large crown 8vo, cloth extra, 7s. 6d. each.

A SHORT HISTORY OF OUR OWN TIMES. One Vol., crown 8vo, cloth extra, 6s.
—Also a CHEAP POPULAR EDITION, post 8vo, cloth limp, 2s. 6d.

A HISTORY OF THE FOUR GEORGES. Four Vols. demy 8vo, cloth extra, 12s. each. [Vols. I. & II. *ready*

Crown 8vo, cloth extra, 3s. 6d. each; post 8vo, illustrated boards, 2s. each.
THE WATERDALE NEIGHBOURS. | MISS MISANTHROPE.
MY ENEMY'S DAUGHTER. | DONNA QUIXOTE.
A FAIR SAXON. | THE COMET OF A SEASON.
LINLEY ROCHFORD. | MAID OF ATHENS.
DEAR LADY DISDAIN. | CAMIOLA: A Girl with a Fortune.

"THE RIGHT HONOURABLE." By JUSTIN MCCARTHY, M.P., and Mrs. CAMPBELL-PRAED. Fourth Edition. Crown 8vo, cloth extra, 6s.

McCARTHY (JUSTIN H., M.P.), WORKS BY.

THE FRENCH REVOLUTION. Four Vols., 8vo, 12s. each. [Vols. I. & II. *ready*.
AN OUTLINE OF THE HISTORY OF IRELAND. Crown 8vo, 1s.; cloth, 1s. 6d.
IRELAND SINCE THE UNION: Irish History, 1798-1886. Crown 8vo, cloth, 6s.
ENGLAND UNDER GLADSTONE, 1880-85. Crown 8vo, cloth extra, 6s.
HAFIZ IN LONDON: Poems. Small 8vo, gold cloth, 3s. 6d.
HARLEQUINADE: Poems. Small 4to, Japanese vellum, 8s.
OUR SENSATION NOVEL. Crown 8vo, picture cover, 1s.; cloth limp, 1s. 6d.
DOOM! An Atlantic Episode. Crown 8vo, picture cover, 1s.
DOLLY: A Sketch. Crown 8vo, picture cover, 1s.; cloth limp, 1s. 6d.
LILY LASS: A Romance. Crown 8vo, picture cover, 1s.; cloth limp, 1s. 6d.

MACDONALD (GEORGE, LL.D.), WORKS BY.

WORKS OF FANCY AND IMAGINATION. Ten Vols., cl. extra, gilt edges, in cloth case, 21s. Or the Vols. may be had separately, in grolier cl., at 2s. 6d. each.
Vol. I. WITHIN AND WITHOUT.—THE HIDDEN LIFE.
" II. THE DISCIPLE.—THE GOSPEL WOMEN.—BOOK OF SONNETS.—ORGAN SONGS.
" III. VIOLIN SONGS.—SONGS OF THE DAYS AND NIGHTS.—A BOOK OF DREAMS.—ROADSIDE POEMS.—POEMS FOR CHILDREN.
" IV. PARABLES.—BALLADS.—SCOTCH SONGS.
" V. & VI. PHANTASTES: A Faerie Romance. | Vol. VII. THE PORTENT.
" VIII. THE LIGHT PRINCESS.—THE GIANT'S HEART.—SHADOWS.
" IX. CROSS PURPOSES.—THE GOLDEN KEY.—THE CARASOYN.—LITTLE DAYLIGHT.
" X. THE CRUEL PAINTER.—THE WOW O' RIVVEN.—THE CASTLE.—THE BROKEN SWORDS.—THE GRAY WOLF.—UNCLE CORNELIUS.

THE COMPLETE POETICAL WORKS OF DR. GEORGE MACDONALD. Collected and arranged by the Author. Crown 8vo, buckram, 6s. [*Shortly.*

MACDONELL.—QUAKER COUSINS: A Novel. By AGNES MACDONELL.
Crown 8vo, cloth extra, 3s. 6d.; post 8vo, illustrated boards, 2s.

MACGREGOR.—PASTIMES AND PLAYERS: Notes on Popular
Games. By ROBERT MACGREGOR. Post 8vo, cloth limp, 2s. 6d.

MACKAY.—INTERLUDES AND UNDERTONES; or, Music at Twilight.
By CHARLES MACKAY, LL.D. Crown 8vo, cloth extra, 6s.

MACLISE PORTRAIT GALLERY (THE) OF ILLUSTRIOUS LITER-
ARY CHARACTERS: 85 PORTRAITS; with Memoirs — Biographical, Critical, Bibliographical, and Anecdotal—illustrative of the Literature of the former half of the Present Century, by WILLIAM BATES, B.A. Crown 8vo, cloth extra, 7s. 6d.

MACQUOID (MRS.), WORKS BY. Square 8vo, cloth extra, 7s. 6d. each.
IN THE ARDENNES. With 50 Illustrations by THOMAS R. MACQUOID.
PICTURES AND LEGENDS FROM NORMANDY AND BRITTANY. With 34 Illustrations by THOMAS R. MACQUOID.
THROUGH NORMANDY. With 92 Illustrations by T. R. MACQUOID, and a Map.
THROUGH BRITTANY. With 35 Illustrations by T. R. MACQUOID, and a Map.
ABOUT YORKSHIRE. With 67 Illustrations by T. R. MACQUOID.

Post 8vo, illustrated boards, 2s. each.
THE EVIL EYE, and other Stories. | **LOST ROSE.**

MAGIC LANTERN, THE, and its Management: including full Practical Directions for producing the Limelight, making Oxygen Gas, and preparing Lantern Slides. By T. C. HEPWORTH. With 10 Illustrations. Cr. 8vo. 1s.; cloth. 1s. 6d.

MAGICIAN'S OWN BOOK, THE: Performances with Cups and Balls, Eggs, Hats, Handkerchiefs, &c. All from actual Experience. Edited by W. H. CREMER. With 200 Illustrations. Crown 8vo. cloth extra. 4s. 6d.

MAGNA CHARTA: An Exact Facsimile of the Original in the British Museum. 3 feet by 2 feet. with Arms and Seals emblazoned in Gold and Colours, 5s.

MALLOCK (W. H.), WORKS BY.
THE NEW REPUBLIC. Post 8vo, picture cover, 2s.; cloth limp, 2s. 6d.
THE NEW PAUL & VIRGINIA: Positivism on an Island. Post 8vo, cloth, 2s. 6d.
POEMS. Small 4to, parchment, 8s.
IS LIFE WORTH LIVING? Crown 8vo, cloth extra, 6s.

MALLORY'S (SIR THOMAS) MORT D'ARTHUR: The Stories of King Arthur and of the Knights of the Round Table. (A Selection.) Edited by B. MONTGOMERIE RANKING. Post 8vo, cloth limp, 2s.

MARK TWAIN, WORKS BY. Crown 8vo, cloth extra, 7s. 6d. each.
THE CHOICE WORKS OF MARK TWAIN. Revised and Corrected throughout by the Author. With Life, Portrait, and numerous Illustrations.
ROUGHING IT, and INNOCENTS AT HOME. With 200 Illusts by F. A. FRASER.
THE GILDED AGE. By MARK TWAIN and C. D. WARNER. With 212 Illustrations.
MARK TWAIN'S LIBRARY OF HUMOUR. With 197 Illustrations.
A YANKEE AT THE COURT OF KING ARTHUR. With 220 Illusts. by BEARD.

Crown 8vo, cloth extra (illustrated), 7s. 6d. each; post 8vo, illust. boards, 2s. each.
THE INNOCENTS ABROAD; or New Pilgrim's Progress. With 234 Illustrations. (The Two-Shilling Edition is entitled **MARK TWAIN'S PLEASURE TRIP.**)
THE ADVENTURES OF TOM SAWYER. With 111 Illustrations.
A TRAMP ABROAD. With 314 Illustrations.
THE PRINCE AND THE PAUPER. With 190 Illustrations.
LIFE ON THE MISSISSIPPI. With 300 Illustrations.
ADVENTURES OF HUCKLEBERRY FINN. With 174 Illusts. by E. W. KEMBLE.

THE STOLEN WHITE ELEPHANT, &c. Cr. 8vo. cl., 6s.; post 8vo, illust. bds., 2s.

MARLOWE'S WORKS. Including his Translations. Edited, with Notes and Introductions, by Col. CUNNINGHAM. Crown 8vo, cloth extra, 6s.

MARRYAT (FLORENCE), NOVELS BY. Post 8vo, illust. boards, 2s. each.
A HARVEST OF WILD OATS. | WRITTEN IN FIRE. | FIGHTING THE AIR.
OPEN! SESAME! Crown 8vo, cloth extra, 3s. 6d.; post 8vo, picture boards, 2s.

MASSINGER'S PLAYS. From the Text of WILLIAM GIFFORD. Edited by Col. CUNNINGHAM. Crown 8vo. cloth extra. 6s.

MASTERMAN.—HALF-A-DOZEN DAUGHTERS: A Novel. By J. MASTERMAN. Post 8vo, illustrated boards, 2s.

MATTHEWS.—A SECRET OF THE SEA, &c. By BRANDER MATTHEWS. Post 8vo, illustrated boards, 2s.; cloth limp, 2s. 6d.

MAYHEW.—LONDON CHARACTERS AND THE HUMOROUS SIDE OF LONDON LIFE. By HENRY MAYHEW. With Illusts. Crown 8vo, cloth, 3s. 6d.

MENKEN.—INFELICIA: Poems by ADAH ISAACS MENKEN. With Biographical Preface, Illustrations by F. E. LUMMIS and F. O. C. DARLEY, and Facsimile of a Letter from CHARLES DICKENS. Small 4to, cloth extra, 7s. 6d.

MEXICAN MUSTANG (ON A), through Texas to the Rio Grande. By A. E. SWEET and J. ARMOY KNOX. With 265 Illusts. Cr. 8vo. cloth extra. 7s. 6d.

MIDDLEMASS (JEAN), NOVELS BY. Post 8vo, illust. boards, 2s. each.
TOUCH AND GO. | MR. DORILLION.

MILLER.—PHYSIOLOGY FOR THE YOUNG; or, The House of Life: Human Physiology, with its application to the Preservation of Health. By Mrs. F. FENWICK MILLER. With numerous Illustrations. Post 8vo, cloth limp, 2s. 6d.

MILTON (J. L.), WORKS BY. Post 8vo, 1s. each; cloth, 1s. 6d. each.
THE HYGIENE OF THE SKIN. With Directions for Diet, Soaps, Baths, &c.
THE BATH IN DISEASES OF THE SKIN.
THE LAWS OF LIFE, AND THEIR RELATION TO DISEASES OF THE SKIN.
THE SUCCESSFUL TREATMENT OF LEPROSY. Demy 8vo, 1s.

MINTO (WM.)—WAS SHE GOOD OR BAD? Cr. 8vo, 1s.; cloth, 1s. 6d.

MOLESWORTH (MRS.), NOVELS BY.
HATHERCOURT RECTORY. Post 8vo, illustrated boards, 2s.
THAT GIRL IN BLACK. Crown 8vo, picture cover, 1s.; cloth, 1s. 6d.

MOORE (THOMAS), WORKS BY.
THE EPICUREAN; and ALCIPHRON. Post 8vo, half-bound, 2s.
PROSE AND VERSE, Humorous, Satirical, and Sentimental, by THOMAS MOORE; with Suppressed Passages from the MEMOIRS OF LORD BYRON. Edited by R. HERNE SHEPHERD. With Portrait. Crown 8vo, cloth extra, 7s. 6d.

MUDDOCK (J. E.), STORIES BY.
STORIES WEIRD AND WONDERFUL. Post 8vo, illust. boards, 2s.; cloth, 2s. 6d.
THE DEAD MAN'S SECRET; or, The Valley of Gold: A Narrative of Strange Adventure. With a Frontispiece by F. BARNARD. Crown 8vo, cloth extra, 5s.; post 8vo, illustrated boards, 2s.

MURRAY (D. CHRISTIE), NOVELS BY.
Crown 8vo, cloth extra, 3s. 6d. each; post 8vo, illustrated boards, 2s. each.
A LIFE'S ATONEMENT. | A MODEL FATHER. | A BIT OF HUMAN NATURE.
JOSEPH'S COAT. | HEARTS. | FIRST PERSON SINGULAR.
COALS OF FIRE. | THE WAY OF THE | CYNIC FORTUNE.
VAL STRANGE. | WORLD. |

BY THE GATE OF THE SEA. Post 8vo, picture boards, 2s.
OLD BLAZER'S HERO. With Three Illustrations by A. McCORMICK. Crown 8vo, cloth extra, 6s.; post 8vo, illustrated boards, 2s.

MURRAY (D. CHRISTIE) & HENRY HERMAN, WORKS BY.
Crown 8vo, cloth extra, 6s. each; post 8vo, illustrated boards, 2s. each.
ONE TRAVELLER RETURNS.
PAUL JONES'S ALIAS. With 13 Illustrations by A. FORESTIER and G. NICOLET.
THE BISHOPS' BIBLE. Crown 8vo, cloth extra, 3s. 6d.

MURRAY.—A GAME OF BLUFF: A Novel. By HENRY MURRAY. Post 8vo, picture boards, 2s.; cloth limp, 2s. 6d.

NISBET (HUME), BOOKS BY.
"BAIL UP!" A Romance of BUSHRANGERS AND BLACKS. Cr. 8vo, cl. ex., 3s. 6d.
LESSONS IN ART. With 21 Illustrations. Crown 8vo, cloth extra, 2s. 6d.

NOVELISTS.—HALF-HOURS WITH THE BEST NOVELISTS OF THE CENTURY. Edit. by H. T. MACKENZIE BELL. Cr. 8vo, cl., 3s. 6d. [Preparing.

O'CONNOR.—LORD BEACONSFIELD: A Biography. By T. P. O'CONNOR, M.P. Sixth Edition, with an Introduction. Crown 8vo, cloth extra, 5s.

O'HANLON (ALICE), NOVELS BY. Post 8vo, illustrated boards, 2s. each.
THE UNFORESEEN. | CHANCE? OR FATE?

OHNET (GEORGES), NOVELS BY.
DOCTOR RAMEAU. Translated by Mrs. CASHEL HOEY. With 9 Illustrations by E. BAYARD. Crown 8vo, cloth extra, 6s.; post 8vo, illustrated boards, 2s.
A LAST LOVE. Translated by ALBERT D. VANDAM. Crown 8vo, cloth extra, 5s.; post 8vo, illustrated boards, 2s.
A WEIRD GIFT. Translated by ALBERT D. VANDAM. Crown 8vo, cloth, 3s. 6d.

OLIPHANT (MRS.), NOVELS BY. Post 8vo, illustrated boards, 2s. each.
THE PRIMROSE PATH. | THE GREATEST HEIRESS IN ENGLAND.
WHITELADIES. With Illustrations by ARTHUR HOPKINS and HENRY WOODS, A.R.A. Crown 8vo, cloth extra, 3s. 6d.; post 8vo, illustrated boards, 2s.

O'REILLY (MRS.).—PHŒBE'S FORTUNES. Post 8vo, illust. bds., 2s.

O'SHAUGHNESSY (ARTHUR), POEMS BY.
LAYS OF FRANCE. Crown 8vo, cloth extra, 10s. 6d.
MUSIC AND MOONLIGHT. Fcap. 8vo, cloth extra, 7s. 6d.
SONGS OF A WORKER. Fcap. 8vo, cloth extra, 7s. 6d.

OUIDA, NOVELS BY. Cr. 8vo, cl., 3s. 6d. each; post 8vo, illust. bds., 2s. each.
HELD IN BONDAGE.
TRICOTRIN.
STRATHMORE.
CHANDOS.
CECIL CASTLEMAINE'S GAGE.
IDALIA.
UNDER TWO FLAGS.
PUCK.
FOLLE-FARINE.
A DOG OF FLANDERS.
PASCAREL.
TWO LITTLE WOODEN SHOES.
SIGNA.
IN A WINTER CITY.
ARIADNE.
FRIENDSHIP.
MOTHS.
PIPISTRELLO.
A VILLAGE COMMUNE.
IN MAREMMA.
BIMBI.
WANDA.
FRESCOES.
PRINCESS NAPRAXINE.
OTHMAR. | GUILDEROY.

Crown 8vo, cloth extra, 3s. 6d. each.
SYRLIN. | RUFFINO.

WISDOM, WIT, AND PATHOS, selected from the Works of OUIDA by F. SYDNEY MORRIS. Post 8vo, cloth extra, 5s. — CHEAP EDITION, illustrated boards, 2s.

PAGE (H. A.), WORKS BY.
THOREAU: His Life and Aims. With Portrait. Post 8vo, cloth limp, 2s. 6d.
ANIMAL ANECDOTES. Arranged on a New Principle. Crown 8vo, cloth extra, 5s.

PASCAL'S PROVINCIAL LETTERS. A New Translation, with Historical Introduction and Notes by T. M'CRIE, D.D. Post 8vo, cloth limp, 2s.

PAUL.—GENTLE AND SIMPLE. By MARGARET A. PAUL. With Frontispiece by HELEN PATERSON. Crown 8vo, cloth, 3s. 6d.; post 8vo, illust. boards. 2s.

PAYN (JAMES), NOVELS BY.
Crown 8vo, cloth extra, 3s. 6d. each; post 8vo, illustrated boards, 2s. each.
LOST SIR MASSINGBERD.
WALTER'S WORD.
LESS BLACK THAN WE'RE PAINTED.
BY PROXY.
HIGH SPIRITS.
UNDER ONE ROOF.
A CONFIDENTIAL AGENT.
A GRAPE FROM A THORN.
FROM EXILE.
SOME PRIVATE VIEWS.
THE CANON'S WARD.
THE TALK OF THE TOWN.
HOLIDAY TASKS.
GLOW-WORM TALES.
THE MYSTERY OF MIRBRIDGE.

Post 8vo, illustrated boards, 2s. each.
HUMOROUS STORIES.
THE FOSTER BROTHERS.
THE FAMILY SCAPEGRACE.
MARRIED BENEATH HIM.
BENTINCK'S TUTOR.
A PERFECT TREASURE.
A COUNTY FAMILY.
LIKE FATHER, LIKE SON.
A WOMAN'S VENGEANCE.
CARLYON'S YEAR. | CECIL'S TRYST.
MURPHY'S MASTER.
AT HER MERCY.
THE CLYFFARDS OF CLYFFE.
FOUND DEAD.
GWENDOLINE'S HARVEST.
A MARINE RESIDENCE.
MIRK ABBEY.
NOT WOOED, BUT WON.
TWO HUNDRED POUNDS REWARD.
THE BEST OF HUSBANDS.
HALVES.
FALLEN FORTUNES.
WHAT HE COST HER.
KIT: A MEMORY. | FOR CASH ONLY

Crown 8vo, cloth extra, 3s. 6d. each.
IN PERIL AND PRIVATION: Stories of MARINE ADVENTURE Re-told. With 17 Illustrations.
THE BURNT MILLION. | THE WORD AND THE WILL.
SUNNY STORIES, and some SHADY ONES. With a Frontispiece by FRED. BARNARD.

NOTES FROM THE "NEWS." Crown 8vo, portrait cover, 1s.; cloth, 1s. 6d.

PENNELL (H. CHOLMONDELEY), WORKS BY. Post 8vo, cl., 2s. 6d. each.
PUCK ON PEGASUS. With Illustrations.
PEGASUS RE-SADDLED. With Ten full-page Illustrations by G. DU MAURIER.
THE MUSES OF MAYFAIR. Vers de Société, Selected by H. C. PENNELL.

PHELPS (E. STUART), WORKS BY. Post 8vo, 1s. each; cloth, 1s. 6d. each.
BEYOND THE GATES. By the Author of "The Gates Ajar."
AN OLD MAID'S PARADISE.
BURGLARS IN PARADISE.

JACK THE FISHERMAN. Illustrated by C. W. REED. Cr. 8vo, 1s.; cloth, 1s. 6d.

PIRKIS (C. L.), NOVELS BY.
TROOPING WITH CROWS. Fcap. 8vo, picture cover, 1s.
LADY LOVELACE. Post 8vo, illustrated boards, 2s.

PLANCHE (J. R.), WORKS BY.
THE PURSUIVANT OF ARMS; or, Heraldry Founded upon Facts. With Coloured Frontispiece, Five Plates, and 209 Illusts. Crown 8vo, cloth, 7s. 6d.
SONGS AND POEMS, 1819-1879. Introduction by Mrs. MACKARNESS. Cr. 8vo, cl., 6s.

PLUTARCH'S LIVES OF ILLUSTRIOUS MEN. Translated from the Greek, with Notes Critical and Historical, and a Life of Plutarch, by JOHN and WILLIAM LANGHORNE. With Portraits. Two Vols., demy 8vo, half-bound, 10s. 6d.

POE'S (EDGAR ALLAN) CHOICE WORKS, in Prose and Poetry. Introduction by CHAS. BAUDELAIRE; Portrait, and Facsimiles. Cr. 8vo, cloth, 7s. 6d.
THE MYSTERY OF MARIE ROGET, &c. Post 8vo. illustrated boards, 2s.

POPE'S POETICAL WORKS. Post 8vo, cloth limp, 2s.

PRICE (E. C.), NOVELS BY.
Crown 8vo, cloth extra, 3s. 6d. each; post 8vo, illustrated boards, 2s. each.
VALENTINA. | THE FOREIGNERS. | MRS. LANCASTER'S RIVAL.
GERALD. Post 8vo, illustrated boards, 2s.

PRINCESS OLGA.—RADNA; or, The Great Conspiracy of 1881. By the Princess OLGA. Crown 8vo, cloth extra, 6s.

PROCTOR (RICHARD A., B.A.), WORKS BY.
FLOWERS OF THE SKY. With 55 Illusts. Small crown 8vo, cloth extra, 3s. 6d.
EASY STAR LESSONS. With Star Maps for Every Night in the Year, Drawings of the Constellations, &c. Crown 8vo, cloth extra, 6s.
FAMILIAR SCIENCE STUDIES. Crown 8vo, cloth extra, 6s.
SATURN AND ITS SYSTEM. With 13 Steel Plates. Demy 8vo, cloth ex., 10s. 6d.
MYSTERIES OF TIME AND SPACE. With Illustrations. Cr. 8vo, cloth extra, 6s.
THE UNIVERSE OF SUNS. With numerous Illustrations. Cr. 8vo, cloth ex., 6s.
WAGES AND WANTS OF SCIENCE WORKERS. Crown 8vo, 1s. 6d.

PRYCE.—MISS MAXWELL'S AFFECTIONS. By RICHARD PRYCE, Author of "The Ugly Story of Miss Wetherby," &c. 2 vols., crown 8vo. [Shortly.

RAMBOSSON.—POPULAR ASTRONOMY. By J. RAMBOSSON, Laureate of the Institute of France. With numerous Illusts. Crown 8vo, cloth extra, 7s. 6d.

RANDOLPH.—AUNT ABIGAIL DYKES: A Novel. By Lt.-Colonel GEORGE RANDOLPH, U.S.A. Crown 8vo, cloth extra, 7s. 6d.

READE (CHARLES), NOVELS BY.
Crown 8vo, cloth extra, illustrated, 3s. 6d. each; post 8vo, illust. bds., 2s. each.
PEG WOFFINGTON. Illustrated by S. L. FILDES, R.A.—Also a POCKET EDITION, set in New Type, in Elzevir style, fcap. 8vo, half-leather, 2s. 6d.
CHRISTIE JOHNSTONE. Illustrated by WILLIAM SMALL.—Also a POCKET EDITION, set in New Type, in Elzevir style, fcap. 8vo, half-leather, 2s. 6d.
IT IS NEVER TOO LATE TO MEND. Illustrated by G. J. PINWELL.
THE COURSE OF TRUE LOVE NEVER DID RUN SMOOTH. Illustrated by HELEN PATERSON.
THE AUTOBIOGRAPHY OF A THIEF, &c. Illustrated by MATT STRETCH.
LOVE ME LITTLE, LOVE ME LONG. Illustrated by M. ELLEN EDWARDS.
THE DOUBLE MARRIAGE. Illusts. by Sir JOHN GILBERT, R.A., and C. KEENE.
THE CLOISTER AND THE HEARTH. Illustrated by CHARLES KEENE.
HARD CASH. Illustrated by F. W. LAWSON.
GRIFFITH GAUNT. Illustrated by S. L. FILDES, R.A., and WILLIAM SMALL.
FOUL PLAY. Illustrated by GEORGE DU MAURIER.
PUT YOURSELF IN HIS PLACE. Illustrated by ROBERT BARNES.
A TERRIBLE TEMPTATION. Illustrated by EDWARD HUGHES and A. W. COOPER.
A SIMPLETON. Illustrated by KATE CRAUFURD.
THE WANDERING HEIR. Illustrated by HELEN PATERSON, S. L. FILDES, R.A., C. GREEN, and HENRY WOODS, A.R.A.
A WOMAN-HATER. Illustrated by THOMAS COULDERY.
SINGLEHEART AND DOUBLEFACE. Illustrated by P. MACNAB.
GOOD STORIES OF MEN AND OTHER ANIMALS. Illustrated E. A. ABBEY, PERCY MACQUOID, R.W.S., and JOSEPH NASH.
THE JILT, and other Stories. Illustrated by JOSEPH NASH.
READIANA. With a Steel-plate Portrait of CHARLES READE.
BIBLE CHARACTERS: Studies of David, Paul, &c. Fcap. 8vo, leatherette, 1s.

SELECTIONS FROM THE WORKS OF CHARLES READE. With an Introduction by Mrs. ALEX. IRELAND, and a Steel-Plate Portrait. Crown 8vo, buckram, 6s.

RIDDELL (MRS. J. H.), NOVELS BY.
Crown 8vo, cloth extra, 3s. 6d. each; post 8vo, illustrated boards, 2s. each.
HER MOTHER'S DARLING. | WEIRD STORIES.
THE PRINCE OF WALES'S GARDEN PARTY.
Post 8vo, illustrated boards, 2s. each.
UNINHABITED HOUSE. | FAIRY WATER. | MYSTERY IN PALACE GARDENS.

RIMMER (ALFRED), WORKS BY. Square 8vo, cloth gilt, 7s. 6d. each.
OUR OLD COUNTRY TOWNS. With 55 Illustrations.
RAMBLES ROUND ETON AND HARROW. With 50 Illustrations.
ABOUT ENGLAND WITH DICKENS. With 58 Illusts. by C. A. VANDERHOOF, &c.

ROBINSON CRUSOE. By DANIEL DEFOE. (MAJOR'S EDITION.) With 37 Illustrations by GEORGE CRUIKSHANK. Post 8vo, half-bound, 2s.

ROBINSON (F. W.), NOVELS BY.
Crown 8vo, cloth extra, 3s. 6d. each; post 8vo, illustrated boards, 2s. each.
WOMEN ARE STRANGE. | THE HANDS OF JUSTICE.

ROBINSON (PHIL), WORKS BY. Crown 8vo, cloth extra, 7s. 6d. each.
THE POETS' BIRDS. | THE POETS' BEASTS.
THE POETS AND NATURE: REPTILES, FISHES, INSECTS. [*Preparing.*

ROCHEFOUCAULD'S MAXIMS AND MORAL REFLECTIONS. With Notes, and an Introductory Essay by SAINTE-BEUVE. Post 8vo, cloth limp, 2s.

ROLL OF BATTLE ABBEY, THE: A List of the Principal Warriors who came from Normandy with William the Conqueror, and Settled in this Country, A.D. 1066-7. With Arms emblazoned in Gold and Colours. Handsomely printed, 5s.

ROWLEY (HON. HUGH), WORKS BY. Post 8vo, cloth, 2s. 6d. each.
PUNIANA: RIDDLES AND JOKES. With numerous Illustrations.
MORE PUNIANA. Profusely Illustrated.

RUNCIMAN (JAMES), STORIES BY.
Post 8vo, illustrated boards, 2s. each; cloth limp, 2s. 6d. each.
SKIPPERS AND SHELLBACKS. | GRACE BALMAIGN'S SWEETHEART.
SCHOOLS AND SCHOLARS. |

RUSSELL (W. CLARK), BOOKS AND NOVELS BY:
Crown 8vo, cloth extra, 6s. each; post 8vo, illustrated boards, 2s. each.
ROUND THE GALLEY-FIRE. | A BOOK FOR THE HAMMOCK.
IN THE MIDDLE WATCH. | MYSTERY OF THE "OCEAN STAR."
A VOYAGE TO THE CAPE. | THE ROMANCE OF JENNY HARLOWE.
ON THE FO'K'SLE HEAD. Post 8vo, illustrated boards, 2s.
AN OCEAN TRAGEDY. Cr. 8vo, cloth extra, 3s. 6d.; post 8vo, illust. bds., 2s.
MY SHIPMATE LOUISE. Crown 8vo, cloth extra, 3s. 6d.

SAINT AUBYN (ALAN), NOVELS BY.
A FELLOW OF TRINITY. With a Note by OLIVER WENDELL HOLMES and a Frontispiece. Crown 8vo, cloth extra, 3s. 6d.; post 8vo, illust. boards, 2s.
THE JUNIOR DEAN. 3 vols., crown 8vo. [*Shortly.*

SALA.—GASLIGHT AND DAYLIGHT. By GEORGE AUGUSTUS SALA. Post 8vo, illustrated boards, 2s.

SANSON.—SEVEN GENERATIONS OF EXECUTIONERS: Memoirs of the Sanson Family (1688 to 1847). Crown 8vo, cloth extra, 3s. 6d.

SAUNDERS (JOHN), NOVELS BY.
Crown 8vo, cloth extra, 3s. 6d. each; post 8vo, illustrated boards, 2s. each.
GUY WATERMAN. | THE LION IN THE PATH. | THE TWO DREAMERS.
BOUND TO THE WHEEL. Crown 8vo, cloth extra, 3s. 6d.

SAUNDERS (KATHARINE), NOVELS BY.
Crown 8vo, cloth extra, 3s. 6d. each; post 8vo, illustrated boards, 2s. each.
MARGARET AND ELIZABETH. | HEART SALVAGE.
THE HIGH MILLS. | SEBASTIAN.
JOAN MERRYWEATHER. Post 8vo, illustrated boards, 2s.
GIDEON'S ROCK. Crown 8vo, cloth extra, 3s. 6d.

SCIENCE-GOSSIP: An Illustrated Medium of Interchange for Students and Lovers of Nature. Edited by Dr. J. E. TAYLOR, F.L.S., &c. Devoted to Geology, Botany, Physiology, Chemistry, Zoology, Microscopy, Telescopy, Physiography Photography, &c. Price 4d. Monthly; or 5s. per year, post-free. Vols. I. to XIX. may be had, 7s. 6d. each; Vols. XX. to date, 5s. each. Cases for Binding, 1s. 6d.

SECRET OUT, THE: One Thousand Tricks with Cards; with Entertaining Experiments in Drawing-room or "White Magic." By W. H. CREMER. With 300 Illustrations. Crown 8vo, cloth extra, **4s. 6d.**

SEGUIN (L. G.), WORKS BY.
THE COUNTRY OF THE PASSION PLAY (OBERAMMERGAU) and the Highlands of Bavaria. With Map and 37 Illustrations. Crown 8vo, cloth extra, **3s. 6d.**
WALKS IN ALGIERS. With 2 Maps and 16 Illusts. Crown 8vo. cloth extra. **6s.**

SENIOR (WM.).—BY STREAM AND SEA. Post 8vo, cloth, 2s. 6d.

SHAKESPEARE, THE FIRST FOLIO.—MR. WILLIAM SHAKESPEARE'S COMEDIES, HISTORIES, AND TRAGEDIES. Published according to the true Originall Copies. London, Printed by ISAAC IAGGARD and ED. BLOUNT. 1623.— A reduced Photographic Reproduction. Small 8vo, half-Roxburghe. **7s. 6d.**
SHAKESPEARE FOR CHILDREN: LAMB'S TALES FROM SHAKESPEARE. With Illustrations, coloured and plain, by J. MOYR SMITH. Crown 4to. cloth, **6s.**

SHARP.—CHILDREN OF TO-MORROW: A Novel. By WILLIAM SHARP. Crown 8vo, cloth extra, **6s.**

SHELLEY.—THE COMPLETE WORKS IN VERSE AND PROSE OF PERCY BYSSHE SHELLEY. Edited, Prefaced, and Annotated by R. HERNE SHEPHERD. Five Vols., crown 8vo, cloth boards, **3s. 6d.** each.
POETICAL WORKS, in Three Vols.;
Vol. I. Introduction by the Editor; Posthumous Fragments of Margaret Nicholson; Shelley's Correspondence with Stockdale; The Wandering Jew; Queen Mab, with the Notes; Alastor, and other Poems; Rosalind and Helen; Prometheus Unbound; Adonai, &c.
Vol. II. Laon and Cythna; The Cenci; Julian and Maddalo; Swellfoot the Tyrant; The Witch of Atlas; Epipsychidion; Hellas.
Vol. III. Posthumous Poems; The Masque of Anarchy; and other Pieces.
PROSE WORKS, in Two Vols.:
Vol. I. The Two Romances of Zastrozzi and St. Irvyne; the Dublin and Marlow Pamphlets; A Refutation of Deism; Letters to Leigh Hunt, and some Minor Writings and Fragments.
Vol. II. The Essays; Letters from Abroad; Translations and Fragments, Edited by Mrs. SHELLEY. With a Bibliography of Shelley, and an Index of the Prose Works.

SHERARD.—ROGUES: A Novel. By R. H. SHERARD. Crown 8vo, picture cover, **1s.**; cloth, **1s. 6d.**

SHERIDAN (GENERAL). — PERSONAL MEMOIRS OF GENERAL P. H. SHERIDAN. With Portraits and Facsimiles. Two Vols., demy 8vo, cloth. **24s.**

SHERIDAN'S (RICHARD BRINSLEY) COMPLETE WORKS. With Life and Anecdotes. Including his Dramatic Writings, his Works in Prose and Poetry, Translations, Speeches, Jokes, &c. With 10 Illusts. Cr. 8vo. cl., **7s. 6d.**
THE RIVALS, THE SCHOOL FOR SCANDAL, and other Plays. Post 8vo, printed on laid paper and half-bound. **2s.**
SHERIDAN'S COMEDIES: THE RIVALS and THE SCHOOL FOR SCANDAL. Edited, with an Introduction and Notes to each Play, and a Biographical Sketch, by BRANDER MATTHEWS. With Illustrations. Demy 8vo, half-parchment, **12s. 6d.**

SIDNEY'S (SIR PHILIP) COMPLETE POETICAL WORKS, including all those in "Arcadia." With Portrait, Memorial-Introduction, Notes, &c. by the Rev. A. B. GROSART, D.D. Three Vols., crown 8vo, cloth boards. **18s.**

SIGNBOARDS: Their History. With Anecdotes of Famous Taverns and Remarkable Characters. By JACOB LARWOOD and JOHN CAMDEN HOTTEN. With Coloured Frontispiece and 94 Illustrations. Crown 8vo, cloth extra. **7s. 6d.**

SIMS (GEORGE R.), WORKS BY.
Post 8vo, illustrated boards, **2s.** each; cloth limp, **2s. 6d.** each.
ROGUES AND VAGABONDS. | MARY JANE MARRIED.
THE RING O' BELLS. | TALES OF TO-DAY.
MARY JANE'S MEMOIRS. | DRAMAS OF LIFE. With 60 Illustrations.
TINKLETOP'S CRIME. With a Frontispiece by MAURICE GREIFFENHAGEN.
Crown 8vo, picture cover, **1s.** each; cloth, **1s. 6d.** each.
HOW THE POOR LIVE; and HORRIBLE LONDON.
THE DAGONET RECITER AND READER: being Readings and Recitations in Prose and Verse, selected from his own Works by GEORGE R. SIMS.
DAGONET DITTIES. From the *Referee.*
THE CASE OF GEORGE CANDLEMAS.

SISTER DORA: A Biography. By MARGARET LONSDALE. With Four Illustrations. Demy 8vo, picture cover, **4d.**; cloth, **6d.**

SKETCHLEY.—A MATCH IN THE DARK. By ARTHUR SKETCHLEY. Post 8vo, illustrated boards, 2s.

SLANG DICTIONARY (THE): Etymological, Historical, and Anecdotal. Crown 8vo, cloth extra, 6s. 6d.

SMITH (J. MOYR), WORKS BY.
THE PRINCE OF ARGOLIS. With 130 Illusts. Post 8vo, cloth extra, 3s. 6d.
TALES OF OLD THULE. With numerous Illustrations. Crown 8vo, cloth gilt, 6s.
THE WOOING OF THE WATER WITCH. Illustrated. Post 8vo, cloth, 6s.

SOCIETY IN LONDON. By A FOREIGN RESIDENT. Crown 8vo, 1s.; cloth, 1s. 6d.

SOCIETY IN PARIS: The Upper Ten Thousand. A Series of Letters from Count PAUL VASILI to a Young French Diplomat. Crown 8vo, cloth, 6s.

SOMERSET. — SONGS OF ADIEU. By Lord HENRY SOMERSET. Small 4to, Japanese vellum, 6s.

SPALDING.—ELIZABETHAN DEMONOLOGY: An Essay on the Belief in the Existence of Devils. By T. A. SPALDING, LL.B. Crown 8vo, cloth extra, 5s.

SPEIGHT (T. W.), NOVELS BY.
Post 8vo, illustrated boards, 2s. each.
| THE MYSTERIES OF HERON DYKE. | THE GOLDEN HOOP. |
| BY DEVIOUS WAYS, and A BARREN TITLE. | HOODWINKED; and THE SANDYCROFT MYSTERY. |

Post 8vo, cloth limp, 1s. 6d. each.
| A BARREN TITLE. | WIFE OR NO WIFE? |

THE SANDYCROFT MYSTERY. Crown 8vo, picture cover, 1s.

SPENSER FOR CHILDREN. By M. H. TOWRY. With Illustrations by WALTER J. MORGAN. Crown 4to, cloth gilt, 6s.

STARRY HEAVENS (THE): A POETICAL BIRTHDAY BOOK. Royal 16mo, cloth extra, 2s. 6d.

STAUNTON.—THE LAWS AND PRACTICE OF CHESS. With an Analysis of the Openings. By HOWARD STAUNTON. Edited by ROBERT B. WORMALD. Crown 8vo, cloth extra, 5s.

STEDMAN (E. C.), WORKS BY.
VICTORIAN POETS. Thirteenth Edition. Crown 8vo, cloth extra, 9s.
THE POETS OF AMERICA. Crown 8vo, cloth extra, 9s.

STERNDALE. — THE AFGHAN KNIFE: A Novel. By ROBERT ARMITAGE STERNDALE. Cr. 8vo, cloth extra, 3s. 6d.; post 8vo, illust. boards, 2s.

STEVENSON (R. LOUIS), WORKS BY. Post 8vo, cl. limp, 2s. 6d. each.
TRAVELS WITH A DONKEY. Eighth Edit. With a Frontis. by WALTER CRANE.
AN INLAND VOYAGE. Fourth Edition. With a Frontispiece by WALTER CRANE.

Crown 8vo, buckram, gilt top, 6s. each.
FAMILIAR STUDIES OF MEN AND BOOKS. Fifth Edition.
THE SILVERADO SQUATTERS. With a Frontispiece. Third Edition.
THE MERRY MEN. Second Edition. | UNDERWOODS: Poems. Fifth Edition.
MEMORIES AND PORTRAITS. Third Edition
VIRGINIBUS PUERISQUE, and other Papers. Fifth Edition. | BALLADS.

NEW ARABIAN NIGHTS. Eleventh Edition. Crown 8vo, buckram, gilt top, 6s.; post 8vo, illustrated boards, 2s.
PRINCE OTTO. Post 8vo, illustrated boards, 2s.
FATHER DAMIEN: An Open Letter to the Rev. Dr. Hyde. Second Edition. Crown 8vo, hand-made and brown paper, 1s.

STODDARD. — SUMMER CRUISING IN THE SOUTH SEAS. By C. WARREN STODDARD. Illustrated by WALLIS MACKAY. Cr. 8vo, cl. extra, 3s. 6d.

STORIES FROM FOREIGN NOVELISTS. With Notices by HELEN and ALICE ZIMMERN. Crown 8vo, cloth extra, 3s. 6d.; post 8vo, illustrated boards, 2s.

STRANGE MANUSCRIPT (A) FOUND IN A COPPER CYLINDER.
With 19 Illustrations by GILBERT GAUL. Third Edition. Crown 8vo. cloth extra, 5s.

STRUTT'S SPORTS AND PASTIMES OF THE PEOPLE OF ENGLAND; including the Rural and Domestic Recreations, May Games, Mummeries, Shows, &c., from the Earliest Period to the Present Time. Edited by WILLIAM HONE. With 140 Illustrations. Crown 8vo, cloth extra, 7s. 6d.

SUBURBAN HOMES (THE) OF LONDON: A Residential Guide. With a Map, and Notes on Rental, Rates, and Accommodation Crown 8vo, cloth, 7s. 6d.

SWIFT'S (DEAN) CHOICE WORKS, in Prose and Verse. With Memoir, Portrait, and Facsimiles of the Maps in "Gulliver's Travels." Cr. 8vo, cl., 7s. 6d.
GULLIVER'S TRAVELS, and **A TALE OF A TUB.** Post 8vo, printed on laid paper and half-bound, 2s.
A MONOGRAPH ON SWIFT. By J. CHURTON COLLINS. Cr. 8vo. cloth, 8s. [*Shortly*.

SWINBURNE (ALGERNON C.), WORKS BY.
SELECTIONS FROM POETICAL WORKS OF A. C. SWINBURNE. Fcap. 8vo, 6s.
ATALANTA IN CALYDON. Cr. 8vo, 6s.
CHASTELARD: A Tragedy. Cr. 8vo. 7s.
NOTES ON POEMS AND REVIEWS. Demy 8vo, 1s.
POEMS AND BALLADS. FIRST SERIES. Crown 8vo or fcap. 8vo, 9s.
POEMS AND BALLADS. SECOND SERIES. Crown 8vo or fcap. 8vo. 9s.
POEMS AND BALLADS. THIRD SERIES. Crown 8vo. 7s.
SONGS BEFORE SUNRISE. Crown 8vo, 10s. 6d.
BOTHWELL: A Tragedy. Crown 8vo, 12s. 6d.
SONGS OF TWO NATIONS. Cr. 8vo, 6s.
GEORGE CHAPMAN. (*See* Vol. II. of G. CHAPMAN's Works.) Crown 8vo, 6s.
ESSAYS AND STUDIES. Cr. 8vo, 12s.
ERECHTHEUS: A Tragedy. Cr. 8vo, 6s.
SONGS OF THE SPRINGTIDES. Crown 8vo, 6s.
STUDIES IN SONG. Crown 8vo, 7s.
MARY STUART: A Tragedy. Cr. 8vo 8s
TRISTRAM OF LYONESSE. Cr. 8vo, 9s.
A CENTURY OF ROUNDELS. Sm. 4to, 8s.
A MIDSUMMER HOLIDAY. Cr. 8vo, 7s.
MARINO FALIERO: A Tragedy. Crown 8vo, 6s.
A STUDY OF VICTOR HUGO. Cr. 8vo, 6s.
MISCELLANIES. Crown 8vo, 12s.
LOCRINE: A Tragedy. Cr. 8vo, 6s.
A STUDY OF BEN JONSON. Cr. 8vo, 7s.

SYMONDS.—WINE, WOMEN, AND SONG: Mediæval Latin Students' Songs. With Essay and Trans. by J. ADDINGTON SYMONDS. Fcap. 8vo, parchment, 6s.

SYNTAX'S (DR.) THREE TOURS: In Search of the Picturesque, in Search of Consolation, and in Search of a Wife. With ROWLANDSON's Coloured Illustrations, and Life of the Author by J. C. HOTTEN. Crown 8vo, cloth extra, 7s. 6d.

TAINE'S HISTORY OF ENGLISH LITERATURE. Translated by HENRY VAN LAUN. Four Vols., medium 8vo, cloth boards, 30s.—POPULAR EDITION, Two Vols., large crown 8vo, cloth extra, 15s.

TAYLOR'S (BAYARD) DIVERSIONS OF THE ECHO CLUB: Burlesques of Modern Writers. Post 8vo, cloth limp, 2s.

TAYLOR (DR. J. E., F.L.S.), WORKS BY. Cr. 8vo, cl. ex., 7s. 6d. each.
THE SAGACITY AND MORALITY OF PLANTS: A Sketch of the Life and Conduct of the Vegetable Kingdom. With a Coloured Frontispiece and 100 Illustrations.
OUR COMMON BRITISH FOSSILS, and Where to Find Them. 331 Illustrations.
THE PLAYTIME NATURALIST. With 366 Illustrations. Crown 8vo, cloth, 5s.

TAYLOR'S (TOM) HISTORICAL DRAMAS. Containing "Clancarty," "Jeanne Darc," "'Twixt Axe and Crown," "The Fool's Revenge," "Arkwright's Wife," "Anne Boleyn," "Plot and Passion." Crown 8vo, cloth extra, 7s. 6d.
* The Plays may also be had separately, at 1s. each.

TENNYSON (LORD): A Biographical Sketch. By H. J. JENNINGS. With a Photograph-Portrait. Crown 8vo, cloth extra, 6s.

THACKERAYANA: Notes and Anecdotes. Illustrated by Hundreds of Sketches by WILLIAM MAKEPEACE THACKERAY, depicting Humorous Incidents in his School-life, and Favourite Characters in the Books of his Every-day Reading. With a Coloured Frontispiece. Crown 8vo, cloth extra, 7s. 6d.

THAMES.—A NEW PICTORIAL HISTORY OF THE THAMES.
By A. S. KRAUSSE. With 340 Illustrations Post 8vo, 1s.; cloth, 1s. 6d.

BOOKS PUBLISHED BY

THOMAS (BERTHA), NOVELS BY. Cr. 8vo, cl., 3s. 6d. ea.; post 8vo, 2s. ea.
CRESSIDA. | THE VIOLIN-PLAYER. | PROUD MAISIE.

THOMSON'S SEASONS, and CASTLE OF INDOLENCE. Introduction by ALLAN CUNNINGHAM, and Illustrations on Steel and Wood. Cr. 8vo. cl., 7s. 6d.

THORNBURY (WALTER), WORKS BY. Cr. 8vo, cl. extra, 7s. 6d. each.
THE LIFE AND CORRESPONDENCE OF J. M. W. TURNER. Founded upon Letters and Papers furnished by his Friends. With Illustrations in Colours.
HAUNTED LONDON. Edit. by E. WALFORD, M.A. Illusts. by F. W. FAIRHOLT, F.S.A.

Post 8vo, illustrated boards, 2s. each.
OLD STORIES RE-TOLD. | TALES FOR THE MARINES.

TIMBS (JOHN), WORKS BY. Crown 8vo, cloth extra, 7s. 6d. each.
THE HISTORY OF CLUBS AND CLUB LIFE IN LONDON: Anecdotes of its Famous Coffee-houses, Hostelries, and Taverns. With 42 Illustrations.
ENGLISH ECCENTRICS AND ECCENTRICITIES: Stories of Wealth and Fashion, Delusions, Impostures, and Fanatic Missions, Sporting Scenes, Eccentric Artists, Theatrical Folk, Men of Letters. &c. With 48 Illustrations.

TROLLOPE (ANTHONY), NOVELS BY.
Crown 8vo. cloth extra, 3s. 6d. each; post 8vo, illustrated boards, 2s. each.
THE WAY WE LIVE NOW. | MARION FAY.
KEPT IN THE DARK. | MR. SCARBOROUGH'S FAMILY.
FRAU FROHMANN. | THE LAND-LEAGUERS.

Post 8vo, illustrated boards, 2s. each.
GOLDEN LION OF GRANPERE. | JOHN CALDIGATE. | AMERICAN SENATOR.

TROLLOPE (FRANCES E.), NOVELS BY.
Crown 8vo. cloth extra, 3s. 6d. each; post 8vo. illustrated boards, 2s. each.
LIKE SHIPS UPON THE SEA. | MABEL'S PROGRESS. | ANNE FURNESS.

TROLLOPE (T. A.).—DIAMOND CUT DIAMOND. Post 8vo, illust. bds., 2s.

TROWBRIDGE.—FARNELL'S FOLLY: A Novel. By J. T. TROWBRIDGE. Post 8vo, illustrated boards, 2s.

TYTLER (C. C. FRASER-).—MISTRESS JUDITH: A Novel. By C. C. FRASER-TYTLER. Crown 8vo, cloth extra, 3s. 6d.; post 8vo. illust. boards, 2s.

TYTLER (SARAH), NOVELS BY.
Crown 8vo. cloth extra, 3s. 6d. each; post 8vo. illustrated boards, 2s. each.
THE BRIDE'S PASS. | BURIED DIAMONDS.
NOBLESSE OBLIGE. | THE BLACKHALL GHOSTS.
LADY BELL. |

Post 8vo, illustrated boards, 2s. each.
WHAT SHE CAME THROUGH. | BEAUTY AND THE BEAST.
CITOYENNE JACQUELINE. | DISAPPEARED.
SAINT MUNGO'S CITY. | THE HUGUENOT FAMILY.

VILLARI.—A DOUBLE BOND. By LINDA VILLARI. Fcap. 8vo, picture cover 1s.

WALT WHITMAN, POEMS BY. Edited, with Introduction, by WILLIAM M. ROSSETTI. With Portrait. Cr. 8vo, hand-made paper and buckram, 6s.

WALTON AND COTTON'S COMPLETE ANGLER; or, The Contemplative Man's Recreation, by IZAAK WALTON; and Instructions how to Angle for a Trout or Grayling in a clear Stream, by CHARLES COTTON. With Memoirs and Notes by Sir HARRIS NICOLAS, and 61 Illustrations. Crown 8vo, cloth antique, 7s. 6d.

WARD (HERBERT), WORKS BY.
FIVE YEARS WITH THE CONGO CANNIBALS. With 92 Illustrations by the Author, VICTOR PERARD, and W. B. DAVIS. Third ed. Roy. 8vo, cloth ex., 14s.
MY LIFE WITH STANLEY'S REAR GUARD. With a Map by F. S. WELLER, F.R.G.S. Post 8vo, 1s.; cloth, 1s. 6d.

WARNER.—A ROUNDABOUT JOURNEY. By CHARLES DUDLEY WARNER. Crown 8vo, cloth extra, 6s.

WALFORD (EDWARD, M.A.), WORKS BY.
  WALFORD'S COUNTY FAMILIES OF THE UNITED KINGDOM (1891). Containing the Descent, Birth, Marriage, Education, &c., of 12,000 Heads of Families, their Heirs, Offices, Addresses, Clubs, &c. Royal 8vo, cloth gilt, 50s.
  WALFORD'S SHILLING PEERAGE (1891). Containing a List of the House of Lords, Scotch and Irish Peers, &c. 32mo, cloth, 1s.
  WALFORD'S SHILLING BARONETAGE (1891). Containing a List of the Baronets of the United Kingdom, Biographical Notices, Addresses, &c. 32mo, cloth, 1s.
  WALFORD'S SHILLING KNIGHTAGE (1891). Containing a List of the Knights of the United Kingdom, Biographical Notices, Addresses, &c. 32mo, cloth, 1s.
  WALFORD'S SHILLING HOUSE OF COMMONS (1891). Containing a List of all Members of Parliament, their Addresses, Clubs, &c. 32mo, cloth, 1s.
  WALFORD'S COMPLETE PEERAGE, BARONETAGE, KNIGHTAGE, AND HOUSE OF COMMONS (1891). Royal 32mo, cloth extra, gilt edges. 5s.
  WALFORD'S WINDSOR PEERAGE, BARONETAGE, AND KNIGHTAGE (1891). Crown 8vo, cloth extra, 12s. 6d.
  TALES OF OUR GREAT FAMILIES. Crown 8vo, cloth extra, 3s. 6d.
  WILLIAM PITT: A Biography. Post 8vo, cloth extra, 5s.

WARRANT TO EXECUTE CHARLES I. A Facsimile, with the 59 Signatures and Seals. Printed on paper 22 in. by 14 in. 2s.
  WARRANT TO EXECUTE MARY QUEEN OF SCOTS. A Facsimile, including Queen Elizabeth's Signature and the Great Seal. 2s.

WEATHER, HOW TO FORETELL THE, WITH POCKET SPECTROSCOPE. By F. W. CORY. With 10 Illustrations. Cr. 8vo, 1s.; cloth, 1s. 6d.

WESTROPP.—HANDBOOK OF POTTERY AND PORCELAIN. By HODDER M. WESTROPP. With Illusts. and List of Marks. Cr. 8vo, cloth, 4s. 6d.

WHIST.—HOW TO PLAY SOLO WHIST. By ABRAHAM S. WILKS and CHARLES F. PARDON. Crown 8vo, cloth extra, 3s. 6d.

WHISTLER'S (MR.) TEN O'CLOCK. Cr. 8vo, hand-made paper, 1s.

WHITE.—THE NATURAL HISTORY OF SELBORNE. By GILBERT WHITE, M.A. Post 8vo, printed on laid paper and half-bound, 2s.

WILLIAMS (W. MATTIEU, F.R.A.S.), WORKS BY.
  SCIENCE IN SHORT CHAPTERS. Crown 8vo, cloth extra, 7s. 6d.
  A SIMPLE TREATISE ON HEAT. With Illusts. Cr. 8vo, cloth limp, 2s. 6d.
  THE CHEMISTRY OF COOKERY. Crown 8vo, cloth extra, 6s.
  THE CHEMISTRY OF IRON AND STEEL MAKING. Crown 8vo, cloth extra, 9s.

WILLIAMSON.—A CHILD WIDOW. By Mrs. F. H. WILLIAMSON. Three Vols., crown 8vo.

WILSON (DR. ANDREW, F.R.S.E.), WORKS BY.
  CHAPTERS ON EVOLUTION. With 259 Illustrations. Cr. 8vo, cloth extra, 7s. 6d.
  LEAVES FROM A NATURALIST'S NOTE-BOOK. Post 8vo, cloth limp, 2s. 6d.
  LEISURE-TIME STUDIES. With Illustrations. Crown 8vo, cloth extra, 6s.
  STUDIES IN LIFE AND SENSE. With numerous Illusts. Cr. 8vo, cl. ex., 6s.
  COMMON ACCIDENTS: HOW TO TREAT THEM. Illusts. Cr. 8vo, 1s.; cl., 1s. 6d.
  GLIMPSES OF NATURE. With 35 Illustrations. Crown 8vo, cloth extra, 3s. 6d.

WINTER (J. S.), STORIES BY. Post 8vo, illustrated boards, 2s. each.
  CAVALRY LIFE. | REGIMENTAL LEGENDS.

WISSMANN.—MY SECOND JOURNEY THROUGH EQUATORIAL AFRICA, from the Congo to the Zambesi, in 1886, 1887. By HERMANN VON WISSMANN. With a Map and 92 Illustrations. Demy 8vo, cloth extra, 16s.

WOOD.—SABINA: A Novel. By Lady WOOD. Post 8vo, boards, 2s.

WOOD (H. F.), DETECTIVE STORIES BY.
  Crown 8vo, cloth extra, 6s. each; post 8vo, illustrated boards, 2s. each.
  PASSENGER FROM SCOTLAND YARD. | ENGLISHMAN OF THE RUE CAIN.

WOOLLEY.—RACHEL ARMSTRONG; or, Love and Theology. By CELIA PARKER WOOLLEY. Post 8vo, illustrated boards, 2s.; cloth, 2s. 6d.

WRIGHT (THOMAS), WORKS BY. Crown 8vo, cloth extra, 7s. 6d. each.
  CARICATURE HISTORY OF THE GEORGES. With 400 Pictures, Caricatures, Squibs, Broadsides, Window Pictures, &c.
  HISTORY OF CARICATURE AND OF THE GROTESQUE IN ART, LITERATURE, SCULPTURE, AND PAINTING. Illustrated by F. W. FAIRHOLT, F.S.A.

YATES (EDMUND), NOVELS BY. Post 8vo, illustrated boards, 2s. each.
  LAND AT LAST. | THE FORLORN HOPE. | CASTAWAY.

BOOKS PUBLISHED BY

LISTS OF BOOKS CLASSIFIED IN SERIES.

** For full cataloguing, see alphabetical arrangement, pp. 1-25.

THE MAYFAIR LIBRARY. Post 8vo, cloth limp, 2s. 6d. per Volume.

A Journey Round My Room. By XAVIER DE MAISTRE.
Quips and Quiddities. By W. D. ADAMS.
The Agony Column of "The Times."
Melancholy Anatomised: Abridgment of "Burton's Anatomy of Melancholy."
The Speeches of Charles Dickens.
Literary Frivolities, Fancies, Follies, and Frolics. By W. T. DOBSON.
Poetical Ingenuities. By W. T. DOBSON.
The Cupboard Papers. By FIN-BEC.
W. S. Gilbert's Plays. FIRST SERIES.
W. S. Gilbert's Plays. SECOND SERIES.
Songs of Irish Wit and Humour.
Animals and Masters. By Sir A. HELPS.
Social Pressure. By Sir A. HELPS.
Curiosities of Criticism. H. J. JENNINGS.
Holmes's Autocrat of Breakfast-Table.
Pencil and Palette. By R. KEMPT.
Little Essays: from LAMB's Letters.
Forensic Anecdotes. By JACOB LARWOOD
Theatrical Anecdotes. JACOB LARWOOD.
Jeux d'Esprit. Edited by HENRY S. LEIGH.
Witch Stories. By E. LYNN LINTON.
Ourselves. By E. LYNN LINTON.
Pastimes & Players. By R. MACGREGOR.
New Paul and Virginia. W.H.MALLOCK.
New Republic. By W. H. MALLOCK.
Puck on Pegasus. By H. C. PENNELL.
Pegasus Re-Saddled. By H. C. PENNELL.
Muses of Mayfair. Ed. H. C. PENNELL.
Thoreau: His Life & Aims. By H. A. PAGE.
Puniana. By Hon. HUGH ROWLEY.
More Puniana. By Hon. HUGH ROWLEY.
The Philosophy of Handwriting.
By Stream and Sea. By WM. SENIOR.
Leaves from a Naturalist's Note-Book. By Dr. ANDREW WILSON.

THE GOLDEN LIBRARY. Post 8vo, cloth limp, 2s. per Volume.

Bayard Taylor's Diversions of the Echo Club.
Bennett's Ballad History of England.
Bennett's Songs for Sailors.
Godwin's Lives of the Necromancers.
Pope's Poetical Works.
Holmes's Autocrat of Breakfast Table.
Holmes's Professor at Breakfast Table.
Jesse's Scenes of Country Life.
Leigh Hunt's Tale for a Chimney Corner.
Mallory's Mort d'Arthur: Selections.
Pascal's Provincial Letters.
Rochefoucauld's Maxims & Reflections.

THE WANDERER'S LIBRARY. Crown 8vo, cloth extra, 3s. 6d. each.

Wanderings in Patagonia. By JULIUS BEERBOHM. Illustrated.
Camp Notes. By FREDERICK BOYLE.
Savage Life. By FREDERICK BOYLE.
Merrie England in the Olden Time. By G. DANIEL. Illustrated by CRUIKSHANK.
Circus Life. By THOMAS FROST.
Lives of the Conjurers. THOMAS FROST.
The Old Showmen and the Old London Fairs. By THOMAS FROST.
Low-Life Deeps. By JAMES GREENWOOD.
Wilds of London. JAMES GREENWOOD.
Tunis. Chev. HESSE-WARTEGG. 22 Illusts.
Life and Adventures of a Cheap Jack.
World Behind the Scenes. P.FITZGERALD.
Tavern Anecdotes and Sayings.
The Genial Showman. By E.P. HINGSTON.
Story of London Parks. JACOB LARWOOD.
London Characters. By HENRY MAYHEW.
Seven Generations of Executioners.
Summer Cruising in the South Seas. By C. WARREN STODDARD. Illustrated.

POPULAR SHILLING BOOKS.

Harry Fludyer at Cambridge.
Jeff Briggs's Love Story. BRET HARTE.
Twins of Table Mountain. BRET HARTE.
A Day's Tour. By PERCY FITZGERALD.
Esther's Glove. By R. E. FRANCILLON.
Sentenced! By SOMERVILLE GIBNEY.
The Professor's Wife. J. H. GRAHAM.
Mrs. Gainsborough's Diamonds. By JULIAN HAWTHORNE.
Niagara Spray. By J. HOLLINGSHEAD.
A Romance of the Queen's Hounds. By CHARLES JAMES.
The Garden that Paid the Rent. By TOM JERROLD.
Cut by the Mess. By ARTHUR KEYSER.
Our Sensation Novel. J. H. MCCARTHY.
Doom! By JUSTIN H. MCCARTHY, M.P.
Dolly. By JUSTIN H. MCCARTHY, M.P.
Lily Lass. JUSTIN H. MCCARTHY, M.P.
Was She Good or Bad? By W. MINTO.
That Girl in Black. MRS. MOLESWORTH.
Notes from the "News." By JAS. PAYN.
Beyond the Gates. By E. S. PHELPS.
Old Maid's Paradise. By E. S. PHELPS.
Burglars in Paradise. By E. S. PHELPS.
Jack the Fisherman. By E. S. PHELPS.
Trooping with Crows. By C. L. PIRKIS.
Bible Characters. By CHARLES READE.
Rogues. By R. H. SHERARD.
The Dagonet Reciter. By G. R. SIMS.
How the Poor Live. By G. R. SIMS.
Case of George Candlemas. G. R. SIMS.
Sandycroft Mystery. T. W. SPEIGHT.
Hoodwinked. By T. W. SPEIGHT.
Father Damien. By R. L. STEVENSON.
A Double Bond. By LINDA VILLARI.
My Life with Stanley's Rear Guard. By HERBERT WARD.

MY LIBRARY.

Choice Works, printed on laid paper, bound half-Roxburghe, **2s. 6d.** each.

Four Frenchwomen. By AUSTIN DOBSON.
Citation and Examination of William Shakspeare. By W. S. LANDOR.
Christie Johnstone. By CHARLES READE. With a Photogravure Frontispiece.
Peg Woffington. By CHARLES READE.

THE POCKET LIBRARY.
Post 8vo, printed on laid paper and hf.-bd., **2s.** each.

The Essays of Elia. By CHARLES LAMB.
Robinson Crusoe. Edited by JOHN MAJOR. With 37 Illusts. by GEORGE CRUIKSHANK.
Whims and Oddities. By THOMAS HOOD. With 85 Illustrations.
The Barber's Chair, and The Hedgehog Letters. By DOUGLAS JERROLD.
Gastronomy as a Fine Art. By BRILLAT-SAVARIN. Trans. R. E. ANDERSON, M.A.
The Epicurean, &c. By THOMAS MOORE.
Leigh Hunt's Essays. Ed. E. OLLIER.
The Natural History of Selborne. By GILBERT WHITE.
Gulliver's Travels, and The Tale of a Tub. By Dean SWIFT.
The Rivals, School for Scandal, and other Plays by RICHARD BRINSLEY SHERIDAN.
Anecdotes of the Clergy. J. LARWOOD.

THE PICCADILLY NOVELS.
LIBRARY EDITIONS OF NOVELS BY THE BEST AUTHORS, many Illustrated, crown 8vo, cloth extra, **3s. 6d.** each.

By GRANT ALLEN.
Philistia.
Babylon
In all Shades.
The Tents of Shem.
For Maimie's Sake.
The Devil's Die.
This Mortal Coil.
The Great Taboo.

By ALAN ST. AUBYN.
A Fellow of Trinity.

By Rev. S. BARING GOULD.
Red Spider. | Eve.

By W. BESANT & J. RICE.
My Little Girl.
Case of Mr. Lucraft.
This Son of Vulcan.
Golden Butterfly.
Ready-Money Mortiboy.
With Harp and Crown.
'Twas in Trafalgar's Bay.
The Chaplain of the Fleet.
By Celia's Arbour.
Monks of Thelema.
The Seamy Side.
Ten Years' Tenant.

By WALTER BESANT.
All Sorts and Conditions of Men.
The Captains' Room.
All in a Garden Fair
The World Went Very Well Then.
For Faith and Freedom.
Dorothy Forster.
Uncle Jack.
Children of Gibeon.
Herr Paulus.
Bell of St. Paul's.
To Call Her Mine.
The Holy Rose.
Armorel of Lyonesse.

By ROBERT BUCHANAN.
The Shadow of the Sword.
A Child of Nature.
The Martyrdom of Madeline.
God and the Man.
Love Me for Ever.
Annan Water.
Matt.
The New Abelard.
Foxglove Manor.
Master of the Mine.
Heir of Linne.

By HALL CAINE.
The Shadow of a Crime.
A Son of Hagar. | The Deemster.

MORT. & FRANCES COLLINS.
Sweet Anne Page. | Transmigration.
From Midnight to Midnight.
Blacksmith and Scholar.
Village Comedy. | You Play Me False

By Mrs. H. LOVETT CAMERON.
Juliet's Guardian. | Deceivers Ever.

By WILKIE COLLINS.
Armadale.
After Dark.
No Name.
Antonina. | Basil.
Hide and Seek.
The Dead Secret.
Queen of Hearts.
My Miscellanies.
Woman in White.
The Moonstone.
Man and Wife.
Poor Miss Finch.
Miss or Mrs?
New Magdalen.
The Frozen Deep.
The Two Destinies.
Law and the Lady.
Haunted Hotel.
The Fallen Leaves.
Jezebel's Daughter.
The Black Robe.
Heart and Science.
"I Say No."
Little Novels.
The Evil Genius.
The Legacy of Cain
A Rogue's Life.
Blind Love.

By DUTTON COOK.
Paul Foster's Daughter.

By WILLIAM CYPLES.
Hearts of Gold.

By ALPHONSE DAUDET.
The Evangelist; or, Port Salvation.

By JAMES DE MILLE.
A Castle in Spain.

By J. LEITH DERWENT.
Our Lady of Tears. | Circe's Lovers.

By Mrs. ANNIE EDWARDES.
Archie Lovell.

By PERCY FITZGERALD.
Fatal Zero.

By R. E. FRANCILLON.
Queen Cophetua. | A Real Queen.
One by One. | King or Knave?

Pref. by Sir BARTLE FRERE.
Pandurang Hari.

By EDWARD GARRETT.
The Capel Girls.

THE PICCADILLY (3/6) NOVELS—continued.

By CHARLES GIBBON.
Robin Gray. | The Golden Shaft.
In Honour Bound. | Of High Degree.
Loving a Dream.
The Flower of the Forest.

By JULIAN HAWTHORNE.
Garth. | Dust.
Ellice Quentin. | Fortune's Fool.
Sebastian Strome. | Beatrix Randolph.
David Poindexter's Disappearance.
The Spectre of the Camera.

By Sir A. HELPS.
Ivan de Biron.

By ISAAC HENDERSON.
Agatha Page.

By Mrs. ALFRED HUNT.
The Leaden Casket. | Self-Condemned.
That other Person.

By JEAN INGELOW.
Fated to be Free.

By R. ASHE KING.
A Drawn Game.
"The Wearing of the Green."

By HENRY KINGSLEY.
Number Seventeen.

By E. LYNN LINTON.
Patricia Kemball. | Ione.
Under which Lord? | Paston Carew.
"My Love!" | Sowing the Wind.
The Atonement of Leam Dundas.
The World Well Lost.

By HENRY W. LUCY.
Gideon Fleyce.

By JUSTIN McCARTHY.
A Fair Saxon. | Donna Quixote.
Linley Rochford. | Maid of Athens.
Miss Misanthrope. | Camiola.
The Waterdale Neighbours.
My Enemy's Daughter.
Dear Lady Disdain.
The Comet of a Season.

By AGNES MACDONELL.
Quaker Cousins.

By FLORENCE MARRYAT.
Open! Sesame!

By D. CHRISTIE MURRAY.
Life's Atonement. | Coals of Fire.
Joseph's Coat. | Val Strange.
A Model Father. | Hearts.
A Bit of Human Nature.
First Person Singular.
Cynic Fortune.
The Way of the World.

By MURRAY & HERMAN.
The Bishops' Bible.

By GEORGES OHNET.
A Weird Gift.

THE PICCADILLY (3/6) NOVELS—continued.

By Mrs. OLIPHANT.
Whiteladies.

By OUIDA.
Held in Bondage. | Two Little Wooden
Strathmore. | Shoes.
Chandos. | In a Winter City.
Under Two Flags. | Ariadne.
Idalia. | Friendship.
CecilCastlemaine's | Moths. | Ruffino.
Gage. | Pipistrello.
Tricotrin. | Puck. | A Village Commune
Folle Farine. | Bimbi. | Wanda.
A Dog of Flanders. | Frescoes.
Pascarel. | Signa. | In Maremma.
Princess Naprax- | Othmar. | Syrlin.
ine. | Guilderoy.

By MARGARET A. PAUL.
Gentle and Simple.

By JAMES PAYN.
Lost Sir Massingberd.
Less Black than We're Painted.
A Confidential Agent.
A Grape from a Thorn.
Some Private Views.
In Peril and Privation.
The Mystery of Mirbridge.
The Canon's Ward.
Walter's Word. | Talk of the Town.
By Proxy. | Holiday Tasks.
High Spirits. | The Burnt Million.
Under One Roof. | The Word and the
From Exile. | Will.
Glow-worm Tales. | Sunny Stories.

By E. C. PRICE.
Valentina. | The Foreigners.
Mrs. Lancaster's Rival.

By CHARLES READE.
It is Never Too Late to Mend.
The Double Marriage.
Love Me Little, Love Me Long.
The Cloister and the Hearth.
The Course of True Love.
The Autobiography of a Thief.
Put Yourself in his Place.
A Terrible Temptation.
Singleheart and Doubleface.
Good Stories of Men and other Animals.
Hard Cash. | Wandering Heir.
Peg Woffington. | A Woman-Hater.
ChristieJohnstone. | A Simpleton.
Griffith Gaunt. | Readiana.
Foul Play. | The Jilt.

By Mrs. J. H. RIDDELL.
Her Mother's Darling.
Prince of Wales's Garden Party.
Weird Stories.

By F. W. ROBINSON.
Women are Strange.
The Hands of Justice.

By W. CLARK RUSSELL.
An Ocean Tragedy.
My Shipmate Louise.

By JOHN SAUNDERS.
Guy Waterman. | Two Dreamers.
Bound to the Wheel.
The Lion in the Path.

CHATTO & WINDUS, 214, PICCADILLY. 29

THE PICCADILLY (3/6) NOVELS—*continued*.
By KATHARINE SAUNDERS.
Margaret and Elizabeth.
Gideon's Rock. | Heart Salvage.
The High Mills. | Sebastian.

By HAWLEY SMART.
Without Love or Licence.

By R. A. STERNDALE.
The Afghan Knife.

By BERTHA THOMAS.
Proud Maisie. | Cressida.
The Violin-player.

By FRANCES E. TROLLOPE.
Like Ships upon the Sea.
Anne Furness. | Mabel's Progress.

THE PICCADILLY (3/6) NOVELS—*continued*.
By ANTHONY TROLLOPE.
Frau Frohmann. | Kept in the Dark.
Marion Fay. | Land-Leaguers.
The Way We Live Now.
Mr. Scarborough's Family.

By IVAN TURGENIEFF, &c.
Stories from Foreign Novelists.

By C. C. FRASER-TYTLER.
Mistress Judith.

By SARAH TYTLER.
The Bride's Pass. | Lady Bell.
Noblesse Oblige. | Buried Diamonds.
The Blackhall Ghosts.

CHEAP EDITIONS OF POPULAR NOVELS.
Post 8vo, illustrated boards, 2s. each.

By ARTEMUS WARD.
Artemus Ward Complete.

By EDMOND ABOUT.
The Fellah.

By HAMILTON AIDE.
Carr of Carrlyon. | Confidences.

By MARY ALBERT.
Brooke Finchley's Daughter.

By Mrs. ALEXANDER.
Maid, Wife, or Widow? | Valerie's Fate.

By GRANT ALLEN.
Strange Stories. | The Devil's Die.
Philistia. | This Mortal Coil.
Babylon. | In all Shades.
The Beckoning Hand.
For Maimie's Sake. | Tents of Shem.

By ALAN ST. AUBYN.
A Fellow of Trinity.

By Rev. S. BARING GOULD.
Red Spider. | Eve.

By FRANK BARRETT.
Fettered for Life.
Between Life and Death.

By SHELSLEY BEAUCHAMP.
Grantley Grange.

By W. BESANT & J. RICE.
This Son of Vulcan. | By Celia's Arbour.
My Little Girl. | Monks of Thelema.
Case of Mr. Lucraft. | The Seamy Side.
Golden Butterfly. | Ten Years' Tenant.
Ready-Money Mortiboy.
With Harp and Crown.
'Twas in Trafalgar's Bay.
The Chaplain of the Fleet.

By WALTER BESANT.
Dorothy Forster. | Uncle Jack.
Children of Gibeon. | Herr Paulus.
All Sorts and Conditions of Men.
The Captains' Room.
All in a Garden Fair.
The World Went Very Well Then.
For Faith and Freedom.

By FREDERICK BOYLE.
Camp Notes. | Savage Life.
Chronicles of No-man's Land.

By BRET HARTE.
Flip. | Californian Stories
Maruja. | Gabriel Conroy.
An Heiress of Red Dog.
The Luck of Roaring Camp.
A Phyllis of the Sierras.

By HAROLD BRYDGES.
Uncle Sam at Home.

By ROBERT BUCHANAN.
The Shadow of the | The Martyrdom of
  Sword. | Madeline.
A Child of Nature. | Annan Water.
God and the Man. | The New Abelard.
Love Me for Ever. | Matt.
Foxglove Manor. | The Heir of Linne.
The Master of the Mine.

By HALL CAINE.
The Shadow of a Crime.
A Son of Hagar. | The Deemster.

By Commander CAMERON.
The Cruise of the "Black Prince."

By Mrs. LOVETT CAMERON.
Deceivers Ever. | Juliet's Guardian.

By AUSTIN CLARE.
For the Love of a Lass.

By Mrs. ARCHER CLIVE.
Paul Ferroll.
Why Paul Ferroll Killed his Wife.

By MACLAREN COBBAN.
The Cure of Souls.

By C. ALLSTON COLLINS.
The Bar Sinister.

MORT. & FRANCES COLLINS.
Sweet Anne Page. | Transmigration.
From Midnight to Midnight.
A Fight with Fortune.
Sweet and Twenty. | Village Comedy.
Frances. | You Play me False.
Blacksmith and Scholar.

BOOKS PUBLISHED BY

Two-Shilling Novels—*continued*.

By WILKIE COLLINS.
Armadale.
After Dark.
No Name.
Antonina. | Basil.
Hide and Seek.
The Dead Secret.
Queen of Hearts.
Miss or Mrs?
New Magdalen.
The Frozen Deep.
Law and the Lady.
The Two Destinies.
Haunted Hotel.
A Rogue's Life.
My Miscellanies.
Woman in White.
The Moonstone.
Man and Wife.
Poor Miss Finch.
The Fallen Leaves.
Jezebel's Daughter
The Black Robe.
Heart and Science.
"I Say No."
The Evil Genius.
Little Novels.
Legacy of Cain.
Blind Love.

By M. J. COLQUHOUN.
Every Inch a Soldier.

By DUTTON COOK.
Leo. | Paul Foster's Daughter.

By C. EGBERT CRADDOCK.
Prophet of the Great Smoky Mountains.

By WILLIAM CYPLES.
Hearts of Gold.

By ALPHONSE DAUDET.
The Evangelist; or, Port Salvation.

By JAMES DE MILLE.
A Castle in Spain.

By J. LEITH DERWENT.
Our Lady of Tears. | Circe's Lovers.

By CHARLES DICKENS.
Sketches by Boz. | Oliver Twist.
Pickwick Papers. | Nicholas Nickleby.

By DICK DONOVAN.
The Man-Hunter. | Caught at Last!
Tracked and Taken.
Who Poisoned Hetty Duncan?
The Man from Manchester.
A Detective's Triumphs.

By CONAN DOYLE, &c.
Strange Secrets.

By Mrs. ANNIE EDWARDES.
A Point of Honour. | Archie Lovell.

By M. BETHAM-EDWARDS.
Felicia. | Kitty.

By EDWARD EGGLESTON.
Roxy.

By PERCY FITZGERALD.
Bella Donna. | Polly.
Never Forgotten. | Fatal Zero.
The Second Mrs. Tillotson.
Seventy-five Brooke Street.
The Lady of Brantome.

ALBANY DE FONBLANQUE.
Filthy Lucre.

By R. E. FRANCILLON.
Olympia.
One by One.
A Real Queen.
Queen Cophetua.
King or Knave?
Romances of Law.

By HAROLD FREDERICK.
Seth's Brother's Wife.
The Lawton Girl.

Pref. by Sir BARTLE FRERE.
Pandurang Hari.

Two-Shilling Novels—*continued*.

By HAIN FRISWELL.
One of Two.

By EDWARD GARRETT.
The Capel Girls.

By CHARLES GIBBON.
Robin Gray.
Fancy Free.
For Lack of Gold.
What will the
World Say?
In Love and War.
For the King.
In Pastures Green.
Queen of Meadow.
A Heart's Problem.
The Dead Heart.
In Honour Bound.
Flower of Forest.
Braes of Yarrow.
The Golden Shaft.
Of High Degree.
Mead and Stream.
Loving a Dream.
A Hard Knot.
Heart's Delight.
Blood-Money.

By WILLIAM GILBERT.
Dr. Austin's Guests. | James Duke.
The Wizard of the Mountain.

By HENRY GREVILLE.
A Noble Woman.

By JOHN HABBERTON.
Brueton's Bayou. | Country Luck.

By ANDREW HALLIDAY.
Every-Day Papers.

By Lady DUFFUS HARDY.
Paul Wynter's Sacrifice.

By THOMAS HARDY.
Under the Greenwood Tree.

By J. BERWICK HARWOOD.
The Tenth Earl.

By JULIAN HAWTHORNE.
Garth.
Ellice Quentin.
Fortune's Fool.
Miss Cadogna.
David Poindexter's Disappearance.
The Spectre of the Camera.
Sebastian Strome.
Dust.
Beatrix Randolph.
Love—or a Name.

By Sir ARTHUR HELPS.
Ivan de Biron.

By Mrs. CASHEL HOEY.
The Lover's Creed.

By Mrs. GEORGE HOOPER.
The House of Raby.

By TIGHE HOPKINS.
'Twixt Love and Duty.

By Mrs. ALFRED HUNT.
Thornicroft's Model. | Self Condemned.
That Other Person. | Leaden Casket.

By JEAN INGELOW.
Fated to be Free.

By HARRIETT JAY.
The Dark Colleen.
The Queen of Connaught.

By MARK KERSHAW.
Colonial Facts and Fictions.

By R. ASHE KING.
A Drawn Game. | Passion's Slave.
"The Wearing of the Green."

CHATTO & WINDUS, 214, PICCADILLY.

Two-Shilling Novels—*continued.*

By HENRY KINGSLEY.
Oakshott Castle.

By JOHN LEYS.
The Lindsays.

By MARY LINSKILL.
In Exchange for a Soul.

By E. LYNN LINTON.
Patricia Kemball. | Paston Carew.
World Well Lost. | "My Love!"
Under which Lord? | Ione.
The Atonement of Leam Dundas.
With a Silken Thread.
The Rebel of the Family.
Sowing the Wind.

By HENRY W. LUCY.
Gideon Fleyce.

By JUSTIN McCARTHY.
A Fair Saxon. | Donna Quixote.
Linley Rochford. | Maid of Athens.
Miss Misanthrope. | Camiola.
Dear Lady Disdain.
The Waterdale Neighbours.
My Enemy's Daughter.
The Comet of a Season.

By AGNES MACDONELL.
Quaker Cousins.

KATHARINE S. MACQUOID.
The Evil Eye. | Lost Rose.

By W. H. MALLOCK.
The New Republic.

By FLORENCE MARRYAT.
Open! Sesame! | Fighting the Air.
A Harvest of Wild Oats.
Written in Fire.

By J. MASTERMAN.
Half-a-dozen Daughters.

By BRANDER MATTHEWS.
A Secret of the Sea.

By JEAN MIDDLEMASS.
Touch and Go. | Mr. Dorillion.

By Mrs. MOLESWORTH.
Hathercourt Rectory.

By J. E. MUDDOCK.
Stories Weird and Wonderful.
The Dead Man's Secret.

By D. CHRISTIE MURRAY.
A Model Father. | Old Blazer's Hero.
Joseph's Coat. | Hearts.
Coals of Fire. | Way of the World.
Val Strange. | Cynic Fortune.
A Life's Atonement.
By the Gate of the Sea.
A Bit of Human Nature.
First Person Singular.

By MURRAY and HERMAN.
One Traveller Returns.
Paul Jones's Alias.

By HENRY MURRAY.
A Game of Bluff.

By ALICE O'HANLON.
The Unforeseen. | Chance? or Fate?

Two-Shilling Novels—*continued.*

By GEORGES OHNET.
Doctor Rameau. | A Last Love.

By Mrs. OLIPHANT.
Whiteladies. | The Primrose Path.
The Greatest Heiress in England.

By Mrs. ROBERT O'REILLY.
Phœbe's Fortunes.

By OUIDA.
Held in Bondage. | Two Little Wooden
Strathmore. | Shoes.
Chandos. | Ariadne.
Under Two Flags. | Friendship.
Idalia. | Moths.
CecilCastlemaine's | Pipistrello.
Gage. | A Village Com-
Tricotrin. | mune.
Puck. | Bimbi.
Folle Farine. | Wanda.
A Dog of Flanders. | Frescoes.
Pascarel. | In Maremma.
Signa. | Othmar.
Princess Naprax- | Guilderoy.
ine. | Ouida's Wisdom.
In a Winter City. | Wit, and Pathos.

MARGARET AGNES PAUL.
Gentle and Simple.

By JAMES PAYN.
Bentinck's Tutor. | £200 Reward.
Murphy's Master. | Marine Residence.
A County Family. | Mirk Abbey.
At Her Mercy. | By Proxy.
Cecil's Tryst. | Under One Roof.
Clyffards of Clyffe. | High Spirits.
Foster Brothers. | Carlyon's Year.
Found Dead. | From Exile.
Best of Husbands. | For Cash Only.
Walter's Word. | Kit.
Halves. | The Canon's Ward
Fallen Fortunes. | Talk of the Town.
Humorous Stories. | Holiday Tasks.
Lost Sir Massingberd.
A Perfect Treasure.
A Woman's Vengeance.
The Family Scapegrace.
What He Cost Her.
Gwendoline's Harvest.
Like Father, Like Son.
Married Beneath Him.
Not Wooed, but Won.
Less Black than We're Painted.
A Confidential Agent.
Some Private Views.
A Grape from a Thorn.
Glow-worm Tales.
The Mystery of Mirbridge.

By C. L. PIRKIS.
Lady Lovelace.

By EDGAR A. POE.
The Mystery of Marie Roget.

By E. C. PRICE.
Valentina. | The Foreigners.
Mrs. Lancaster's Rival.
Gerald.

TWO-SHILLING NOVELS—*continued.*

By CHARLES READE.
It is Never Too Late to Mend.
Christie Johnstone.
Put Yourself in His Place.
The Double Marriage.
Love Me Little, Love Me Long.
The Cloister and the Hearth.
The Course of True Love.
Autobiography of a Thief.
A Terrible Temptation.
The Wandering Heir.
Singleheart and Doubleface.
Good Stories of Men and other Animals.
Hard Cash. | A Simpleton.
Peg Woffington. | Readiana.
Griffith Gaunt. | A Woman-Hater.
Foul Play. | The Jilt.

By Mrs. J. H. RIDDELL.
Weird Stories. | Fairy Water.
Her Mother's Darling.
Prince of Wales's Garden Party.
The Uninhabited House.
The Mystery in Palace Gardens.

By F. W. ROBINSON.
Women are Strange.
The Hands of Justice.

By JAMES RUNCIMAN.
Skippers and Shellbacks.
Grace Balmaign's Sweetheart.
Schools and Scholars.

By W. CLARK RUSSELL.
Round the Galley Fire.
On the Fo'k'sle Head.
In the Middle Watch.
A Voyage to the Cape.
A Book for the Hammock.
The Mystery of the "Ocean Star."
The Romance of Jenny Harlowe.
An Ocean Tragedy.

GEORGE AUGUSTUS SALA.
Gaslight and Daylight.

By JOHN SAUNDERS.
Guy Waterman. | Two Dreamers.
The Lion in the Path.

By KATHARINE SAUNDERS.
Joan Merryweather. | Heart Salvage.
The High Mills. | Sebastian.
Margaret and Elizabeth.

By GEORGE R. SIMS.
Rogues and Vagabonds.
The Ring o' Bells.
Mary Jane's Memoirs.
Mary Jane Married.
Tales of To-day. | Dramas of Life.
Tinkletop's Crime.

By ARTHUR SKETCHLEY.
A Match in the Dark.

By T. W. SPEIGHT.
The Mysteries of Heron Dyke.
The Golden Hoop. | By Devious Ways.
Hoodwinked, &c.

TWO-SHILLING NOVELS—*continued.*

By R. A. STERNDALE.
The Afghan Knife.

By R. LOUIS STEVENSON.
New Arabian Nights. | Prince Otto.

BY BERTHA THOMAS.
Cressida. | Proud Maisie.
The Violin-player.

By WALTER THORNBURY.
Tales for the Marines.
Old Stories Re-told.

T. ADOLPHUS TROLLOPE.
Diamond Cut Diamond.

By F. ELEANOR TROLLOPE.
Like Ships upon the Sea.
Anne Furness. | Mabel's Progress.

By ANTHONY TROLLOPE.
Frau Frohmann. | Kept in the Dark.
Marion Fay. | John Caldigate.
The Way We Live Now.
The American Senator.
Mr. Scarborough's Family.
The Land-Leaguers.
The Golden Lion of Granpere.

By J. T. TROWBRIDGE.
Farnell's Folly.

By IVAN TURGENIEFF, &c.
Stories from Foreign Novelists.

By MARK TWAIN.
Tom Sawyer. | A Tramp Abroad.
The Stolen White Elephant.
A Pleasure Trip on the Continent.
Huckleberry Finn.
Life on the Mississippi.
The Prince and the Pauper.

By C. C. FRASER-TYTLER.
Mistress Judith.

By SARAH TYTLER.
The Bride's Pass. | Noblesse Oblige.
Buried Diamonds. | Disappeared.
Saint Mungo's City. | Huguenot Family.
Lady Bell. | Blackhall Ghosts.
What She Came Through.
Beauty and the Beast.
Citoyenne Jaqueline.

By J. S. WINTER.
Cavalry Life. | Regimental Legends.

By H. F. WOOD.
The Passenger from Scotland Yard.
The Englishman of the Rue Cain.

By Lady WOOD.
Sabina.

CELIA PARKER WOOLLEY.
Rachel Armstrong; or, Love & Theology

By EDMUND YATES.
The Forlorn Hope. | Land at Last.
Castaway.

www.ingramcontent.com/pod-product-compliance
Lightning Source LLC
Chambersburg PA
CBHW020247240426
43672CB00006B/660